IERI Monograph Series

Issues and Methodologies in Large-Scale Assessments

VOLUME 2

October 2009

A joint publication between the International Association for the Evaluation of Educational Achievement (IEA) and Educational Testing Service (ETS)

ISBN 978-0-88685-404-1

Copies of this publication can be obtained from:

IERInstitute
IEA Data Processing and Research Center
Mexikoring 37
22297 Hamburg,
Germany

IERInstitute
Educational Testing Service
Mail Stop 02-R
Princeton, NJ 08541,
United States

By email: ierinstitute@iea-dpc.de
Free downloads: www.ierinstitute.org

Copyedited by Paula Wagemaker Editorial Services, Christchurch, New Zealand
Design and production by Becky Bliss Design and Production, Wellington, New Zealand

IERI Monograph Series

Issues and Methodologies in Large-Scale Assessments

Volume 2	2009

TABLE OF CONTENTS

Introduction

Matthias von Davier (Editor)
Educational Testing Service

Dirk Hastedt (Editor)
IEA Data Processing and Research Center

We are pleased to present Volume 2 of the *IERI Monograph Series*.

In 2007, IEA and ETS decided to establish the IEA-ETS Research Institute (IERI) with a focus on improving the science of large-scale assessments. IERI undertakes activities around three broad areas of work that include research studies related to the development and implementation of large-scale assessments; professional development and training; and dissemination of research findings and information gathered through large-scale assessments. Since IERI's establishment, many activities have taken place in the pursuit of the institute's mission.

One such activity is the institute's biannual training academies, which typically see 20 to 25 researchers from around the world attending each session. These academies provide researchers with training on the use of international large-scale assessment databases, and on more advanced statistical techniques for analyzing these data. To date, a total of six academies have been held. By the time this volume reaches you, the seventh academy will have taken place.

In addition to the academies, IERI has sponsored training on the use of large-scale assessment databases at a number of international education research conferences, such as those conducted by the American Educational Research Association (AERA), the Comparative & International Education Society (CIES), the European Educational Research Association (EERA), the International Association for Educational Assessment (IAEA), the International Meeting of the Psychometric Society (IMPS), and the National Council for Measurement in Education (NCME). IERI staff have also conducted similar training seminars for a number of other organizations in a variety of countries.

This monograph series represents, in part, the outcome of the training and research activities undertaken and supported by IERI. This volume begins with an examination of the use and usefulness of plausible values. In this paper, Matthias von Davier,

Eugenio Gonzalez, and Robert J. Mislevy present the rationale for using plausible values when estimating ability distributions in large-scale assessments. They discuss examples drawn from existing large-scale assessments, as well as examples based on simulations. The authors also offer arguments in support of the use of plausible values and the use of plausible value methodology.

The research paper by Ruth Zuzovsky deals with the interrelations between teacher preparation and professional development as it relates to student achievement. In her paper, Zuzovsky validates some assumptions regarding the interrelationship among these variables through reference to data from the Trends in International Mathematics and Science Study 2003 (TIMSS 2003). Results from this paper help inform the current debate surrounding teacher preparation and professional development and its effect on student achievement.

The paper by Aletta Grisay, Eugenio Gonzalez, and Christian Monseur tackles a topic that is at the heart of the comparability of large-scale assessments. The paper examines the equivalence of item difficulties across national versions of international large-scale assessments. The authors conducted their analyses using data from the Programme for International Student Assessment 2000 (PISA 2000) and Progress in Reading Literacy 2001 (PIRLS 2001) reading surveys.

The paper by Juliane Hencke, Leslie Rutkowski, Oliver Neuschmidt, and Eugenio Gonzalez focuses on the relationship between curriculum coverage and the results of TIMSS 2003. The extent to which results are comparable across participating countries is also at the heart of questions related to comparability in international assessments. This paper provides evidence to help us better understand the effect of curriculum coverage as it relates to the stability and comparability of results from these cross-national assessments.

The paper by Wolfram Schulz presents us with a study on construct validation in the International Civics and Citizenship Education Study. The paper presents and describes some of the procedures used in this study to validate the scales used during the pilot administration, and provides us with some preliminary results. The authors discuss the extent to which classical item statistics, factor analysis, and item response modeling help us assess the construct validity of questionnaire data obtained from international studies.

The final two papers, "Cluster Analysis for Cognitive Diagnosis: An Application to the 2001 PIRLS Reading Assessment," by Chia-Yi Chiu and Minhee Seo, and "Variance Estimation for NAEP Data Using a Resampling-based Approach: An Application of Cognitive Diagnostic Models," by Chueh-an Hsieh, Xueli Xu, and Matthias von Davier close this issue. The two papers present state-of-the-art statistical procedures that provide answers to the demands imposed on large-scale assessments to report more diagnostic information about the groups of examinees, and their cognitive profiles.

While Chiu and Seo focus on the cognitive diagnostic methods themselves, Hsieh, Xu, and von Davier present, via use of a multidimensional model for item response data, an application of a jackknifing approach to variance estimation of ability inferences for group of students. The data utilized to demonstrate the approach came from the

National Assessment of Educational Progress (NAEP). In contrast to the operational approach used in NAEP, where plausible values are used to make ability inferences, the approach presented in this paper re-estimates all parameters of the model, and makes ability inferences based on replicate samples using jackknife estimates without using plausible values.

We hope you enjoy reading and learning from the papers in this volume. Comments may be sent directly to contributing authors, or to the IERI email address: ierinstitute@iea-dpc.de. Information on submitting papers can be found on the last two pages of this volume or online at http://www.ierinstitute.org.

ABOUT THE IEA

The International Association for the Evaluation of Educational Achievement (IEA) is an independent, non-profit, international cooperative of national research institutions and governmental research agencies. Through its comparative research and assessment projects, IEA aims to:

• Provide international benchmarks that may assist policymakers identify the comparative strengths and weaknesses of their education systems;

• Provide high-quality data that will increase policy-makers' understanding of key school-based and non-school-based factors that influence teaching and learning;

• Provide high-quality data that will serve as a resource for identifying areas of concern and action, and for preparing and evaluating educational reforms;

• Develop and improve the capacity of educational systems to engage in national strategies for educational monitoring and improvement; and

• Contribute to development of the worldwide community of researchers in educational evaluation.

Additional information about IEA is available at www.iea.nl and www.iea-dpc.de.

ABOUT ETS

ETS is a non-profit institution whose mission is to advance quality and equity in education by providing fair and valid assessments, research, and related services for all people worldwide. In serving individuals, educational institutions and government agencies around the world, ETS customizes solutions to meet the need for teacher professional development products and services, classroom and end-of-course assessments, and research-based teaching and learning tools. Founded in 1947, ETS today develops, administers, and scores more than 24 million tests annually in more than 180 countries, at over 9,000 locations worldwide.

Additional information about ETS is available at www.ets.org.

What are plausible values and why are they useful?

Matthias von Davier
Educational Testing Service, Princeton, New Jersey, United States

Eugenio Gonzalez
Educational Testing Service, Princeton, New Jersey, United States

Robert J. Mislevy
University of Maryland, College Park, Maryland, United States

This paper shows some of the adverse effects that can occur when plausible values are not used or are used incorrectly during analysis of large-scale survey data. To ensure that the uncertainty associated with measures of skills in large-scale surveys is properly taken into account, researchers need to follow the procedures outlined in the article and in more detail in, for example, Little and Rubin (1987) and Schafer (1997). There is no need to rely on computational shortcuts by averaging plausible values before calculations: analytical shortcuts such as averaging plausible values produce biased estimates and should be discouraged. All analyses using survey assessment results need not only use the data as provided by the different assessment organizations but also adhere to the appropriate procedures described in this article and the included references, as well as in the guides provided for users of international survey assessment databases.

INTRODUCTION

The use of large-scale assessment data to describe what students know and can do has increased, as has the extent to which this information is used to describe group performance and develop educational interventions and policy. International large-scale assessments administer large numbers of items in limited time to representative samples of students, and provide comparable information about student skills and knowledge in content domains such as reading, mathematics, and science. The goal of large-scale educational survey assessments is to collect data on skills assessed in representative samples of student or adult populations. The data are used to describe groups within a population of interest with respect to broadly defined areas of school- or work-relevant skills. They are not used to assign individual test scores to test-takers or to employ scores for individual decision-making.

Large-scale assessments achieve a broad coverage of the targeted content domain by dividing the pool of items into blocks or clusters of items. Each student is then given one or more of these blocks, and thus receives only a subset of what constitutes the total assessment pool. As an example of how such an assessment might look, consider a national assessment of mathematics administered to Grade 9 students. Let us assume that 270 minutes worth of test items are necessary to cover the topics specified in the assessment framework document. Test administration can only take place during a two-hour period that includes preparing for administration, distribution of the test booklets, and answering a few background questions. This limitation on testing time is based on considerations with respect to reducing student burden, minimizing interruptions of the school schedule, and other factors. As a consequence, the 270 minutes worth of items are organized into six 45-minute blocks, each with 24 items, named with the letters A through F, and with each student administered two blocks according to the design depicted in Table 1.

Table 1: Booklet structure for six blocks combined into two-block booklets

	Booklet					
	1	2	3	4	5	6
First Part	A	B	C	D	E	F
Second Part	B	C	D	E	F	A

Under this design, each student responds to only a fraction of the entire assessment in the form of a booklet. These test booklets are partially linked through blocks that occur in multiple test booklets. In our example, Block A appears with Block B, which appears with Block C, and so on. Block A appears as the first block in Booklet 1 and as the second block in Booklet 6. Likewise, all other blocks appear once in the first and once in the second block-order position.

The relatively small number of items per block and the relatively small number of blocks per test booklet mean that the accuracy of measurement at the individual level of these assessments is considerably lower than is the level of accuracy common for individual tests used for diagnosis, tracking, and/or admission purposes. In tests for individual reporting, the number of items administered is considerably more than the number contained in a typical booklet in a large-scale survey assessment.

Because students are measured with only a subset of the total item pool, the measurement of individual proficiency is achieved with a substantial amount of measurement error. Traditional approaches to estimating individual proficiency, such as marginal maximum likelihood (MML) and expected-a-posteriori (EAP) estimates, are point estimates optimal for individual students, not for group-level estimation. These approaches consequently result in biased estimates of group-level results, as we show through examples later in this article.

One way of taking the uncertainty associated with the estimates into account, and of obtaining unbiased group-level estimates, is to use multiple values representing the likely distribution of a student's proficiency. These so-called plausible values provide us with a database that allows unbiased estimation of the plausible range and the location of proficiency for groups of students. Plausible values are based on student responses to the subset of items they receive, as well as on other relevant and available background information (Mislevy, 1991). Plausible values can be viewed as a set of special quantities generated using a technique called multiple imputations. Plausible values are not individual scores in the traditional sense, and should therefore not be analyzed as multiple indicators of the same score or latent variable (Mislevy, 1993).

In this article, we use simulated data to show and explain, in a non-formal way, the advantages of using plausible values over using traditional point estimates of individual proficiency. We do this by analyzing simulated response data under different conditions, using different estimation methods, and then comparing the results. We finish by summarizing how researchers need to analyze the statistics they obtain when using plausible values so that they can derive unbiased estimates of the quantities of interest.

We have organized this article as follows: the next section presents an illustrative example based on a small sample and an area of human behavior where the relationship between observed variables and the quantity of interest is direct. Our aim in this section is to introduce some important concepts at a basic, non-technical level. These concepts form the basis of statistical tools utilized in data analysis for large-scale survey assessments. We then introduce another example that takes the concepts developed in the first example to the next level. This second example is a much more realistic one: the design is similar to the one above, but it remains compact enough to allow us to discuss the central concepts in a way that focuses on the main ideas.

A SIMPLE EXAMPLE

Assume we want to predict the score of a basketball free-throw contest,[1] and assume we have students from two different schools. Students from School A tend to succeed, on average, on 50% of the free-throw trials, and the success rates across students is normally distributed. Students from School B tend to succeed, on average, on 70% of the free-throw trials, and the success rate across students is also normally distributed. Let us now assume that within each school the standard deviation of a student's success rate in free throws is 10%. Thus, only a few students in School A are likely to have a "true" free-throw success rate as high as 70%, and only a few of the students from School B are likely to have a free-throw success rate as low as 50%.

We want to come up with a good estimate of a student's "true" free-throw success rate based on a limited number of observations and our knowledge of the school she attends. Note that we can only observe the trials of a student selected for the tryouts, and we can observe the school the student belongs to (we can ask her). The "true" success rate of 50% cannot be "seen," and a "true" rate of 50% means that the student does not have to succeed at a rate of 50% in all cases; it simply means that the student with this success rate should succeed in 50% of throws over the long run, and that with each single shot, the student stands a chance of succeeding or failing.

Let us now assume that a student who wants to participate in the tryout learns that each applicant gets only three shots, so he tries to find out what results he can expect. Table 2 presents the results of this student's practice with three shots, which he repeats 10 times.

Table 2: Results for 10 repetitions of three-throw tryouts of a student from School A with an average long-term success rate of 50%

Trial	1	2	3	4	5	6	7	8	9	10
1	0	1	1	0	1	1	1	1	0	1
2	0	0	1	0	0	1	1	0	0	0
3	0	1	1	1	1	1	0	1	0	0
Rate	00	67	100	33	67	100	67	67	00	33

The first thing we notice is that, for three free-throws, we can observe only 0%, 33%, 67%, and 100% levels of success, and no other percentages in between. The average percentage across the 10 repetitions, though, lies between these numbers, and is 53% for the data given in Table 2.

The standard deviation of our 10 averages is 36 when basing the try-out sample on three free-throws only, again using the data in Table 2 for calculations. From

---

1   Note that the estimates in this example are based on very small sample sizes. Statistics based on such small samples would not be reported in large-scale survey assessments because the errors associated with such estimates would be too large. The example presented in this section is for demonstration purposes only and intended to explain concepts rather than actual procedures.

inspection of this table, we also see that this student would be quite successful in 6 out of 10 cases and produce a success rate of either 100% or 67%. However, there are also two cases with 0% success. Obviously, three throws is a small number from which to accurately estimate the success rate of a player. What happens when the number of throws is increased by a factor of four? Table 3 contains the data for a student with the same actual long-term success rate (50% success rate), who throws 10 repeats of 12 trials each.

Table 3: Results for 10 repetitions of 12-throw tryouts of a student from School A with a long-term success rate of 50%

Trial	1	2	3	4	5	6	7	8	9	10
1	1	0	1	1	0	0	1	0	1	0
2	0	0	0	1	1	0	0	1	1	0
3	1	1	0	1	0	1	0	0	1	1
4	0	1	1	0	1	0	0	1	0	1
5	1	1	1	0	1	0	0	1	0	0
6	0	0	0	1	0	1	1	1	0	0
7	0	1	0	1	1	0	0	0	0	1
8	1	0	1	1	0	0	1	1	1	1
9	1	1	0	1	1	1	1	0	1	0
10	1	0	1	1	1	1	0	1	0	0
11	1	0	1	1	0	1	0	0	0	0
12	0	0	1	1	1	0	1	0	0	1
Rate	58	42	58	83	58	42	42	50	42	42

The 10 averages of 12 trials appear in the last row of Table 3. Notice that there are no cases where all trials were successful (100%) or unsuccessful (0%). The largest success rate in this sample is 83% (repeated trial number 4); the smallest success rate is 42% in the repeated trials 2, 6, 7, 9, and 10. The average success rate of these 12 trials is 52%, and the standard deviation of these averages over 12 trials is 13.5. Note that this is still not exactly 50%, even though this player threw 120 times. This outcome is not an error, but is due to the fact that the actual results of a limited number of trials generally vary somewhat from the long-term expected success rate. Some trials will be slightly below the expected value; some will be slightly above.

We can determine the theoretical standard deviation of the averages mathematically in this simple experiment. The standard deviation of a single trial is 50 in this case, and this number needs to be divided by the square root of the number of trials, which gives us a theoretical standard deviation of the average percentage, that is, the standard error (s. e.) of the estimate of average percentage of success. For a three-throw tryout, the standard deviation of the percentage is 28.87; for the 12-throw trials, it is 14.43. Intuitively, these differences in standard deviations of averages make considerable sense in that more trials per tryout seem to lead to more consistent results.

Unfortunately, this approach to obtaining higher accuracy and reducing uncertainty about the estimate seems to be a rather inefficient one. For a target of a standard error of 5%, we would need 100 free-throws per tryout; a standard error of 1% would require 2,500 throws.

Using What We Know about the Student

While it would be good to use other students' tryout throws from the same school as evidence of what we could expect if a student from this school comes to a tryout, how much can we gain from this type of information? Given our knowledge about student averages, and their variability, relative to the long-term success rates from the different schools, we might be able to "stabilize" or "improve" what we know if we could see a very small number of trial free-throws.

What, then, would be our best guess of a student's success rates on the free throws if we had not seen this student perform any free throws but knew which school he was attending? Our guess would be that this student would have a success rate of 70% if he came from School B. And if he were from School A, his success rate would be 50%, right? So what would we guess if this student threw once and succeeded, and is from School A? Still 50%, or would we guess 100% based on a single trial, or somewhere in between? When we have only a very limited number of observations, it is hard to judge how a player will perform in the long run. In such instances, including information on additional variables, for example, the school the student comes from, can help.

Note that we may not do the right thing for an individual student because we can get lucky in terms of finding a student from School A who has an actual long-term success performance of 70%. We can also find students from School B who have an actual long-term success rate of only 50%. However, this situation changes drastically if we compare groups of students or selections involving multiple students (as in teams, for example).

Group-level Considerations

The person putting together a team and the individual player chosen (or not) as part of that team operate from different perspectives. The person who selects multiple players for a team is interested mostly in how that set of players will perform on average, and how much variability this team will show in terms of performance. The individual player, however, wants his or her actual performance reflected in the most accurate terms.

As a continuation of the tryout example, let us assume that we are in the process of selecting a bunch of new players from the two Schools—A and B. How should we proceed in that case? Let us say we have observed the actual performance on 10 trials for 20 players from each of the two schools. Figure 1 shows a distribution of observed scores generated based on the information we know about the schools and the number of successful free-throws for the two groups. Also shown in the graph in parentheses are the numbers we are interested in but cannot directly see: the actual long-term success rates of each of the students next to their actual score based on the 10 throws. As an example of how to read the graph, Score 4 is observed in two cases in School A and two cases in School B. The students from A who scored 4 have an actual long-run success rate of 39% and 53%, whereas the students from School B with Score 4 have success rates in the long-run of 71% and 43%. Also note that no student from School A scored higher than 8, and no student from School B scored lower than 4.

Figure 1: Distribution of 20 students from each school scoring on 10 free-throws in a tryout for a new team

School A: E=50%, S=10%	Score	School B: E=70%, S=10%
-/-	0	-/-
-/-	1	-/-
(43%) (33%)	2	-/-
(39%) (58%)	3	-/-
(39%) (53%)	4	(71%) (43%)
(56%) (47%) (43%) (54%)	5	(58%) (55%) (62%) (67%)
(39%) (64%) (54%) (56%) (49%)	6	(70%) (64%) (62%) (70%)
(51%) (49%) (67%)	7	(66%) (67%) (65%) (85%)
(53%) (69%)	8	(65%) (68%) (71%)
-/-	9	(72%) (84%)
-/-	10	(73%)

What is particularly interesting about Figure 1 is the fact that students with rather different "true" success rates get the same observed score on the 10 trials, and that the average "true" success rate by school is also different for the same score level. For example, the group of students with Score 6 has an average "true" success rate of 52.4% ($1/5$*(39+64+54+56+49)) for School A, and an average of 66.5% ($1/4$*(70+64+62+70)) for students from School B. While readers might think these results are fabricated to make a point,[2] these numbers are indeed based on data generated using random draws calculated with a spreadsheet fed with only the basic long-term success rates determined for Schools A and B. We later show how the same phenomenon is observed when we use simulated student response data from an assessment.

Let us now look at the same data from a different perspective. Table 4 gives the means of the "true" success rates of the (admittedly small) groups of students in the percentage metric. It also gives the observed score expressed as a percentage, as well

---

2 We did not fabricate the values in Figure 1 but obtained them by using a spreadsheet and available statistical functions that allowed us to conduct random draws from a uniform distribution, a function that allows calculation of inverse normal function values, and a Boolean logic function.

as the difference between the two. In Table 4, we observe, as we move away from the school average "true" success rate, larger differences between the observed score and the average "true" score of those who obtained it.

Table 4: Observed scores expressed as percentages on 10 trials, average "true" success rates in the score groups by school, and differences between observed scores and averages

Score	Mean A	Difference A	Mean B	Difference B
20	38.0	-18.0	-/-	-/-
30	48.5	-18.5	-/-	-/-
40	46.0	- 6.0	57.0	-17.0
50	50.0	0.0	60.5	-10.5
60	52.4	+7.6	66.5	- 6.5
70	55.7	+14.3	70.8	+0.8
80	61.0	+19.0	68.0	+12.0
90	-/-	-/-	78.0	+12.0
100	-/-	-/-	73.0	+27.0

These differences seem to be centered on the average skill we identified for the two schools. The smallest difference between the observed score and the average "true" skill of students from School A is found for score 50 (which is also the average percentage of success for School A). The smallest difference between the observed scores and the average "true" skill of students from School B is found at score level 70 (which is the average success rate overall for students in School B).

Given these observations, we would substantially misjudge the situation if we were to state that students from School A with a score of 60 (6/10 successful throws x 100) have the same average success rate compared to students from School B with a score of 60. In our example, the average success rate based on the long-term rates for students with this score is 52.4% for students from School A and 66.5% for students from School B. (We will show this effect again later with our simulated assessment data from a much larger sample.) For the person forming a new team, the best decision would be to select students from School B at a higher rate than students from School A, even if those students have the same observed score, because the long-term success rate of students seems to be higher for students in School B than for those in School A.

There is a way of taking into account the fact that we know, from previous trials, how students from these different school teams perform, on average, and how their performance varies. Table 5 provides an example of how this might look. Note that, for only one throw, we would remain very close to the school-based long-term averages as our guess for the student's expected long-term success rate. Because we do not know much after seeing just one successful throw, all we can do is estimate that a student who throws once and succeeds will have a expected long-term success rate of 51.92% if she is from School A and an estimated long-term success rate of 71.36% if she is from School B.

Table 5: Average long-term success rate used to derive expected success rates given the successes on a number of throws, Schools A and B

	A	B	A	B	A	B	A	B
Throws	1	1	10	10	100	100	500	500
0.00	48.08	66.82	35.71	47.42	10.00	12.15	2.38	2.82
10.00	-/-	-/-	38.57	50.65	18.00	20.41	11.90	12.42
20.00	-/-	-/-	41.43	53.87	26.00	28.68	21.43	22.02
30.00	-/-	-/-	44.29	57.10	34.00	36.94	30.95	31.61
40.00	-/-	-/-	47.14	60.32	42.00	45.21	40.48	41.21
50.00	-/-	-/-	50.00	63.55	50.00	53.47	50.00	50.81
60.00	-/-	-/-	52.86	66.77	58.00	61.74	59.52	60.40
70.00	-/-	-/-	55.71	70.00	66.00	70.00	69.05	70.00
80.00	-/-	-/-	58.57	73.23	74.00	78.26	78.57	79.60
90.00	-/-	-/-	61.43	76.45	82.00	86.53	88.10	89.19
100.00	51.92	71.36	64.29	79.68	90.00	94.79	97.62	98.79

Note: Values given are for one throw, 10 throws, 100 throws, 500 throws.

This situation changes markedly when we increase the number of throws for each of the candidates. After completing 100 throws, a student from School A who succeeded on 70% of the throws would have an estimated success rate of 66%, quite close to the 70% he has shown. This estimate is 16 percentage points away from what we would expect if we only knew which school the student came from. A student from School B who succeeded in 50 out of 100 cases would get an estimated success rate of 53.47%, much closer to the 50% he has shown than to the 70% we would expect if all we knew was which school he came from. The values for our expectations after 500 throws would be even closer to the observed percentages.

In our comparison between the schools, we had each student throw 10 times, which obviously presents us with a better picture than if that student had thrown just once, but is still not as informative as seeing 100 throws. We have tabulated the result for 20 students each from School A and School B based on 10 throws. Table 6 shows the relationship between the expected values, the observed values, and the actual values obtained from our sample of students from each school.

Table 6: Observed scores based on 10 throws, expected values based on the observed score and prior information about school-players' average long-term performance and variability of players within schools

Observed	Expected	Mean A	Diff A	Observed	Expected	Mean B	Diff B
00	35.7	-/-	-/-	00	50.0	-/-	-/-
10	38.6	-/-	-/-	10	52.9	-/-	-/-
20	41.4	38.0	-3.4	20	55.7	-/-	-/-
30	44.3	48.5	- 4.2	30	58.6	-/-	-/-
40	47.1	46.0	+1.1	40	61.4	57.0	4.4
50	50.0	50.0	+0.0	50	64.3	60.5	3.8
60	52.8	52.4	+0.4	60	67.1	66.5	0.6
70	55.7	55.7	+0.0	70	70.0	70.8	-0.8
80	58.6	61.0	-2.4	80	72.9	68.0	4.9
90	61.4	-/-	-/-	90	75.7	78.0	-2.3
100	64.3	-/-	-/-	100	78.6	73.0	5.6

In order to derive these expected scores based on observed data (free throws) and prior knowledge (long-term school average and within-school variability), we used Bayesian methods as the tool of choice. Without going into the mathematical details and formal introductions of the concepts involved, we endeavor, through the text box below, to give a little more detail for interested readers. By using some simplifying assumptions that allow us to approximate the discrete observed success rate variable with a continuous normally distributed variable, we can derive the expected long-term proficiency for each observed score, given the known school-team membership of each student.

Likelihoods, Prior Information, and Posteriors

Figures 2 and 3 illustrate how we obtained the numbers in Table 6. The two figures show an abscissa (x-coordinate) axis that represents the long-term success rate expressed as a percentage. The ordinate (y-coordinate) axis represents the function value of the continuous probability densities in the figures.

The figures include a dashed line that represents the probability density based on the assumption that the long-term success rate is normally distributed, with an expectation of 70% and a standard deviation of 10% in School B. The two dotted plots in the figures represent different amounts of information gathered (the likelihood) from observing 10 throws and four successes (represented in Figure 2), or from observing 100 throws and 40 successes (represented in Figure 3).

Figure 2: Relationship between *a priori* distribution of a measure in School B, the likelihood of the observed data (10 throws), and the derived posterior distribution of the given observations

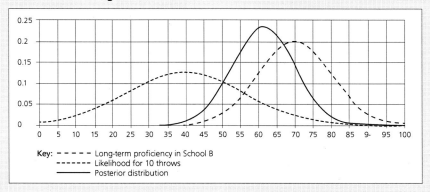

Figure 3: Relationship between *a priori* distribution of a measure in School B, the likelihood of the observed data (100 throws), and the derived posterior distribution of the given observations

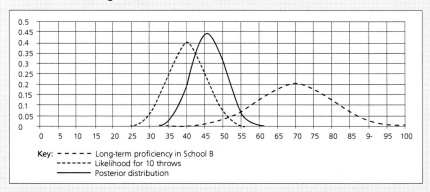

The product of the ordinate (y-coordinate) values of the dashed and the dotted lines are calculated, normalized, and plotted as a solid line. The solid lines depict the resulting posterior distribution, which integrates our observations and prior knowledge about the long-term success rates in a given school. Note how in both figures the solid line is between the prior distribution given for the school and the curve depicting the likelihood of success for the 10-throw trial as well as for the 100-throw trial.

The two figures show that the best guess we have might be located between what we observe in the student try-out and what we know about the school in terms of long-term success rate. For only 10 trials and 4 successes, the posterior expectation for a student is much closer to the school-based distribution, which means our best prediction for the student's long-term success would be about 60%. If 100 throws are observed, our best guess is much closer to the observed value of 40 out of 100 successful trials; for a student from School B, our best guess after 100 throws would be about 45%.

Note that the differences between the "expected" columns and the averages of the actual long-term performance from our sample in Table 6 are much smaller than the differences between the observed score and the average long-term success in Table 4. Note also that this method gives us expected values even for extreme observed scores such as 0 or 10 successes, which would not qualify as a reasonable estimate of the long-term success rate. For 10/10 successful throws, we get an expected long-term success rate of 64.3% for students from School A and 78.6% for School B, which in both is 64.3%-50% = 14.3 and 78.6%-70% = 8.6 percentage points higher than the respective average school performances, but is still not quite at 100%. The same occurs for 0/10 successful throws. Here, we would expect that students who show this performance and are from School A would have, on average, an actual long-term success rate of only 35%, while students from School B would still have a long-term success rate of 50%, even if they had not scored once during 10 trials. These are 14.3 and 20 percentage points lower than the respective school averages, but not quite 0%. We could argue that these estimates make more sense because an estimate of 0% seems too extreme given that we observed only 10 throws, and given that we know how the students from each school tend to perform in the long run.

Recall that the goal is not to assign a mark, grade, or score to individual students, but to describe a group of students in terms of their long-term expected success rate and the variability of the success rate based on the data we have. The expected values presented in Table 6 do seem to perform well in terms of tracking the expected long-term success rates given school membership and the observed number of successes during 10 throws. Note, however, that the expected values do not represent the fact that we have variability of long-term success rates even for the same given number of observed successes. Figure 4 gives an impression of the variability of scores if they were based on the expected values (rounded to save space in the figure) compared to the distribution of observed score-based percentages. The values in the figure are based on School A only; the results for School B would be similar.

Figure 4: Distribution of observed score-based percentages and expected percentages for the 20 students from School A

Observed score percentages	Score	Expected score percentages
-/-	0	-/-
-/-	1	-/-
(20%) (20%)	2	(41%) (41%)
(30%) (30%)	3	(44%) (44%)
(40%) (40%)	4	(47%) (47%)
(50%) (50%) (50%) (50%)	5	(50%) (50%) (50%) (50%)
(60%) (60%) (60%) (60%) (60%)	6	(53%) (53%) (53%) (53%) (53%)
(70%) (70%) (70%)	7	(56%) (56%) (56%)
(80%) (80%)	8	(59%) (59%)
-/-	9	-/-
-/-	10	-/-

In Figure 4, the score obtained in the 10-throw tryout for students from School A is associated with either the observed score-based percentage (on the left-hand side) or the expected values given in Table 5 on the right-hand side. When we calculate the variability of these measures based on the 20 values obtained from the left-hand side of Figure 4, we arrive at an estimate of 17.57 for the standard deviation of the observed score-based percentages, and an estimate of 5.01 for the standard deviation of the expected value-based measures on the right-hand side. The actual standard deviation of the sample, as given in Figure 1, is 9.5; the observation-only-based values over-estimate this value, while the expectation-based values under-estimate the actual variability of the long-term success rate in our sample.

Uncertainty Where Uncertainty Is Due

The expected values obtained from the free-throw score and prior knowledge based on school performance are useful in establishing that a result from a short tryout may not be the best predictor of long-term performance. This is especially the case when groups are concerned: we need to describe them in terms of statistical characteristics that are free from undesirable effects introduced by observing only a very small selection of the behavior of interest (as with the few trials in our example).

The "expected" values presented in Table 5 are surprisingly close to the actual average of the players given their observed performance. However, we found that the expected values did not reflect the reality of only a few trials; the true long-term success rate of students with the same number of successes on a short trial was still quite variable.

Unfortunately, the actual long-term success rates are not something we would have available. So how can we make up for the fact that the observed values do not serve our purpose, while the expected values do not vary "enough"? Note that Figure 4 reveals something peculiar about our use of the expectations we generated. We always replace the same observed score for a given school with the same expected percentage. In contrast, the actual long-term performances of students vary, even if they have the same observed number of successful throws. There is a way to reintroduce the knowledge that the long-term rate estimates are not certain even for the same observed score. This possibility also involves an application of Bayesian statistical methods.

We thus derived, in similar fashion to how we produced the expected values, a measure of variability around these expected values. Figures 3 and 4 showed that while we were able to derive an expected value for each set of numbers of throws, for successful throws, and for a given school, we still witnessed considerable variability around this expected value. A more appropriate representation of this remaining uncertainty can be gained by generating values that follow these posterior distributions. The values, randomly drawn from the posterior distribution show that, after 10 throws and knowing which school a student comes from, a considerable amount of uncertainty remains about this student's probable long-term success rate. Even after 100 throws, we still see some uncertainty.

Within the context of large-scale survey assessments, random draws from posterior distributions are referred to as *plausible values*. We use this term here even though the plausible values in our example are based on a much reduced statistical model and are derived via our use of a number of simplifying assumptions. Table 7 shows the two sets of plausible values that were generated according to the procedure described above. The posterior distribution for each of the 20 students was generated as illustrated in Figure 3. The values in that figure drawn from the posterior distribution are depicted as solid lines.

Table 7: Examples of plausible values representing the expected values by observed score and the remaining variability of long-term expectations

First set of "plausible values"							Second set of "plausible values"				
						0					
						1					
			38.2	43.9		2	38.8	36.2			
			45.1	36.1		3	47.1	39.1			
			58.5	43.1		4	45.5	48.5			
	42.6	47.5	39.8	47.0		5	39.6	55.3	49.0	45.7	
43.5	65.4	66.8	50.1	54.8		6	37.5	34.6	31.4	42.9	56.7
			55.4	67.5		7	65.4	61.0			
			57.9	48.2		8	58.9	59.5			
						9					
						10					

Note: The two sets of plausible values are based on observed scores in School A.

As can be deduced from the information in Table 7, the mean for the first set of values is 50.1, and the standard deviation is 10.1. The mean for the second set is 47, and the standard deviation is 10.0. The values for the standard deviations are much closer to the value obtained for the actual long-term averages given in Figure 1 (9.5) when compared to the standard deviation based on expected values or observed score-based percentages.

The point that we want to make here is that the sets of plausible values give a more realistic representation of the expected values in subgroups as well as of the variances within actual results for these subgroups. Because the true values or, in our case, long-term averages are in most cases unknown, and because we do not have accurate estimates of individual performance on short tests, plausible values are a very useful tool for generating values that have more accurate statistical properties than do observed scores for subgroup comparisons. In our simple example, we had the true values available all along, and therefore did not need to use made-up plausible values. However, if we do not have the true values (and that is generally the case in real applications), plausible values can help us represent how the true distribution of proficiencies (in basketball or other areas) might look in those instances where we have substantial information about groups of students, but not enough observations on each individual student.

In practice, more than two sets of plausible values are generated; most national and international assessments use five, in accordance with recommendations put forward by Little and Rubin (1987). These five plausible values can be used to generate estimates of the statistics of interest, and then combined using the appropriate expressions for the variance of these statistics of interest (see Equation 1 below; also Little & Rubin, 1987). In closing the example presented in this section, we note again that the size of the samples we used is much smaller than what would be considered a minimal group size suitable for reporting in operational settings.

Working with Plausible Values

As is evident from the example above, we can repeat the drawing of plausible values several times, each time obtaining a slightly different result for the individuals, yet each time obtaining unbiased estimates of the mean and the standard deviation of the distribution overall, and of the subgroups. So what should we consider to be our results? While plausible values are simply random draws from the posterior distributions, and any one set of plausible values will give us unbiased estimates of group distributions and differences between subgroups, these values are not suitable "scores" for the individuals in our sample. The average of these estimates across the subgroups will give us the best estimates of the group-level statistics of interest. In general, for each application, five sets of plausible values are drawn, although more can be drawn. Summarizing the results using the plausible values requires calculating the statistic of interest using each of the plausible values, and then finally averaging the results. (We refer, later in this article, to this method as PV-R—"R" for right, that is, correct.)

Computing the variance within groups properly requires us to use K sets of plausible values (we often find $K=5$ sets of plausible values in public-use databases), and the appropriate expressions for the imputation variance as articulated by Little and Rubin (1987):

$$\hat{V}_{IMP} = \left(1 + \frac{1}{K}\right)\left[\frac{1}{K-1}\ \Sigma_i(M_{PVi} - \bar{M}_{PV})^2\right] + \frac{1}{K}\ \Sigma_i \hat{V}(M_{PVi}) \tag{1}$$

This expression is one that is commonly found for variance decompositions into the average of variance estimates $\hat{V}(M_{PVi})$ of the statistic M_{PVi} for each group of plausible values i and variance of the K plausible values-based statistics M_{PVi} between the K groups,

$$\frac{1}{K-1}\ \Sigma_i(M_{PVi} - M_{PV})^2.$$

We might be tempted to take a shortcut by averaging the plausible values for each individual student and then calculating the statistics of interest only once by using these averages of the plausible values. (We refer to this method later in the article as PV-W—"W" for wrong, not correct.) Although this method allows us to obtain the same mean as is evident with the PV-R method, the variance and percentile estimates will be biased because the distribution will have shrunk.

In the next section, we take the conceptual descriptions based on the first example and put the developed concepts to work in a more realistic setting. We use, in this example, larger, more realistic sample sizes. We also use a data structure as well as models and derived statistics that are closer to the actual analytical procedures used in large-scale survey assessments.

A MORE COMPLEX EXAMPLE

How plausible values are generated in large-scale surveys is somewhat more complex than the procedure in the illustration presented above. The reason for this is that survey assessments use a much more complex test design than the 10-free-throw basketball test, which assumes all students are examined by repeating the same task multiple times. As we explained in the introduction, survey assessments include a large number of cognitive tasks or test items, which are administered to a sample of students, with each student taking only a subset of these items. Each of the several test booklets contains a fraction of the total set of test items. The items are systematically arranged into blocks and then combined into booklets, so that each item appears in exactly one block, and each block of items appears once in each of the several block-order positions within the booklets administered to students.

The large number of booklets containing different block combinations establishes an assessment design with many test forms. Because of the large number of blocks being used to cover a broad construct domain such as Grade 9 mathematics, it is often impossible to combine every block with all other blocks. This complex design of survey assessments makes traditional observed-score methods rather difficult or impossible to apply. Methods from modern test theory are applied to analyze the data and link the booklets, enabling reporting of results on one common scale. More specifically, methods based on the Rasch model (Rasch, 1980) or item response theory (IRT) (Lord & Novick, 1968) are applied and extended to allow the integration of covariates collected in background questionnaires alongside data from the test booklets.

Details about the assessment design used in international and national educational survey assessments can be found in, for example, Beaton, Mullis, Martin, Gonzalez, Kelly, and Smith (1996). Von Davier, Sinharay, Oranje, and Beaton (2007) consider current operational analyses methods for these assessments, and describe how these approaches integrate IRT and regression models for latent variables in order to facilitate reporting and the drawing of plausible values. Relatively complex models such as these used in large-scale surveys can be viewed as constrained but fine-grained versions of multiple-group IRT models. For our current purpose, however, these extensions of IRT models form the basis on which we can draw plausible values in practice.

Using Plausible Values and Background Data

Here, we use a simulated dataset to demonstrate the statistical difficulties encountered when aggregating individual "scores" for reporting group-level results. The advantage of using a simulated dataset is that we know the exact values (the "truth") on which we based our simulation. Knowing the truth is useful when comparing different estimates that try to recapture these true values.

For our example, we generated mathematics proficiency-skill-levels for 4,000 cases crossing two "known" background characteristics: school type with levels A and B; and parental socioeconomic status (SES), also with two levels, H and L. This approach resulted in four (2x2) distinct groups, each with 1,000 cases. The average difference in mathematics skills between School Types A and B was 0.000 in our simulation, while the average difference based on parental SES was magnitude 1.414. The average for the high (H) SES group was +0.707, and -0.707 for the low (L) SES group. Let us ignore for now considerations as to whether these assumptions are particularly realistic or unrealistic, especially given that these variables may bear different effects in different populations. Table 8 presents the means and standard deviations used to generate the response data. We set the standard deviation within each of these groups to 0.707, which yielded a variance within each of the four groups of about 0.5 (or 0.707^2), and an overall variance and standard deviation of 1.000.

Table 8: Means and standard deviations (in parenthesis) used to generate the simulated dataset

SES	School		
	A	*B*	*Average*
L	- 0.707 (0.707)	- 0.707 (0.707)	- 0.707 (0.707)
H	+0.707 (0.707)	+0.707 (0.707)	+0.707 (0.707)
Total	0.000 (1.000)	0.000 (1.000)	0.000 (1.000)

For this example, we simulated the responses to a pool of 56 items for all the students in our dataset. The responses were simulated under three different conditions:

1. Items were randomly assigned to one of seven blocks, named A, B, C, D, E, F, and G. Every student responded to three of these blocks (24 items in total) in the assessment pool. The design organized the blocks according to this pattern: (ABD) (BCE) (CDF) (DEG) (EFA) (FGB) (GAC).

2. Using the same blocks composed for (1), every student responded to two of the blocks (16 items in total) in the assessment pool. The blocks were organized in seven pairs as follows: (AB) (BC) (CD) (DE) (EF) (FG) (GA).

3. Items were randomly assigned to one of 14 blocks, named A through N. Every student responded to two of these blocks (eight items in total) in the assessment pool. These blocks were organized in 14 pairs: (AB) (BC) (CD) (DE) (EF) (FG) (GH) (HI) (IJ) (JK) (KL) (LM) (MN) (NA).

We then calibrated the items using Parscale Version 4.1 (Muraki & Bock, 1997), and assigned scores to students via four different methods:

1. Expected-a-posteriori using Parscale (EAP);

2. Expected-a-posteriori using DESI (Gladkova, Moran, & Blew, 2006), taking into account group membership (EAP–MG);

3. Warm's maximum likelihood estimates using Parscale (WML); and

4. Plausible values using DESI (PV-W and PV-R). Note that in our example each student was assigned five plausible values. For illustrative purposes, we can compute and present group statistics using plausible values in two ways. The first, PV-W (W for "wrong"), is calculated by taking the average of the plausible values for each student and using this value for our calculations. The second, PV-R (R for "right"), is calculated using each of the plausible values to compute the statistic of interest and then averaging the results over the five calculations.

We will begin by taking a look at the simulated data in order to determine the presence of any of the peculiarities we described earlier in this article. We will use our most extreme simulations, the ones in which each student was administered only 16 or 8 items, and where the number of correct scores could accordingly range from 0 through 16 in one case, and between 0 and 8 in the other. Keep in mind that in our simulation there is no school effect, so the overall school means are the same. However, remember also that we built in an SES effect such that those in the group SES Type H scored higher than those in SES Type L.

Table 9 shows, for each school type, the number of students in our simulated dataset obtaining each "number correct" score on the 16-item test. We also show these students' average true score by school type and the difference between the average true score for the students obtaining the same number correct.

Notice from the table how the students for each score point come from both school types, in quite similar numbers for most observed scores. Those who score 0 are 41 students from School A and 38 students from School B. As we go down the table, we observe only small differences for most score points. We can also see that the average difference in the average generating ability is close to 0 across the range of number correct scores.

Table 10 shows similar results for the simulated students from School Types A and B who took only 8 items. Again, we observe that the students are fairly evenly distributed across the two school types for each number correct score, and that the average true score differences between schools is again close to 0. We can expect this outcome, because, as we mentioned earlier, we did not introduce differences between school types in our simulation. We also found that where there were no differences between school types, our estimates were fairly consistent when we compared the results of the 16-item test and the 8-item test. If we wanted to obtain the mean by school type, we would simply, in both cases, multiply the average generating ability for each number correct group by the number of cases, and divide by the total number of cases.

Table 9: Average generating ability and number of cases, by school type on the simulated 16-item test

Number correct	Average generating ability (or "truth")		Number of cases		Average difference
	School Type A	School Type B	School Type A	School Type B	
0	-1.668	-1.825	41	38	0.157
1	-1.562	-1.564	91	83	0.002
2	-1.274	-1.257	119	122	- 0.017
3	- 0.979	-1.008	140	137	0.029
4	- 0.852	- 0.823	127	125	- 0.028
5	- 0.652	- 0.611	123	139	- 0.041
6	- 0.457	- 0.455	125	139	- 0.002
7	- 0.272	- 0.215	156	125	- 0.057
8	- 0.054	- 0.058	136	141	0.004
9	0.160	0.111	125	128	0.049
10	0.349	0.391	133	111	- 0.042
11	0.514	0.462	134	130	0.052
12	0.696	0.703	133	129	- 0.007
13	0.929	0.924	127	136	0.006
14	1.139	1.254	131	128	- 0.115
15	1.491	1.465	108	133	0.026
16	1.660	1.802	51	56	- 0.142

Table 10: Average generating ability and number of cases, by school type on the simulated 8-item test

Number correct	Average generating ability (or "truth")		Number of cases		Average difference
	School Type A	School Type B	School Type A	School Type B	
0	-1.458	-1.409	138	139	- 0.048
1	-1.065	-1.141	239	205	0.077
2	- 0.735	- 0.787	243	248	0.052
3	- 0.414	- 0.391	240	250	- 0.023
4	- 0.046	- 0.036	255	241	- 0.010
5	0.335	0.328	245	257	0.006
6	0.624	0.629	271	230	- 0.005
7	1.068	1.075	223	264	- 0.007
8	1.386	1.398	146	166	- 0.013

What happens when we take a look at the same simulated dataset, but by SES type? Table 11 shows these results for the 16-item test. The table contains several features of note. First, the number of students by SES type is nowhere near evenly distributed across the observed raw scores. Of the 79 students scoring 0 on the test, three students are from SES Type H and 76 students are from SES Type L, whereas in Table 9 they were fairly evenly distributed across the schools. We observe a similar pattern of different frequencies in each raw score group, until a raw score of 8 is reached; here, we begin to see a change in the contribution of cases from each of the SES types. When we look at the average difference in true ability, we also notice a consistent difference in true ability between the students of SES Type L and those of SES Type H, with the difference always favoring the students of SES Type H. This difference is quite consistent across the range of scores, indicating that for students with the same number correct score, those coming from SES Type H have, on average, a higher true ability than those coming from SES Type L, even though both sets of students have the same number correct score.

Table 11: Average generating ability and number of cases, by SES type on the simulated 16-item test

| Number correct | Average generating ability (or "truth") | | Number of cases | | |
	SES Type H	SES Type L	SES Type H	SES Type L	Average difference
0	-1.538	-1.752	3	76	- 0.214
1	-1.095	-1.580	6	168	- 0.485
2	- 0.890	-1.282	10	231	- 0.392
3	- 0.796	-1.016	28	249	- 0.220
4	- 0.529	- 0.876	28	224	- 0.347
5	- 0.325	- 0.717	58	204	- 0.393
6	- 0.195	- 0.550	70	194	- 0.355
7	- 0.031	- 0.373	104	177	- 0.342
8	0.091	- 0.196	135	142	- 0.287
9	0.275	- 0.047	143	110	- 0.322
10	0.472	0.139	168	76	- 0.332
11	0.552	0.283	202	62	- 0.269
12	0.742	0.450	224	38	- 0.292
13	0.959	0.618	238	25	- 0.341
14	1.217	0.732	248	11	- 0.484
15	1.495	1.127	229	12	- 0.368
16	1.738	1.389	106	1	- 0.349

When we look at the results for the 8-item test (Table 12), we first notice that the distribution of students by number correct score by SES type is uneven. We then notice that the average differences between the average true ability of the students of SES Type H and those of SES Type L are consistently larger than the average differences found in the 16-item test, with the direction of these differences always favoring the students of SES Type H.

Table 12: Average generating ability and number of cases, by SES type on the simulated 8-item test

| Number correct | Average generating ability (or "truth") | | Number of cases | | |
	SES Type H	SES Type L	SES Type H	SES Type L	Average difference
0	- 0.870	-1.466	15	262	- 0.595
1	- 0.711	-1.135	36	408	- 0.424
2	- 0.323	- 0.844	78	413	- 0.521
3	0.004	- 0.587	153	337	- 0.590
4	0.214	- 0.297	248	248	- 0.511
5	0.495	- 0.002	337	165	- 0.496
6	0.749	0.193	391	110	- 0.555
7	1.119	0.537	447	40	- 0.582
8	1.432	0.706	295	17	- 0.726

In conclusion, and providing evidence similar to that in our earlier basketball example, if we were to assign ability estimates based only on number correct scores, and if we were to ignore SES membership in this case, we would be able to estimate the differences between schools accurately, because there are no differences to estimate. However, we would underestimate the differences between groups based on SES type. The underestimation of these differences increases as the number of items decreases, as our example shows.

Let us now take a look at the estimates we obtained using methods that rely only on the item responses students gave (WML, EAP), and those that rely on item responses and group membership (PV-W and PV-R). Table 13 shows the overall means and standard deviations under each of the four conditions simulated, based on the number of items. The column denoted by "Truth" shows the marginal means of the generating ability.

Table 13: Overall means and standard deviations of the simulated scores

Number of items	Mean						Standard deviation					
	Truth	EAP	EAP-(MG)	WML	PV-W	PV-R	Truth	EAP	EAP-(MG)	WML	PV-W	PV-R
24	-0.01	0.01	0.01	0.01	0.01	0.01	0.99	0.96	0.95	1.05	0.95	0.99
16	-0.01	0.01	0.02	0.02	0.02	0.02	0.99	0.94	0.93	1.06	0.94	0.99
8	-0.01	0.00	0.01	0.00	0.00	0.00	0.99	0.87	0.87	1.02	0.88	0.97

Notice that while the means in Table 13 have been predicted fairly accurately regardless of the number of items and the scoring method used, this is not the case for the estimated standard deviations. Except for the value in the column headed PV-R, the standard deviation (and, as a consequence, the overall estimate of the variance) is generally under-predicted, with a noticeable deterioration as the number of items decreases.

Notice also that although the mean estimates using PV-W and PV-R are identical, this is not the case for the estimates of the standard deviations under these two conditions. PV-R (the averaged results from each of the five plausible values) provides an estimate that is indeed almost identical to the standard deviation of the generating ability. However, when we estimate the standard deviation using the averaged plausible values (PV-W), we consistently underestimate the true standard deviation. The WML estimates start by overestimating the standard deviation, but as the number of items decreases, the standard deviation is underestimated, as it is with the EAP method and the EAP-MG method. When we use plausible values the "right" way (PV-R), we do obtain a relatively good and stable estimate of the standard deviation, even as the number of items reaches down to 8.

Tables 14 and 15 show the marginal means and standard deviations for each of the groups as obtained from the simulated data. The values shown are the sample means for the marginal distributions by school type and by SES.

Table 14: Marginal averages and standard deviations in subgroups defined by school type, and the corresponding EAP, WML, and PV aggregates

Number of items	School type	Mean						Standard deviation					
		Truth	EAP	EAP-(MG)	WML	PV-W	PV-R	Truth	EAP	EAP-(MG)	WML	PV-W	PV-R
24	A	-0.03	0.01	0.01	0.01	0.01	0.01	0.98	0.95	0.94	1.03	0.94	0.98
16	A	-0.03	0.00	0.00	0.00	0.00	0.00	0.98	0.93	0.92	1.05	0.93	0.98
8	A	-0.03	-0.01	-0.02	-0.02	-0.02	-0.02	0.98	0.86	0.86	1.01	0.87	0.95
24	B	0.01	0.02	0.02	0.02	0.02	0.02	1.01	0.96	0.95	1.06	0.96	1.00
16	B	0.01	0.03	0.03	0.04	0.03	0.03	1.01	0.94	0.94	1.07	0.95	1.01
8	B	0.01	0.02	0.03	0.02	0.03	0.03	1.01	0.87	0.88	1.03	0.90	0.98

In Table 14 we observe a similar pattern to that observed in Table 13. The means are estimated fairly well by all methods used, with the PV-W and the PV-R coinciding exactly. But when we look at the standard deviations, we again see a deterioration in these estimates as the number of items decreases. In particular, notice how, when we use the plausible values in the correct way (PV-R), our estimates of the subgroup means and the standard deviations of the groups are estimated consistently.

When using any of the other methods, we are able to estimate only the mean correctly, but not the standard deviation. This is also why plausible values are crucial for estimating proportion-above-point scores, such as proportion of students at or above proficient, which is what so many large-scale assessment program inferences are based on. However, keep in mind that when conducting our simulation, we specified that there should be no differences between the school types, and this is what we observed. This is not the case when we look at the results for the SES types shown in Table 15.

Table 15: Marginal averages and standard deviations in subgroups defined by SES, and the corresponding EAP, WML, and PV aggregates

		Mean						Standard deviation					
Number of items	SES type	Truth	EAP	EAP-(MG)	WML	PV-W	PV-R	Truth	EAP	EAP-(MG)	WML	PV-W	PV-R
24	H	0.69	0.66	0.71	0.71	0.71	0.71	0.72	0.71	0.64	0.79	0.66	0.71
16	H	0.69	0.63	0.71	0.70	0.71	0.71	0.72	0.72	0.64	0.84	0.65	0.73
8	H	0.69	0.56	0.69	0.64	0.68	0.68	0.72	0.66	0.53	0.80	0.56	0.69
24	L	-0.71	-0.64	-0.69	-0.68	-0.68	-0.68	0.70	0.70	0.63	0.77	0.65	0.70
16	L	-0.71	-0.60	-0.68	-0.66	-0.67	-0.67	0.70	0.69	0.61	0.78	0.63	0.70
8	L	-0.71	-0.55	-0.68	-0.63	-0.67	-0.67	0.70	0.67	0.54	0.80	0.57	0.69

In this table, we observe a somewhat different pattern to the one observed in the previous tables. Keep in mind that Table 15 shows us the marginal means and standard deviations for the groups as defined by the grouping variable SES, and that we simulated differences between these two groups. Unlike the previous tables, the EAP and WML results in Table 15 show a bias of the subgroup means toward the overall mean (0.00) as the number of items decreases. However, the results for the EAP-MG, PV-W, and PV-R provide us with means that are fairly close to the means of the generating distribution. When we look at the standard deviations by subgroups, we again see that the only method by which we obtain standard deviations consistent with the generating distribution, and regardless of the number of items administered, is when we compute these statistics using plausible values in the prescribed way (PV-R). In conclusion, it seems that plausible values, when analyzed properly, give us unbiased estimates for the overall mean and the standard deviations of the subgroups of interest.

Let us go back again to our example to see whether using the plausible values as estimates of the average group performance allows us to reproduce the results presented at the beginning of this section. For this purpose, we compute the average raw score for each of the subgroups of interest and compare these with the results observed from the generating or true scores.

As we can see in Table 16, extremely small to no differences by school type are evident in our simulated data (column "Truth"), and there are no differences relative to the estimates we calculated in our analysis. However, when we look at the same data analyzed by SES type (Table 17), we notice a different pattern. For example, while the true scores show differences between SES Type L and SES Type H for each number correct score, the difference always favors SES Type H. Neither WML nor the EAP estimates is able to capture this difference. While the differences slightly favor the SES Type H group, these are clearly underestimates when compared with what we would expect to find based on the true scores used to generate the data. When we look at the EAP-(MG) and the PV-W and PV-R results, we notice that the difference between the groups, while not reflected exactly, does show up fairly well in our analysis. Curiously, but not unexpectedly, the results using PV-W and PV-R are exactly the same because the computation of these means is algebraically equivalent. However, remember that in our previous tables the results we obtained using PV-W underestimated the variances for the subgroups.

Table 16: Difference in average scores between School Type A and School Type B, by number correct on the 8-item test

Number correct	Truth	WML	EAP	EAP-(MG)	PV-W	PV-R
0	- 0.048	0.001	- 0.005	- 0.005	0.028	0.028
1	0.077	0.006	0.003	0.008	0.036	0.036
2	0.052	- 0.006	- 0.005	- 0.022	0.006	0.006
3	- 0.023	0.007	0.009	- 0.010	- 0.033	- 0.033
4	- 0.010	0.018	0.015	0.013	- 0.002	- 0.002
5	0.006	0.010	0.010	0.020	0.011	0.011
6	- 0.005	0.010	0.010	- 0.018	- 0.007	- 0.007
7	- 0.007	- 0.024	- 0.018	- 0.055	- 0.087	- 0.087
8	- 0.013	0.010	0.006	- 0.030	- 0.073	- 0.073

Table 17: Difference in average scores between SES Types L and H, by number correct on the 8-item test

Number correct	Truth	WML	EAP	EAP-(MG)	PV-W	PV-R
0	0.595	-0.011	0.025	0.678	0.651	0.651
1	0.424	0.084	0.067	0.609	0.611	0.611
2	0.521	0.080	0.072	0.554	0.524	0.524
3	0.590	0.094	0.086	0.532	0.542	0.542
4	0.511	0.082	0.077	0.513	0.490	0.490
5	0.496	0.072	0.065	0.511	0.503	0.503
6	0.555	0.068	0.060	0.541	0.529	0.529
7	0.582	0.097	0.076	0.607	0.517	0.517
8	0.726	0.109	0.054	0.684	0.736	0.736

One last inspection of the data will help us see the advantages of using the plausible values in the correct way, even if the EAP-(MG) and the PV-W give point estimates quite similar to those given by PV-R. Table 18 shows the percentiles of the distribution of scores using the 8-item test, calculated with each one of the estimates obtained from the simulated data. The sum of the squared difference gives us a measure of how different our estimated percentiles are over the distribution. Notice that when we look at the distribution of scores, the squared differences between percentiles are relatively small and the percentile estimates using PV-R come closest to the percentiles from the true distribution. Notice also that the estimates obtained using PV-R more closely estimate the extreme percentiles (10th and 90th).

Table 18: Percentiles of the distribution and the sum of the squared differences between the estimated scores and the truth

Percentile	Truth	WML	EAP	EAP-(MG)	PV-W	PV-R
10	-1.295	-1.256	-1.149	-1.161	-1.188	-1.276
20	- 0.912	- 0.870	- 0.829	- 0.871	- 0.855	- 0.872
30	- 0.611	- 0.554	- 0.542	- 0.597	- 0.580	- 0.565
40	- 0.307	- 0.266	- 0.260	- 0.294	- 0.285	- 0.280
50	- 0.023	0.015	0.014	0.026	0.018	0.008
60	0.267	0.266	0.267	0.305	0.298	0.289
70	0.561	0.538	0.535	0.591	0.576	0.569
80	0.887	0.857	0.837	0.889	0.858	0.884
90	1.305	1.350	1.217	1.191	1.203	1.271
		Sum of the squared differences between truth and estimated percentiles				
		0.013	0.047	0.037	0.030	0.007

Table 19 shows the same percentiles by SES type, and the sum of the squared differences between estimates and true values. Again, the estimates obtained using PV-R come the closest to the percentiles obtained for true values. The percentiles obtained using the WML procedure are those of a distribution that is more spread out than is the true distribution, whereas the estimates obtained under both EAP methods and PV-W seem to indicate a distribution that has shrunk toward the mean.

Table 19: Percentiles of the distribution and the sum of the squared differences between the estimated scores and the truth, by SES type

Percentile	SES type	Truth	WML	EAP	EAP-(MG)	PV-W	PV-R
10	H	- 0.217	- 0.317	- 0.300	- 0.015	- 0.056	- 0.203
20	H	0.083	- 0.003	0.001	0.228	0.186	0.098
30	H	0.308	0.219	0.224	0.403	0.389	0.320
40	H	0.490	0.397	0.400	0.576	0.552	0.498
50	H	0.689	0.604	0.595	0.730	0.704	0.676
60	H	0.867	0.797	0.764	0.888	0.854	0.864
70	H	1.059	1.036	0.979	1.049	1.007	1.044
80	H	1.296	1.265	1.175	1.191	1.203	1.267
90	H	1.627	1.871	1.462	1.392	1.399	1.575
10	L	-1.584	-1.949	-1.455	-1.401	-1.400	-1.561
20	L	-1.286	-1.231	-1.147	-1.161	-1.187	-1.271
30	L	-1.076	-1.042	-0.956	-1.027	-1.014	-1.042
40	L	- 0.885	- 0.795	-0.769	- 0.870	- 0.853	- 0.851
50	L	- 0.717	- 0.622	-0.597	- 0.731	- 0.708	- 0.683
60	L	- 0.538	- 0.444	-0.422	- 0.571	- 0.554	- 0.503
70	L	- 0.343	- 0.235	-0.227	- 0.410	- 0.384	- 0.317
80	L	- 0.127	0.033	0.026	- 0.203	- 0.172	- 0.091
90	L	0.175	0.367	0.362	0.061	0.114	0.223
			Sum of the squared differences between truth and estimated percentiles				
	H		0.107	0.097	0.147	0.111	0.005
	L		0.237	0.164	0.076	0.056	0.010

In summary, these results show that the plausible value methodology provides estimates that are closer to the generating parameters when it comes to estimating the means differences and standard deviations for selected subgroups and, as a consequence, for estimating the significance of these differences. In addition, the plausible value methodology provides estimates that are closer to the truth when it comes to estimating percentiles of the distribution.

We should mention that while some of the differences found in these comparisons might seem small or even trivial, we need to keep two issues in mind when interpreting them. First, because the data used in these analyses are simulated and are based on a relatively simple model of group differences, the results are substantially more stable than those that would be found in real-life data. We can expect to find a greater and more noticeable effect when using real data with much larger amounts of background data, because these are collected in large-scale survey assessments. Second, and perhaps of more importance, large-scale assessment data are used to make educational policy decisions that affect many in the population. So, for example, when calculating the percentage of students reaching a benchmark in the population, a 2% difference can translate into many students classified as proficient or not proficient. Using appropriate statistical techniques can minimize the amount of misclassification.

CONCLUSION

In this article, we compared group-level estimates based on commonly used estimators of individual student scores with group-level estimates based on five separate calculations using plausible values. We found that both individual score-based methods (EAP and WML) bear undesirable effects that adversely affect their utility as a basis for accurate group-level statistics. First, we observed a noticeable bias toward more extreme values when generating student scores based on Warm's maximum likelihood estimates (WML) using small numbers of items. Second, we showed that the expected a-posteriori (EAP) score of a student, given his or her set of responses and a (prior) distribution based on a sample of students from the same population, is biased toward the mean of this reference distribution.

Why do we see these undesirable effects in group-level variance estimates? As we stated above, maximum likelihood estimates tend to be "too extreme" when only a few item responses are involved. Our results have shown that the values in column "WML" of the relevant tables are comparably too large, indicating that the WMLs vary too much (are more extreme than the truth). With EAP-based standard deviations, these estimates are much smaller than the truth. From the point of view of individuals, EAPs "pull" toward the group mean in such a way that their expected value is the correct mean over individuals. From the point of view of individuals, PVs add noise. But from the point of view of groups, they add exactly the right amount of variability to make the distribution of the PVs in the group match the distribution of the true values in the group.

The use of plausible values for group-level reporting has been advocated since the National Assessment of Educational Progress (NAEP) started utilizing this imputation technique. However, we stress here that plausible values are not suitable as individual scores, and they were never intended as such. They are a tool that enables official reporting and allows secondary analysts to operate on the same data.

One common misconception among those using plausible values is that the mean of plausible values can be used instead of the average over five calculations with the given set of plausible values. However, as evident from the examples in this article, the variance is severely underestimated for group-level calculations when this method

(PV-W(wrong)) or EAP scores are used. The EAP is the value that we can expect when we have at hand item responses and background data, and it is about the value we can expect to get when averaging the five plausible values of a given student. Thus, using the average of five plausible values should result in the same severe underestimation of group-level variability as using the EAP, a situation that we should obviously avoid.

As we stated at the beginning of this article, analysts do not need to rely on computational shortcuts by averaging plausible values before conducting calculations: analytical shortcuts such as averaging plausible values produce biased estimates and should therefore be discouraged. The procedures developed in the relevant literature should be followed or software employed that is already set up to use plausible values with the appropriate procedures.[3] These tools, which have become increasingly easy to use, provide analysts with appropriate methodologies and procedures for analyzing the information contained in large-scale survey databases.

References

Beaton, A. E., Mullis, I. V. S., Martin, M. O., Gonzalez, E. J., Kelly, D. L., & Smith, T. A. (1996). *Mathematics achievement in the middle school years: IEA's Third International Mathematics and Science Study*. Chestnut Hill, MA: Boston College.

Gladkova, L., Moran, R., & Blew, T. (2006). *Direct Estimation Software Interactive (DESI) manual*. Princeton, NJ: Educational Testing Service.

Little, R. J. A., & Rubin, D. B. (1987). *Statistical analysis with missing data*. New York: J. Wiley & Sons.

Lord, F. M., & Novick, M. R. (1968). *Statistical theories of mental test scores*. Reading, MA: Addison-Wesley.

Mislevy, R. J. (1991). Randomization-based inference about latent variables from complex samples. *Psychometrika, 56*(2), 177–196.

Mislevy, R. J. (1993). Should "multiple imputations" be treated as "multiple indicators"? *Psychometrika, 58*(1), 79–85.

Muraki, E., & Bock, R. D. (1997). *PARSCALE: IRT item analysis and test scoring for rating-scale data* (computer software). Chicago: Scientific Software.

Rasch, G. (1980). *Probabilistic models for some intelligence and attainment tests*. Chicago: The University of Chicago Press.

Schafer, J. L. (1997). *Analysis of incomplete multivariate data*. London: Chapman & Hall.

von Davier, M., Sinharay, S., Oranje, A., & Beaton, A. (2007). The statistical procedures used in National Assessment of Educational Progress: Recent developments and future directions. In C. R. Rao & S. Sinharay (Eds.), *Handbook of statistics: Vol. 26. Psychometrics* (pp. 1039–1055). Amsterdam: Elsevier.

---

3 Several software programs allow the use of multiple imputations, or are already set up to allow various analyses of information contained in the databases of large-scale survey assessments. Examples are the NAEP Data Explorer available at http://nces.ed.gov/nationsreportcard/nde/ through the National Center for Education Statistics (NCES); the latest version of the HLM software (http://www.ssicentral.com/hlm/index.html); AIR's AM software (http://am.air.org/); and the SPSS-based International Association for the Evaluation of Educational Achievement International Database Analyzer (IEA IDB Analyzer) (http://www.iea.nl/iea_studies_datasets.html).

Teachers' qualifications and their impact on student achievement: Findings from TIMSS 2003 data for Israel

Ruth Zuzovsky
Center for Science and Technology Education, Tel Aviv University, Tel Aviv, Israel

Data collected as part of the Trends in International Mathematics and Science Study 2003 (TIMSS 2003) in Israel make it possible to validate several assumptions regarding the relationship between certain teacher characteristics and student achievement. We need this validation if we want to take a stance in the debate, occurring in Israel and elsewhere, regarding the nature of the reforms needed in the selection and preparation of teachers, opportunities for professional development, and the reward mechanisms and incentives that affect teachers' career structures.

INTRODUCTION

International comparative studies of educational achievement have become an important source of information for those involved in educational policymaking. Although many commentators view these studies as "horse races" that focus mainly on the relative position of one country's attainment to that of others, there are those who appreciate their educational role (Bryk & Hermanson, 1993; Darling-Hammond, 1992, 1994; Kellaghan, 1996) and the opportunity these studies provide to clarify and reassess local policy assumptions. Diane Shorrocks-Taylor (2000, p. 18) sees the benefit of participating in international comparative studies as the challenge these present to existing local policies: "The process of participation requires self-evaluation which in turn may lead to assumptions being questioned and what previously understood only implicitly now being made explicit and so examined in a more critical way." This article illustrates the relevance of data obtained as part of the Trends in International Mathematics and Science Study 2003 (TIMSS 2003) for local policymaking in Israel.

The policy issue at the heart of this article relates to the need to ensure the presence of "highly qualified teachers in every classroom" and to determine how best to define and prepare these "qualified" teachers. Quality teachers are often seen simply as "good" teachers and are considered to be those who exhibit desirable traits and uphold the standards and norms of the profession. But quality teachers are also considered to be those who bring about "student learning." These teachers are called "effective" (Berliner, 1987, 2005) or "successful" (Fenstermacher & Richardson, 2005). Fenstermacher and Richardson (cited in Berliner, 2005, p. 207) distinguish between *good* teaching and *successful* teaching as follows:

> By "good teaching" we mean that the content taught accords with disciplinary standards of adequacy and completeness and the methods employed are age appropriate, morally defensible and undertaken with the intention of enhancing the learner's competence with respect to content. By "successful teaching" we mean that the learner actually acquires some reasonable and acceptable level of proficiency from what the teacher is engaged in teaching.

Because of psychometric difficulties in assessing teachers by their normative attributes—the logical, the psychological, and (especially) the ethical, which are defined differently across cultures (Alexander, 2000)—the tendency to evaluate teacher qualities on the basis of student performance is given even greater emphasis. With the increased demands for accountability in line with performance standards and with the growing demand for evidence-based policymaking, student achievement is considered an accurate measure of teacher effectiveness and has become a basis for value-added teacher assessment systems (Braun, 2005; McCaffrey, Lockwood, Koretz, Louis, & Hamilton, 2004; Sanders, 2000; Sanders & Rivers, 1996).

These notions have also found favor in regard to the effectiveness of teacher education systems. After tracing the development and reform of teacher education in terms of the major questions shaping this field of education, Cochran-Smith (2001) argues that "the outcome" question is what currently motivates teacher education research and policymaking. She set down three ways in which the outcomes of teacher education are constructed. One of them, *long-term impact outcomes*, refers to the relationships between teacher qualifications and student learning. Teachers' qualifications encompass teachers' scores on tests and examinations, their years of experience, the extent of their preparation in subject matter and in pedagogy, what qualifications they hold in their area of expertise, and their ongoing professional development. Student learning is taken simply as the gain scores students attain on achievement tests. Cochran-Smith (2001, p. 531) went on to posit the relationship between teacher qualification and student learning as the percentage of variance in student scores accounted for by teacher qualifications when other variables are held constant or adjusted.

In many countries, teacher qualifications that are considered to be related to student learning have become targets of education reform. However, the nature of this reform is under debate. Some perceive the main problem to be the low academic and cognitive level of those who go into the teaching profession and call for policies aimed at attracting more capable candidates through shorter, less regulated alternative routes (Ballou & Podgursky 1997, 1999, 2000; Goldhaber & Brewer, 2000; United States Department of Education, 2002). Others view the problem mainly as the result of inadequate teacher preparation and call for the "professionalization" of teacher education by making it longer, upgrading it to graduate programs, and regulating it through mechanisms of licensure, certification, and promotion aligned with standards (Darling-Hammond, 1998, 1999, 2000a; Darling-Hammond, Berry, & Thorenson, 2001; Darling-Hammond, Chung, & Frelow, 2002; National Commission on Teaching and America's Future, 1996).

The impact of these different approaches on student learning have been explored in several meta-analytic studies based mainly on United States data but also drawing from the databases of other countries (see, in this regard, Darling-Hammond, 1999, 2000b; Greenwald, Hedges, & Laine, 1996; Organisation for Economic Co-operation and Development, 2005; Santiago, 2002; Wayne & Youngs, 2003; Wilson, Floden, & Ferrini-Mundy, 2001). Other relevant studies have drawn more on local sources of data and have been targeted at specific (country-based) policies (Harris & Sass, 2007; Ingersoll, 2003; Wilson, Darling-Hammond, & Berry, 2001). In Israel, too, teacher qualifications have become the target of several recent reforms, such as those announced by different teacher unions (2004), the National Task Force for the Advancement of Education in Israel (Dovrat Committee, 2005), and the Committee of the Commission for Higher Education (Ariav, Olshtain, Alon, Back, Grienfeld, & Libman, 2006). The reforms suggested in Israel are more in line with the advocacy to professionalize teacher preparation. All suggestions thus far envision improving the candidate selection process, upgrading the disciplinary preparation of teachers, opening advanced degree Master of Education (M.Ed) or Master of Teaching (M.Teach) programs, and providing opportunities for professional development.

Given the relatively few studies conducted in Israel on the impact of these recommended policies on student learning, and because of the conflicting results obtained from the many studies conducted elsewhere, the study documented in this article attempted to validate some of the assumptions at the basis of the suggested policies. More specifically, the study re-examined the extent to which advanced academic degrees, majoring in the field of teaching, years of teaching experience, and intensive participation in professional development activities—all assumed to be cardinal teacher qualifications—are indeed positively associated with student achievement in mathematics and science.

LITERATURE REVIEW

This section offers a summary of research findings related to each of the teacher qualifications considered in this study.

Teachers' Formal Education

Findings related to teachers' academic degrees (Bachelor's, Master's, doctorate, and other) are inconclusive. Some studies show positive effects of advanced degrees (Betts, Zau, & Rice, 2003; Ferguson & Ladd, 1996; Goldhaber & Brewer, 1997, 2000;

Rowan, Chiang, & Miller, 1997); others show negative effects (Ehrenberg & Brewer, 1994; Kiesling, 1984). Some researchers maintain that the requirement for teachers to have a second degree raises the cost, financially as well as in time, of teacher education, which may prevent quality candidates from choosing this profession (Murnane, 1996).

Teacher Education in the Subject Matter of Teaching (in-field preparation)

This characteristic is related to the subject-matter knowledge teachers acquire during their formal studies and pre-service teacher education courses. The evidence from different studies is contradictory. Several studies show a positive relationship between teachers' preparation in the subject matter they later teach and student achievement (Darling-Hammond, 1999, 2000b; Goldhaber & Brewer, 2000; Guyton & Farokhi, 1987), while others have less unequivocal results. Monk and King (1994) found both positive and negative effects of teachers' in-field preparation on student achievement. Goldhaber and Brewer (2000) found a positive relationship for students' mathematics achievement but no such relationship for science. Rowan et al. (1997) reported a positive relationship between student achievement and teachers with a major in mathematics. Monk (1994), however, found that while having a major in mathematics had no effect on student achievement in mathematics, having a substantial amount of under- or post-graduate coursework had a significant positive effect on students in physics but not in life sciences.

Ingersoll (2003) considered the widespread phenomenon in the United States of teachers teaching subjects other than those for which they had formal qualifications. His study of out-of-field teaching (as it is known) portrayed a severe situation where 42% to 49% of public Grades 7 to 12 teachers of science and mathematics lacked a major and/or full certification in the field they were teaching (1999/2000 data). In Israel, a recent survey (Maagan, 2007) placed the corresponding percentages even higher for elementary teachers—42% for mathematics and 63% for science (2005/2006 data).

Teacher Education in Pedagogical Studies

The literature shows a somewhat stronger, and more consistently positive, influence of education and pedagogical coursework on teacher effectiveness (e.g., Ashton & Crocker, 1987; Everston, Hawley, & Zlotnik, 1985; Ferguson & Womack, 1993, Guyton & Farokhi, 1987). Some of these studies compare the effect on student achievement of courses in pedagogical subject matter with the effect of courses in the subject matter itself, and present evidence in favor of the former. An example is a study conducted by Monk (1994) related to mathematics achievement. Other studies reveal no impact of education courses on students' achievement (see, for example, Goldhaber & Brewer, 2000, in relation to science achievement).

Duration of Pre-service Education

Despite evidence that five-year programs result in a higher retention rate and career satisfaction of their graduates than do four-year programs (Andrew, 1990), there is no evidence that graduates of the longer programs become more effective teachers. Data collected in TIMSS 2003 in Israel cannot contribute to this consideration, as the information collected on teachers' pre-service education did not differentiate between consecutive teacher preparation programs at universities (one- to two-year programs taken after completion of the first degree in a discipline) and concurrent programs at teachers' colleges (four- to five-year integrated disciplinary and pedagogy programs).

Certification and Licensing Status

Certified teachers are usually those who have graduated from accredited teacher education programs. Some of these teachers are also required to complete an induction program or pass a national teacher examination test in order to obtain a license. There is debate in the USA between those in favor of full certification (Darling-Hammond, 1999; Darling Hammond et al., 2001) and those who argue that students of teachers who hold full certification achieve similarly to those who study under teachers with temporary "emergency" credentials (Goldhaber & Brewer, 2000). These authors also argue that relaxing requirements for certification is a way not only of attracting academically talented college graduates to teaching but also of recruiting a more diverse pool of candidates needed for a diverse student population. The TIMSS 2003 data at hand for Israel prevented examination of this issue, as all participating teachers were fully certified.

Years of Experience

Studies on the effect of teacher experience on student learning have found a positive relationship between teachers' effectiveness and their years of experience, but the relationship observed is not always a significant or an entirely linear one (Klitgaard & Hall, 1974; Murnane & Phillips, 1981). The evidence currently available suggests that while inexperienced teachers are less effective than more senior teachers, the benefits of experience level off after a few years (Rivkin, Hanushek, & Kain, 2000).

The relationship between teacher experience and student achievement is difficult to interpret because this variable is highly affected by market conditions and/or motivation of women teachers to work during the child-rearing period. Harris and Sass (2007) point to a selection bias that can affect the validity of conclusions concerning the effect of teachers' years of experience: if less effective teachers are more likely to leave the profession, this may give the mistaken appearance that experience raises teacher effectiveness. Selection bias could, however, work in the opposite direction if the more able teachers with better opportunities to earn are those teachers most likely to leave the profession.

Participation in Professional Development Activities

Professional development activities can be conducted by many different organizations, in school and out of school, on the job or during sabbatical leave. On these occasions, practicing teachers update their content knowledge and teaching skills so they can meet the requirements of new curricula, consider new research findings on teaching and learning, and adapt to changes in the needs of the student population, and so on. Criticism has been leveled against the episodic nature of these activities and concern expressed that very little is known about what these activities really comprise and involve.

Conclusions in the literature on the relationship between teachers' participation in professional development activities and student outcomes are mixed. Some studies on in-service professional development have found no relationship to student achievement (see, in regard to mathematics and reading, Jacob & Lefgren, 2004). Other studies have found higher levels of student achievement linked to teachers' participation in professional development activities directly related to the area in which they are teaching (see, in regards to mathematics, Brown, Smith, & Stein, 1995; Cohen & Hill, 1977; Wiley & Yoon, 1995; and in regard to language and mathematics, Angrist & Lavy, 2001). Wenglinsky (2000) found a positive correlation between professional development activities aimed at the needs of special education students, and students' higher-order skills and laboratory skills in science. More recently, Harris and Sass (2007) identified what they call the "lagged effect of professional development," that is, the larger effect of teachers' professional development on student outcomes not becoming apparent until three years after the teachers had completed their courses.

The interpretation of the positive effect of participation in teacher professional development activities is not clear cut, as this variable is confounded with other teacher attributes, that is, teachers who participate in these activities are also likely to be more motivated and, usually, more specialized in the subjects they teach.

METHOD

Sample

The sample of teachers who participated in TIMSS 2003 in Israel comprised 371 mathematics teachers and 317 science teachers, who taught about 4,000 students in 149 sampled classes, each class in a different school. It became evident that in only about one quarter of the mathematics classes and about one third of the science classes all students were taught by a single teacher. In the rest of the classes, all students either were taught by more than one teacher, or students in one class were divided into groups, each of which was taught by one, or sometimes more than one, teacher.

In the present study, which examines the relationship between teacher characteristics and student achievement, it was essential to link teachers exclusively to the class or group of students they taught. Thus, a preliminary step in the analysis was identification of these specific learning units. In the process of preparing such a file, the sample of students who participated in the study was first reduced due to missing data on student or teacher variables relevant to this study. The resulting dataset was then used to identify the specific learning unit. Because grouping of students is very common in Israel, and frequently occurs within several same-grade classes, there were occasions when some students, originally studying with same-grade students from other classes, were identified in the sampled classes. These students, who were part of interclass groups and comprised a too small learning unit, were omitted from the analysis. The number of students omitted for this reason in mathematics (where grouping is very common) reached 625; in science, the number of omissions was 277. Table 1 presents the distribution of the remaining learning units according to the number of teachers assigned to teach each such unit (group of students) and the number of students studying in these groups.

Table 1: Learning units by number of teachers teaching them

Type of group according to number of teachers assigned to teach	Mathematics		Science	
	No. of groups	*No. of students*	*No. of groups*	*No. of students*
Groups taught by one teacher	143	2,036	110	1,656
Groups taught by two teachers	12	232	33	683
Groups taught by three (or more) teachers	1	22	11+(2)	298
Total	156	2,290	156	2,637
Missing		625		277
Total		2,915		2,914

We tested the representativeness of the reduced post-exclusions sample by comparing the achievement of students who remained in the analysis with the achievement of students in the sample before the exclusions. The result of a *t*-test showed a small but significant difference (5 to 6 points; 0.05–0.06 of a standard deviation of student score distribution) in favor of the "pre-exclusion" students. We considered this difference educationally meaningless, and the process of excluding students from the interclass groups did not seriously violate the representativeness of the sample. Table 2 presents the comparisons.

Table 2: Achievement of students before and after excluding students in small groups

The comparison groups	Science scores	t-value and sig.	Mathematics scores	t-value and sig.
Students in the groups left for the analysis	493 (80) n = 2,914	3.3**	498 (79) n = 2,915	3.9***
Students before excluding those from small groups	498 (77) n = 2,637		504 (78) n = 2,290	

Note: ** = $p \leq 001$, *** = $p \leq 0001$.

Data Source

We used the responses of teachers and principals to questions in the teacher and school questionnaires to determine the independent teacher variables. Six variables came from the teacher questionnaires; the remaining two came from the school questionnaire. Those variables already known to be associated with science and mathematics achievement (see, for example, extensive reviews by Darling-Hammond, 1999; Greenwald et al., 1996; Wayne & Youngs, 2003) describe teachers' academic preparation, their highest level of education, their preparedness for and feelings of readiness to teach subject matter(s), their years of teaching experience, and their participation in professional development activities. The variables that we drew from the TIMSS' questionnaires were:

1. The ethnic affiliation of the teacher (ISRARB), as inferred from the language used by the teacher with his or her students: 0–*Arabic speaking*; 1–*Hebrew speaking*.

2. Teacher's gender (TSEX): 0–*male*; 1–*female*.

3. Seniority as inferred from the number of years of teaching (TAUT), a continuous variable.

4. Teachers' highest levels of education (MA): 0–*up to and including first university degree*; 1–*beyond first university degree*.

5. Teachers' major areas of study in the field they teach (INFLD): 0–*study in areas other than the subject they teach*; 1–*study in the areas they teach*—mathematics or mathematics education, and, in the sciences, at least one of five relevant areas— biology, physics, chemistry, earth sciences, and science education; and 2–*study in at least one of the areas they teach and in addition in science or in mathematics education*.

6. Teachers' feeling of readiness to teach the content of instruction (READY), an index based on teachers' average responses toward a list of topics in mathematics and in science, on a scale of 1–*not feeling ready to teach the topics* to 3–*feeling highly ready to teach the topics*. The index was cut into three categories, indicating low, medium, and high readiness.

7. Extent of participation in professional development activities focusing on **content knowledge** (PDICK), on a scale of 1–*never or once or twice per year* to 4–*more than 10 times per year* (data from school questionnaire).

8. Extent of participation in professional development activities focusing on **pedagogy** (PEDAG), an index describing teachers' participation in four professional development activities: implementation of the national curriculum, improving school's own goals, improving teaching skills, and using ICT, on a scale of 1–*never or once or twice per year* to 4–*more than 10 times per year* (data from school questionnaire). The index was recoded into three categories indicating low participation (1), medium participation (2), and high participation (3).

The dependent variables used were the average estimates of the five plausible scores in mathematics or science.

Analyses

Two main analyses were carried out in this study. The first involved breaking down the group means of student achievement (dependent variable) by the categories of the different teacher variables (independent variables). We used the differences in achievement scores of students taught by teachers characterized by the extreme variable categories as the measures of teachers' effectiveness. The second analysis that we conducted was a multilevel regression analysis using hierarchical linear modeling software (HLM6) (Raudenbush, Bryk, Cheong, & Congdon, 2000), carried out using all five estimates of individual plausible values in mathematics or science.

The models specified for the analysis were two-level models of students nested in groups taught exclusively by one or more teachers. At their first level, the models contained three variables describing student characteristics. The first of these was *Number of books in student's home* (BOOK) on a scale of 1–*up to 10 books* to 5–*more than 200 books*. This variable provides a proxy of the socioeconomic and cultural background of each participating student's home. The second variable was *Student's self-confidence in learning the subject taught* (SCM/S1), a dummy variable derived from an index constructed for the TIMSS 2003 survey (Martin, Mullis, & Chrostowski, 2004). This variable indicated whether a student had *a lot of confidence* (1) or *not* (0). The third variable described the level of education students aspired to complete (ASPIR) on a scale of 1–*finish high school* to 5–*finish university beyond initial level*. At their second level, the models contained the eight above-described teacher variables. In cases where several teachers were teaching the same group of students, we averaged and sometimes rounded the values of their relevant variables.

To avoid problems of multicollinearity and to maximize interpretability, the second-level teacher variables were centered and standardized around their grand mean (Aiken & West, 1991, p. 43). Thus, their regression coefficients represent the change in achievement score points due to an increase by one standard deviation above the standardized mean of the relevant teacher variable.

The regression analyses were carried out separately for the two dependent variables. For each analysis, we specified three models. The first model was a "null" variance component model with no predictors. This model provided estimates of the variance components at each of the model's levels, indicating an upper limit to the explanatory power of the different models specified later. The second model included only the student-level variables; the third model also contained the second-level variables, that is, the teacher variables. The models specified for each dependent variable contained the same predictors at each level.

The most important outputs of this analysis were estimates of the regression coefficients of the predictors that indicate their effect on student achievement (the slopes of the predictor's regression lines). Allowing the coefficients of the first-level variables (student variables) to be modeled as random yields a "slope as outcome" model (Raudenbush & Bryk, 1986) in which the slope (regression coefficient) of a student-level variable is itself regressed over the higher-level teacher variables. This "slope as outcome" model is formally equivalent to an interaction model, indicating the existence of an interaction between a student-level variable, which varies randomly among the second-level units of analysis, and relevant second-level teacher variables.

The significant slope variation revealed for all student-level variables in our analysis justified our decision to look for interactions between these variables and the teacher variables or—to state this another way—to determine if student-level variables buffer the effect of teacher variables on achievement. In this study, we looked for interactions related to only one student-level variable—*Student's aspiration to finish a high level of academic education* (ASPIR). This variable is usually associated with both a student's intellectual capabilities and his or her socioeconomic background. The effects of the two other student variables were specified as fixed effects.

RESULTS

1. Breakdown of Group Achievement Scores by Categories of Teacher Variables

Table 3 presents the group mean achievement and its standard deviation as well as the gaps in the mean achievement of groups of students taught by teachers belonging to the distal categories of each teacher variable. In those cases where there were only a few groups in the distal categories, the categories were collapsed with others to render a more accurate picture. Large gaps indicate that the relevant teacher variable is associated with achievement (i.e., is effective).

Among the mathematics teacher variables, we found the following ones to be the most effective in terms of their association with student achievement.

- *Ethnic affiliation* (ISRARB): Students in groups taught by Hebrew-speaking mathematics teachers achieve more—almost three quarters of a standard deviation of the group's mean mathematics scores ($SD = .57$)—than do students studying in groups taught by Arabic-speaking teachers.

- *Gender* (TSEX): Students taught by female teachers achieve more—about a third of a group standard deviation—than do students taught by male teachers.

- *Seniority* (TAUT): Students studying in groups taught by mathematics teachers with more than 15 years of experience achieve more—by about a half of a group standard deviation—than do students studying in groups taught by mathematics teachers with less experience (five years or fewer).

Table 3: Breakdown of group mean achievement in mathematics and science by the categories of teacher variables

Teacher variables	Mathematics		Science	
	No. of groups 156	Group mean and SD	No. of groups 156	Group mean and SD
Ethnic affiliation (ISRARB)				
0 Arabic-speaking	40	465 (48)	35	464 (39)
1 Hebrew-speaking	116	507 (55)	121	490 (48)
Gap: Hebrew-speaking vs. Arabic-speaking	42		26	
Teacher's gender (TSEX)				
0 Male	30	480 (53)	26	477 (47)
1 Female	113	501 (57)	130	486 (47)
Gap: Female vs. male	21		9	
Second degree (MA)				
0 First degree or less	119	498 (55)	108	481 (45)
1 Second degree or more	37	493 (63)	48	491 (52)
Gap: Second degree vs. first degree	-5		10	
Seniority (TAUT)				
Up to 5 years	55	482 (55)	53	479 (45)
5–15 years	48	450 (56)	53	475 (46)
15+ years	53	507 (58)	50	499 (48)
Gap: High vs. low seniority	25		20	
Participation in content-oriented prof. development (PDICK)				
Never/Once or twice a year	20	485 (57)	18	465 (39)
3–5 times a year	55	493 (49)	49	482 (50)
6–10 times a year	43	507 (62)	46	492 (47)
More than 10 times a year	38	496 (51)	43	487 (47)
Gap: More than 10 times a year vs. never	11		22	
Participation in pedagogically-oriented prof. development (PEDAG)				
Never /Once or twice a year	60	506 (51)	62	488 (42)
3–10 times a year	59	491 (53)	39	486 (42)
More than 10 times a year	37	490 (69)	55	478 (56)
Gap: More than 10 times a year vs. never	-16		-4	
Major in subject-area being taught (INFLD)				
0 no major	10	502 (78)	3	466 (36)
1 majoring in at least one relevant content area	68	496 (55)	51	489 (43)
2 majoring in at least one relevant content area and in ped. content knowledge	78	497 (55)	102	482 (49)
Gap: Major in content and pedagogy vs. no major	-5		16	
Feeling ready to teach topics included in the list				
1 Low	55	492 (58)	75	477 (44)
2 Medium	32	502 (55)	29	478 (50)
3 High	69	497 (57)	52	498 (48)
Gap: High readiness vs. low readiness	5		21	

We found the rest of the mathematics teacher variables to be less associated with achievement. The mean group achievement of students taught by mathematics teachers who had a second degree or by teachers who had majored in at least one relevant subject area (e.g., mathematics or mathematics education) was slightly lower (about one tenth of a group standard deviation) than that for students studying in groups taught by teachers with a first or no academic degree, and lower again for those taught by teachers without a major in a relevant subject area. Teachers' feelings of readiness to teach mathematics topics seemed to have almost no effect on student outcomes in mathematics.

The results also revealed a slight advantage in achievement (about one fifth of a group standard deviation) in favor of students studying in groups taught by mathematics teachers who had participated frequently during the last year (more than 10 times) in **content-oriented** professional development activities over students of mathematics teachers who had either participated only once or twice a year in these types of activity or who had not participated at all. However, there was no apparent advantage in achievement—and, in fact, there was a slight disadvantage—for students who had intensively participated in **pedagogically-oriented** professional development activities over students of mathematics teachers who had rarely, if ever, participated in this type of professional development.

The picture regarding the achievement of students taught by science teachers was only partially similar. The effects of ethnic affiliation, gender, and seniority for students studying with science teachers were smaller than those detected in groups studying with mathematics teachers. However, the students studying in groups taught by Hebrew-speaking science teachers attained higher scores than the students in groups taught by Arabic-speaking science teachers, but only by about half a standard deviation of the group's mean distribution of science scores ($SD = .47$). Students in groups taught by female science teachers did better, but only moderately so (about a fifth of a group standard deviation) than students in groups studying with male science teachers.

The effect of seniority was almost the same in the two school subjects. Students studying in groups taught by teachers with more than 15 years of experience gained higher achievement scores than students studying in groups taught by teachers with fewer years of experience (about 0.4 of a group standard deviation).

Students taught by science teachers with a second degree or by teachers who had majored in at least one of five relevant subject areas and in **pedagogy** (science education) had achievement levels that were slightly higher (about one fifth to one third of a group standard deviation) than those of students studying in groups taught by science teachers with a first degree or less. Students taught by teachers who had majored in the field they taught also did better than those students taught by teachers who had not majored in the field they were teaching. This pattern contrasts with the pattern that emerged relative to mathematics teachers. There, having a second degree or majoring in the field of study was negatively associated with student achievement.

Students in groups taught by science teachers who felt highly ready to teach science topics outperformed students in groups taught by science teachers who did not feel the same degree of readiness (about half a group standard deviation).

We also found from our analyses that students in groups taught by science teachers who participated more than 10 times per year in content-oriented professional development activities had an achievement level about half a group standard deviation higher than that for students in groups taught by science teachers who had either minimally participated or had not participated at all in such activities. This effect was more profound among the science teachers than among the mathematics teachers. As was the case with the mathematics teachers, students studying with science teachers who intensively participated in pedagogically-oriented professional development activities had a lower level of achievement than students studying with science teachers who had not participated in such activities. This negative effect was less profound among the science teachers than among the mathematics teachers.

2. Multi-Level Regression Analysis

Table 4 sets out the results of the HLM analyses. The upper part of the table presents estimates of the variance components of each of the following models—the "null" or "basic" model with no explanatory variable, the "student-level" model, and the "full" model, which also included the teacher variables as well as a "slope as outcome" part, where the coefficients of the student-academic-aspiration variable were regressed on all teacher variables. Table 4 also presents the added explained variance to the between-group variance (BGV), in percentages beyond that explained by the student model, and the cumulative percentage of BGV explained, indicating the total explanatory power of the models. The lower part of the table presents the intercept of each regression equation, the estimated coefficients of all predictors, and the standard error of measurement.

In the full models, the coefficients of the teacher variables indicating main effects appeared first. Their second appearance indicated the effect of these variables on the slope of student academic aspiration. The statistically significant coefficients in the table reveal the interaction effect between teacher variables and student variables that can explain the differential effect of teacher variables on the achievement of students who differ in their academic aspirations.

As is evident from the table, the percentage of BGV relative to the total variance in outcomes was higher in mathematics (41.7%) than in science (27.4%), suggesting that grouping in mathematics is more likely to be based on ability than is grouping in science. In general, the explanatory power of the specified model was higher for mathematics than for science. Student variables, in both school subjects, explained only a small portion of the BGV (about 6.2% to 6.5%). The added percentage of the BGV that could be explained once we had included the teacher variables in the model amounted to almost 16 in mathematics but only about 6 in science. Also, the ratio between the added explanatory power of the BGV offered by the teacher variables compared to that offered by the student variables was 2.5:1 (15.5: 6.2)

Table 4: Results of the multilevel regression analysis of mathematics and science outcomes: Average of five plausible values

	Mathematics	N = 2,290 students in 156 groups		Science	N = 2,637 students in 156 groups	
	Null model	Students	Teachers	Null model	Students	Teachers
Variance components						
• Between-group variance	2,829 (41.7%)	2,653 (45.2%)	2,214 (36.8%)	1848 (27.4%)	1,728 (29.6%)	1,631 (21.4%)
• GHFSG1 Slope	–	43	33	–	20	15
• Within-group variance	3,958	3,167	3,173	4,896	4,085	4,082
• Total variance	6,787	5,863	6,020	6,744	5,833	5,728
• % of BSV explained beyond Model 1			16.5			5.6
• % of added BGV explained			15.5			5.2
• Cumulative % of BGV explained		6.2	21.7		6.5	11.7
Final estimation of student var. main effects						
Intercept	501.2 (4.5)***	417.9 (6.9)***	409.7 (12.9)***	491.7(3.8)***	400.1 (6.3)***	394.0 (15.0)***
Book slope #		5.9 (1.2)***	5.8 (1.2)***		6.9 (1.6)***	7.0 (1.6)***
SCM1 slope #		43.4 (2.8)***	43.3 (2.8)***		39.9 (4.4)***	39.9 (4.4)***
ASPIR slope		9.6 (1.2)***	5.4 (2.3)		11.3 (1.1)***	9.2 (3.5)*
MA			-11.6 (14.4)			10.1 (12.9)
ISRARB			36.2 (15.9)*			17.5 (14.3)
T_SEX			-18.8 (15.0)			-12.5 (15.0)
ZTAUT_M/S			4.2 (5.6)			0.1 (5.1)
ZMRDY_M/S			6.2 (5.7)			8.2 (6.6)
ZMPEDG_M/S			-22.4 (9.0)*			-16.1 (7.6)*
ZGPDIK_M/S			20.4 (9.4)*			8.7 (8.4)
ZNSINFLD			-6.7 (6.4)			1.9 (5.6)

Table 4: Results of the multilevel regression analysis of mathematics and science outcomes: Average of five plausible values (contd.)

	Mathematics			Science		
	Null model	N = 2,290 pupils in 156 students		Null model	N = 2,637 students in 156 groups	
		Students	Teachers		Students	Teachers
Final estimation for GHFSG1 slope						
MA			-1.0 (2.9)			-1.8 (2.5)
ISRARB			1.3 (3.1)			-0.3 (2.7)
T_SEX			7.0 (3.0)*			3.1 (3.1)
ZTAUT_M/S			0.6 (1.2)			0.6 (1.0)
ZMRDY_M/S			-1.1 (1.1)			-2.1 (1.5)
ZMPEDG_M/S			3.7 (1.8)*			3.1 (1.4)*
ZGPDK_M/S			-3.9 (1.9)*			-1.0 (1.7)
ZNSINFLD			0.7 (1.3)			-0.8 (1.1)

Notes:

BGV = Between-group variance

* = $p \leq .05$, · .08, ** = $p \leq .01$, *** = $p \leq .001$

= fixed effect

in mathematics and 0.8:1 (5.2: 6.5) in science. This finding indicates that the set of teacher variables chosen as measures of quality explained more of the BGV in mathematics than they did in science.

The HLM findings also supported the findings of the breakdown analysis. The relationship between teachers' ethnic affiliation and student achievement was found in both school subjects, although it reached significance only in mathematics. We also found, for both school subjects, a significant negative association between frequent participation in pedagogically-oriented professional development activities and student achievement. We furthermore found a positive main association between frequent participation in content-oriented professional development activities and achievement, but this relationship was significant only for mathematics. Teachers' feelings of readiness to teach science or mathematics showed a positive but non-significant relationship with student achievement.

Many of the variables describing teachers' qualifications did not yield similar relationships with student achievement in both school subjects. Mathematics teachers' advanced academic degrees and teachers having a major in the field of teaching seemed to have a negative association with students' outcomes in mathematics. However, in the case of science teachers, these variables showed a positive relationship with students' science outcomes. Teachers' years of experience had a positive, although not significant, relationship with student achievement in the case of mathematics teachers, but there was almost no such relationship in respect of science teachers. Although these relationships were not significant, the contrast is clear.

Teacher's gender was positively associated with student achievement in favor of female teachers, according to the breakdown analysis, and also when fitted as a single predictor in the multilevel analysis. However, when fitted with other teacher-level variables, teacher gender appeared to have a negative relationship with student outcomes, albeit not a statistically significant one, indicating that its effect was probably mediated by other teacher variables.

The analyses thus reveal that some of the teacher variables, such as having second degrees, majoring in the field of teaching, participating in content-oriented professional development activities, and seniority, which are taken as indicators of quality and considered desirable teacher qualifications and criteria for remuneration and reward systems, appear not to have a consistent positive association with student achievement in different school subjects. These associations, as will be elaborated in the next section, were also inconsistent for different students.

3. Interactions between Teacher Variables and Student Variables

Interesting significant interactions were found between teachers' participation in professional development activities and students' academic aspirations. The negative relationship between frequent participation in pedagogically-oriented professional activities and student achievement and the positive relationship between frequent participation in content-oriented professional development activities and student achievement were more profound for students with low academic aspirations. This pattern was significant in the case of mathematics but less clear in the case of science.

Plotting predicted mathematics and science group mean scores as a function of frequent participation of the students' teachers (low [minimal], mean, and high [maximal]) in pedagogically-oriented professional development activities (Figures 1 and 2) and plotting predicted mathematics group mean scores dependent on the frequent participation of the students' teachers in content-oriented professional development activities (Figure 3) for three values of students' academic aspiration (low, mean, and high) helps us to visualize and understand the interaction effect between students' characteristics and their teacher's attributes. The plots chosen refer only to the significant interactions found.

Figure 1: The relationship of frequent participation in pedagogically-oriented professional development activities with the achievement of students with different levels of academic aspiration (ASPIR), science

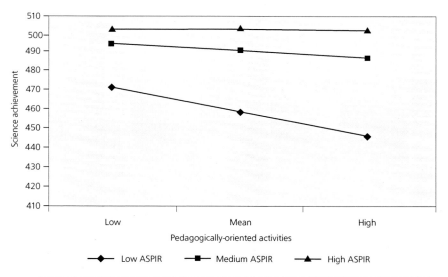

	Low	Mean	High
Low ASPIR	472.350	459.440	446.530
Medium ASPIR	495.151	491.311	487.471
High ASPIR	504.018	503.705	503.393

When students who score low on the scale of academic aspirations are taught by mathematics or science teachers who frequently participate in pedagogically-oriented professional development activities, they achieve less than when taught by teachers who do not, or only rarely, participate in such activities. This negative association is weak for students with mean academic aspirations and even weaker for students with high academic aspirations. Thus, intensity of participation of both mathematics and science teachers in pedagogically-oriented professional development activities seems to increase the achievement gap between high and low academically-motivated students.

Figure 2: The relationship of frequent participation in pedagogically-oriented professional development activities with the achievement of students with different levels of academic aspiration (ASPIR), mathematics

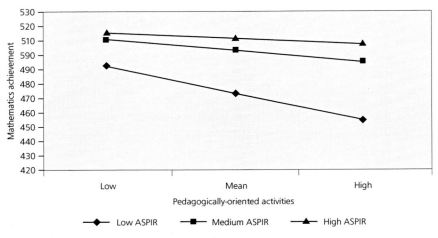

	Low	Mean	High
Low ASPIR	492.850	474.135	455.421
Medium ASPIR	509.915	502.178	494.440
High ASPIR	516.147	512.418	508.689

In contrast, mathematics teachers' frequent participation in content-oriented professional development activities has the opposite association with achievement of students with different academic aspirations. Teachers' frequent participation in content-oriented professional development activity was positively related to achievement of students with low academic aspirations, had a small positive association with the achievement of students with medium academic aspirations, and had almost no association with the achievement of students with medium or high academic aspirations. Thus, intensity of participation in content-oriented professional development activities narrows the gap between high and low academically-motivated students.

A positive interaction effect (significant only in the case of mathematics) was found between level of students' academic aspirations and another teacher variable—gender: achievement of students with high academic aspirations was fostered by female teachers. This interaction effect buffers the negative main association between teacher's gender and student achievement found in the full multilevel regression model.

Figure 3: The relationship of frequent participation in content-oriented professional development activities with the achievement of students with different levels of academic aspirations (ASPIR), mathematics

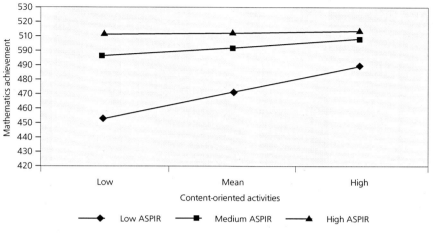

	Low	Mean	High
Low ASPIR	450.679	467.38	484.087
Medium ASPIR	490.112	495.426	500.739
High ASPIR	504.512	505.666	506.820

DISCUSSION

The results of these analyses are disappointing in terms of providing a clearer indication not only for policymakers in Israel but elsewhere on how best to improve the recruitment, education, and remuneration of teachers. Most of the teacher variables commonly regarded as desired qualifications or as indicators of quality, such as advanced academic degrees, securing a major in the subject being taught, and years of teaching experience that were adopted as reform targets in teacher policy and as criteria for remuneration, had only marginal and statistically non-significant positive relationships with student achievement. These associations, moreover, were inconsistent across the two subject areas and varied according to different student groupings. In interpreting these results, we begin with substantive explanations and later bring in others that are more methodological in nature.

Two variables had opposite (although not significant) influences in the two subject areas. The first was *having an advanced degree* and the second was *majoring in the field of teaching*. Both variables were *positively* but not significantly associated with achievement in science. However, they had a negative (but again not significant) association with achievement in mathematics, a result contrary to other findings (Goldhaber & Brewer, 1997, 2000; Rowan et al., 1997).

Rowan, Correnti, and Miller (2002) reported similar findings relative to teachers having advanced degrees. They found that neither teachers' mathematics certification nor teachers having post-graduate degrees in mathematics improved the achievement of their students (who, in this case, were in the upper grades of schools). Struggling to interpret their findings, the authors suggested that advanced academic training in mathematics somehow interferes with effective teaching, either because it limits time spent on professional pedagogical training or because it produces teachers who somehow cannot simplify and clarify their advanced understanding of mathematics for school students.

A possible explanation for the differential effects on student achievement brought about by the students' mathematics teachers or science teachers having advanced qualifications, a major in the subject of teaching, and a good number of years of experience could be found in the fundamental differences between these two subject areas. Because science is a constantly developing domain, science teachers with advanced and frequently updated education in their field of teaching may have a greater advantage. Mathematics, however, is regarded as a classic domain of knowledge, which means that what is taught in schools tends to be basic, and so teaching experience is more important than updated knowledge of the domain. Indeed, the positive main effect of experience in teaching mathematics confirms this.

The fact that the positive main association between frequent participation in content-oriented professional development activities and student achievement reached significance only for mathematics and the fact that the negative association between participating in pedagogically-oriented professional activities and student achievement reached significance in both mathematics and science could point to initial differences between teachers—those who prefer to upgrade their content knowledge and those who prefer to learn new pedagogical tools. Preference for content might indicate higher teacher qualifications.

The opposite associations were more profound for students with low academic aspirations. Teachers' intensive participation in pedagogically-oriented professional development activities appeared to contribute to outcome inequality among students with different academic aspirations, which usually is associated with level of socioeconomic status. The opposite occurred with respect to teachers' participation in content-oriented professional development activities, in that it appeared to narrow the achievement gap between students with different academic aspirations.

The relationships between the two types of professional development opportunities and the achievement of students differing in terms of their academic aspirations can be interpreted in the following way: highly motivated students (who are usually more able) are less sensitive to teachers' input; in many cases, they can manage on their own. The problems that students with low academic aspirations (usually less able) face require more focus on the content teachers teach, and this cannot be replaced by instructional strategies.

The findings in this study on the positive relationship between content-focused professional development activities and student achievement, at least for mathematics teachers, support policy interventions aimed at providing more such opportunities. The findings in this study on the negative association between participating in pedagogically-focused professional development activities (which are very popular in Israel) and student achievement suggest we should investigate what actually happens in such in-service training and how the knowledge gained in these courses is translated into action in classrooms. Another conclusion from our study is that policies related to recommended reforms in teacher education, rather than being broadly applicable and generic, need to account for the manner in which these effects vary across subject areas and across different types of students.

We also wish to offer some methodological explanations for the findings regarding the ineffectiveness of many teacher variables commonly regarded as relevant. One possible explanation could be the lack of variability in some teacher variables, which results in underestimation of their correlation with achievement. This is the case, for instance, with level of certification, which (according to the TIMSS 2003 data for Israel) did not correlate with student achievement because all teachers in Israel are fully certified. The non-linear effects or the low threshold effect that some teacher variables exhibit is another explanation. For instance, if a teacher has a first academic degree in mathematics, he or she is much more likely to have students gaining the higher scores on achievement tests than if he or she has only a non-university education. However, teachers' further education—for a second academic degree in mathematics—had no relationship with student achievement.

Multicollinearity between teacher variables can also mask the relationship between some of these variables and student achievement. Wayne and Youngs (2003) used the following example to illustrate this problem: analysis may show that having a Master's degree matters, but it is likely that teachers with a Master's degree also have more teaching experience. Thus, what appears attributable to a Master's degree may instead be attributable to experience. Studies, such as this present one, that assess multiple teacher characteristics simultaneously are therefore more reliable. Wayne and Youngs (2003) also posit that "failing to reject the null hypothesis [i.e., that the relationship can occur by chance] does not rule out a relationship. Perhaps the study's sample size was too small—the measurement error too great—to provide statistical confirmation. These issues prevent rejection of the possibility that differences occurred randomly, even if the qualification being studied does influence student achievement" (p. 93). For these reasons, Wayne and Youngs sum up by saying, "Studies may establish that an observed teacher quality indicator matters but cannot convincingly show that an observed teacher quality indicator does not matter" (p. 93).

These explanations provide cautions for policymakers who tend to conclude that teachers' formal education, certification, and procurement of a major in the subject of teaching are not indicators of quality. The teacher qualifications covered by this present study should therefore not be dismissed. However, there is also an obvious need to look for other important and more sensitive indicators of quality. Although not always easy to measure, attributes such as enthusiasm, motivation, charisma, ability to convey ideas clearly, and verbal ability should be added to the models that try to associate teachers' required qualifications with students' achievement outcomes.

References

Aiken, L. S., & West, S. G. (1991). *Multiple regression: Testing and interpreting interactions.* London, Newbury Park, New Delhi: Sage.

Alexander, R. (2000). *Culture and pedagogy: International comparisons in primary education.* Oxford: Basil Blackwell.

Andrew, M. D. (1990). Difference between graduates of 4-year and 5-year teacher preparation programs. *Journal of Teacher Education, 41*, 45–51.

Angrist, J. D., & Lavy, V. (2001). Does teacher training affect pupil learning? Evidence from matched pairings in Jerusalem public schools. *Journal of Labor Economics, 19*(2), 343–369.

Ariav, T., Olshtain, E., Alon, B., Back, S., Grienfeld, N., & Libman, Z. (2006). *Committee for guidelines for teacher education: Report on programs in higher education institutions in Israel.* Jerusalem: Council for Higher Education (in Hebrew).

Ashton, P., & Crocker, L. (1987). Systematic study of planned variation: The essential focus of teacher education reform. *Journal of Teacher Education*, May–June, 2–8.

Ballou, D., & Podgursky, M. (1997). Reforming teacher training and recruitment: A critical appraisal of the recommendations of the National Commission on Teaching and America's Future. *Government Unit Review, 17*(4).

Ballou, D., & Podgursky, M (1999). Teacher training and licensure: A layman's guide. In M. Kansteroo & C. Finn (Eds.), *Better teachers, better schools*. Washington, DC: The Thomas Fordham Foundation.

Ballou, D., & Podgursky, M. (2000). Reforming teacher preparation and licensing: What is the evidence? *Teacher College Records, 102*(1), 5–22.

Berliner, D. C. (1987). Simple views of effective teaching and a simple theory of classroom instruction. In D. C. Berliner & B. Rosenshine (Eds.), *Talks to teachers* (pp. 93–110). New York: Random House.

Berliner, D. C. (2005). The near impossibility of testing for teacher quality. *Journal of Teacher Education, 56*(3), 205–213.

Betts, J., Zau, A., & Rice, L. (2003). *Determinants of student achievement: New evidence from San Diego*. San Francisco, CA: Public Policy Institute of California.

Braun, H. J. (2005). *Using student progress to evaluate teachers: A primer on value-added models*. Princeton, NJ: Educational Testing Service. Available online at: http://www.ets.org/research/pic.

Brown, C. A., Smith, M. S., & Stein, M. K. (1995). *Linking teacher support to enhanced classroom instruction.* Paper presented at the annual conference of the American Educational Research Association, New York.

Bryk, S., & Hermanson, K. L. (1993). Educational indicator systems and observations on their structure, interpretation, and use. *Review of Research in Education, 19*, 451–484.

Cochran-Smith, M. (2001). The outcomes question in teacher education. *Teaching and Teacher Education, 17*, 527–546.

Cohen, D. K., & Hill, H. (1977). *Instructional policy and classroom performance: The mathematics reform in California*. Paper presented at the annual conference of the American Educational Research Association, Chicago, IL.

Darling-Hammond, L. (1992). Educational indicators and enlightened policy. *Educational Policy*, September, 235–265.

Darling-Hamond, L. (1994). Policy uses and indicators in making education count. *Developing and using international indicators* (pp. 357–378). Paris: Organisation for Economic Co-operation and Development.

Darling-Hammond, L. (1998). Teachers and teaching: Testing hypotheses from a national commission report. *Educational Researcher, 27*(1), 5–15.

Darling-Hammond, L. (1999). *Teacher quality and student achievement: A review of state policy evidence* (Research Report R-99-1). Washington DC: Center for the Study of Teaching and Policy, University of Washington.

Darling-Hammond, L. (2000a). How teacher education matters. *Journal of Teacher Education, 51*(3), 166–173.

Darling-Hammond, L. (2000b). Reforming teacher preparation and licensing: Continuing the debate. *Teachers College Record, 102*(1), 5–27.

Darling-Hammond, L., Berry, B., & Thorenson, A. (2001). Does teacher certification matter? Evaluating the evidence. *Educational Evaluation and Policy Analysis, 23*(1) 57–77.

Darling-Hammond, L., Chung, R., & Frelow, F. (2002). Variation in teacher preparation: How well do different pathways prepare teachers to teach? *Journal of Teacher Education, 53*(4), 286–302.

Dovrat Committee (Israel) Task Force for the Advancement of Education in Israel. (2005). *National plan for education*. Jerusalem: Government of Israel.

Ehrenberg, R. G., & Brewer, D. J. (1994). Do school and teacher characteristics matter? Evidence from high school and beyond. *Economics of Education Review, 13*, 1–17.

Everston, C. W., Hawley, W., & Zlotnik, M. (1985). Making a difference in educational quality through teacher education. *Journal of Teacher Education, 36*(3), 2–12.

Fenstermacher, G. D., & Richardson, V. (2005). On making determinations of quality in teaching. *Teachers College Record, 107*(1), 186–213.

Ferguson, R. F., & Ladd, H. F. (1996). How and why money matters: An analysis of Alabama schools. In H. F. Ladd (Ed.), *Holding schools accountable: Performance-based reform in education* (pp. 265–298). Washington, DC: Brooking Institution.

Ferguson, P., & Womack, S. T. (1993). The impact of subject matter and education coursework on teaching performance. *Journal of Teacher Education, 44*(1), 155–163.

Goldhaber, D. D., & Brewer, D. J. (1997). Evaluating the effect of teacher degree level on educational performance. In W. J. Fouler (Ed.), *Development in school finance, 1996* (pp. 197–210). Washington, DC: National Center for Education Statistics, US Department of Education.

Goldhaber, D. D., & Brewer, D. J. (2000). Does teacher certification matter? High school teacher certification status and student achievement. *Educational Evaluation and Policy Analysis, 22*(2), 129–145.

Greenwald, R., Hedges, L. V., & Laine, R. D. (1996). The effect of school resources on student achievement. *Review of Educational Research, 66*(3), 361–396.

Guyton, E., & Farokhi, F. (1987). Relationships among academic performance, basic skills, subject-matter knowledge, and teaching skills of teaching education graduates. *Journal of Teacher Education, 38*, 37–42.

Harris, D. N., & Sass, T. R. (2007). *Teacher training, teacher quality and student achievement.* Unpublished manuscript, Grant R305M04121 from US Department of Education.

Ingersoll, R. M. (2003). *Out of field teaching and the limits of teachers' policy: A research report.* Washington DC: Center for the Study of Teaching and Police, University of Washington.

Jacob, B. A., & Lefgren, L. (2004). The impact of teacher training on student achievement: Quasi-experimental evidence from school reform efforts in Chicago. *Journal of Human Resources, 39*(1), 50–79.

Kellaghan, T. (1996). IEA studies and educational policy. *Assessment in Education: Principles, Policy, and Practice, 3*(3), 143–160.

Kiesling, H. J. (1984). Assignment practices and the relationship of instructional time to the reading performance of elementary school children. *Economics of Education Review, 3*, 341–350.

Klitgaard, R. H., & Hall, G. R. (1974). Are there unusually effective schools? *Journal of Human Resources, 10*(3), 40–106.

Maagan, D. (2007). *Teaching staff survey in elementary schools (2005/6).* Jerusalem: Israel Central Bureau of Statistics (in Hebrew)

Martin, M. D., Mullis, I. V. S., & Chrostowski, S. J. (2004). *TIMSS 2003 technical report.* Boston, MA: Boston College.

McCaffrey, D. F., Lockwood, J. R., Koreetz, D., Louis, T. A., & Hamilton, L. (2004). Models for value-added modeling of teacher effects. *Journal of Educational and Behavioral Statistics, 29*(1), 67–101.

Monk, D. H. (1994). Subject area preparation of secondary mathematics and science: Teachers and student achievement. *Economics of Education Review, 13*, 125–145.

Monk, D. H., & King, J. (1994). Multilevel teacher resource effects on pupil performance in secondary mathematics and science. In R. G. Ehrenberg (Ed.), *Contemporary policy issues: Choices and consequences in education* (pp. 29–58). Ithaca, NY: ILR Press.

Murnane, R. J. (1996). Staffing the nation's schools with skilled teachers. In E. Hanushek & D. Jorgenson (Eds.), *Improving America's schools: The role of incentives* (pp. 241–256). Washington, DC: National Research Council, National Academy.

Murnane, R. J., & Phillips, B. (1981). Learning by doing, vintage, and selection: Three pieces of the puzzle relating teaching experience and teaching performance. *Economics of Education Review, 1*(4), 453–465.

National Commission on Teaching and America's Future (NCTAF). (1996). *What matters most: Teaching for America's future*. New York: Author.

Organisation for Economic Co-operation and Development (OECD). (2005). *Attracting, developing and retaining effective teachers. Final report: Teachers matter*. Paris: OECD Publishing.

Raudenbush, S. W., & Bryk, A. S. (1986). A hierarchical linear model: A review. *Sociology of Education, 59*, 1–17.

Raudenbush, S. W., Bryk, A. S., Cheong, Y. E., & Congdon, R. (2000). *Hierarchical linear and nonlinear modeling*. Lincolnwood, IL: Scientific Software International.

Rivkin, S. G., Hanushek, E. A., & Kain, J. F. (2000). *Teachers, schools and academic achievement* (working paper 6691, revised). Cambridge, MA: National Bureau of Economic Research.

Rowan, B., Chiang, F. S., & Miller, R. J. (1997). Using research on employees' performance to study the effects of teachers on students' achievement. *Sociology of Education, 70*, 256–285.

Rowan, B., Correnti, R., & Miller, R. (2002). What large scale survey research tells us about teacher effects on student achievement: Insights from the prospects study of elementary schools. *Teachers College Record, 104*(8), 1525–1567.

Sanders, W. L. (2000). Value-added assessment from student achievement data: Opportunities and hurdles. *Journal of Personnel Evaluation in Education, 14*(4), 329–339.

Sanders, W. L., & Rivers, J. C. (1996). *Cumulative and residual effects of teachers on future academic achievement*. Knoxville, TN: Value-Added Research and Assessment Center, University of Tennessee.

Santiago, P. (2002). *Teacher demand and supply: Improving teaching quality and addressing teacher shortage* (OECD Education Working Paper No. 1). Paris: OECD Head of Publication Service.

Shorrocks-Taylor, D. (2000). International comparisons of pupil performance: An introduction and discussion. In D. Shorrocks-Taylor & E.W. Jenkins (Eds.), *Learning from others* (pp. 13–28). Dordrecht: Kluwer.

United States Department of Education. (2002). *Meeting the highly qualified teachers' challenge*. Washington, DC: Author.

Wayne, A. J., & Youngs, P. (2003). Teacher characteristics and student achievement gains: A review. *Review of Educational Research, 73*(1), 89–122.

Wenglinsky, H. (2000). *How teaching matters: Bringing the classroom back into discussion of teacher quality policy*. Princeton, NJ: Educational Testing Services.

Wiley, D., & Yoon, B. (1995). Teacher reports of opportunity to learn analyses of the 1993 California learning assessment system. *Educational Evaluation and Policy Analysis, 17*(3), 355–370.

Wilson, S. M., Darling-Hammond, L., & Berry, B. (2001). Steady work: The story of Connecticut's reform. *American Educator, 25*(3), 34–39, 48.

Wilson, S. M., Floden, R. E., & Ferrini-Mundy, J. (2001). *Teacher preparation research: Current knowledge, gaps, and recommendations. A research report.* Washington DC: Center for the Study of Teaching and Policy, in collaboration with Michigan State University, University of Washington.

Equivalence of item difficulties across national versions of the PIRLS and PISA reading assessments

Aletta Grisay
University of Liège, Belgium

Eugenio Gonzalez
Educational Testing Service, Princeton, New Jersey, United States

Christian Monseur
University of Liège, Belgium

International comparisons of reading literacy are often considered to depend more than international comparisons of mathematics and science do on the quality of the translations into the various languages that are used for instruction in the participating countries. Major cross-language differences in factors related to reading can make it difficult to maintain cognitive requirement equivalence of the test items, thus affecting their relative difficulty for students assessed in different languages. The study presented in this article used Rasch item parameters from two large-scale reading assessments— the Progress in International Reading Literacy Study (PIRLS) 2001 and the Programme for International Student Assessment (PISA) 2000—to develop two indicators aimed at exploring the equivalence of item difficulties obtained across the various national versions of both tests. The results appeared to be rather similar in PIRLS and PISA. First, in both studies, about 80% of the variance of item difficulties could be explained by a common factor, and the mean absolute magnitude of differential item functioning (DIF) was about one third of a logit. There was no evidence that the impact of language differences might have been greater for the younger PIRLS examinees than for the older students assessed in PISA. Second, both the PIRLS and the PISA data confirmed a general pattern previously observed (Grisay & Monseur, 2007) wherein lower levels of equivalence in item difficulties are found for most versions in non-Indo-European languages and/or versions used in low-GDP countries. Third, as expected, the PIRLS and PISA countries that used versions in a same language (either the English source version or a common version developed co-operatively by several countries sharing the same language) typically obtained more equivalent item difficulties than countries using versions in different languages. The "cost" of translation, in terms of equivalence, could be tentatively assessed by comparing the values of the indicators obtained in the various regions of a single English-speaking country (Australia) to other relevant groups of countries. Finally, it was observed that equivalence issues mainly concerned individual items rather than the sets of items associated with particular reading passages—a finding which does not confirm the common criticism that the selection of passages is a major source of bias in international reading assessments.

INTRODUCTION AND BACKGROUND TO THE STUDY

Since the International Association for the Evaluation of Educational Achievement (IEA) began conducting its activities in the 1960s, various commentators have expressed concern about whether reading assessments that use translated instruments in countries with diverse cultures can be considered comparable. In the report of the findings of the first IEA Reading Comprehension Study (Thorndike, 1973), the author commented that while reading could probably be considered a less curriculum-oriented domain than mathematics and science, cultural and linguistic differences were likely to pose a greater threat to the equivalence of reading assessments:

> In the field of reading, there seems to be much more consensus [than in other subject areas] as to the objectives of instruction. Each country would accept without question, we believe, the proposition that it is desirable that children learn to read with complete comprehension materials of a variety of styles and contents and to read them at a relatively rapid rate. The particular emphasis on different types of reading materials—expository as opposed to literary, prose as opposed to poetry, etc.—might vary to some extent from country to country and from school to school within a country, but there would be general agreement that children should be able to get meaning efficiently from written material of various styles and content areas. On the other hand, the preparation of genuinely equivalent tests in reading, where the essence of the task involves very intimately the language of a particular country, would seem to present very serious difficulties. (p. 14)

Interestingly, the group of researchers who conducted the IEA Six Subject Study considered that splitting mother language achievement into two components (reading comprehension and understanding literature) would be a more appropriate method than including both aspects in a single reading literacy assessment, as has been the case in more recent assessments such as the IEA Reading Literacy Study (RLS), IEA Progress in Reading Literacy Study (PIRLS), and the Organisation for Economic Co-operation and Development (OECD) Programme for International Student Assessment (PISA). One of the reasons the researchers gave when debating this matter was that literature is a particularly risky domain because "... aesthetic nuances of style seemed difficult to preserve from one language to another," whereas reading comprehension allows one "to focus upon the cognitive content of the passage, and to forego most efforts to get at any appraisal of style, feeling, tone, or literary techniques" (Thorndike, 1973, p. 19).

Accordingly, the reading comprehension material of the first IEA/RCS study was mainly composed of expository prose passages, with the student primarily expected to understand the information conveyed by the text, and it comprised only items that would be classified as "locate information" and "interpret" in the PISA 2000 reading framework. In contrast, it was anticipated that the students' patterns of response would be culturally variable in the IEA/Literature study, which comprised six literary passages, with items that mainly assessed dimensions defined in PISA as "reflect on the content of the text" and "reflect on the form of the text."

In both these early IEA studies, the researchers conducted detailed analyses on all items that showed unusual statistics in specific countries (e.g., when one or more of the distractors used in a multiple-choice item attracted a significantly higher or lesser proportion of respondents in one or more countries than in other countries). The authors also checked if the instruments had approximately the same spread of item difficulties in each country and about the same alpha reliability.

In discussing the psychometric properties of the reading comprehension test, Thorndike (1973) concluded that there was a "slight tendency for the reliabilities to be higher in the English-speaking countries" (p. 54). He attributed this outcome to the fact that "the basic and editorial work on the items was done on the English language version" (p. 54) and that only some of the materials had been field-trialled in each of the other languages. In his view, however, "the tests functioned relatively satisfactorily in translation" (p. 55), except in two countries—India and Iran. There, the reliabilities were much lower, and, for too many items, the percentage of correct answers did not fall above the chance level, possibly because of the low performance of the Indian and Iranian students, or because of translation or cultural problems.

In the literature study, and contrary to the test-developers' expectations, the test items appeared to have rather similar psychometric characteristics in most countries (i.e., the items with low discrimination in English countries also tended to show poor discrimination in other languages), and to be less sensitive than anticipated to curricular or cultural differences (Purves, 1973). In this respect, the items functioned much like the items comprising the reading comprehension instrument. In fact, the correlation between the literature and the reading comprehension scores was extremely high in all countries, as was the case in PISA 2000 for the correlations between the "reflect" scale scores and the other reading scale scores. Moreover, the researchers found no clear correlation between the levels of proficiency of students relative to groups of literature items measuring particular aspects of their response to a text (e.g., test items related to readers' perception of text style) and the dominant "patterns of response to literature" in their countries (e.g., teachers' emphasis on text style), as measured by the students' and the teachers' questionnaire instruments.

Two decades after the Six Subject Study, Rasch analyses were conducted for the first time in an international reading assessment, namely, the IEA Reading Literacy Study (Elley, 1992), in order to identify and drop items with differential item functioning (DIF). Half of the items initially developed survived the field trial phase, and a few additional ones were deleted during the main study phase. As a further check, the national difficulties of the items (expressed as percentages of correct answers) were plotted against the international difficulties for each country. The mean rank order correlation of item difficulties was 0.92 for Population A (9-year-old students) and 0.91 for Population B (14-year-old students). The results of these analyses led Elley (1992) to draw this conclusion:

> While some minor features may still be found to exist which a few observers would perceive as lending a cultural bias, the statistics reveal that students in each country did in fact respond in a similar fashion to the items, allowing for differences in ability. Moreover, the items did behave in similar fashion in each country. ... The reader can have reasonable confidence that the test results were as comparable across countries as in any standardised test within a single country. (p. 97)

However, this inference was perhaps overly optimistic. In both populations, the rank correlations between national and international item difficulties tended to be slightly higher in the English-speaking and most of the European countries than in the Asian and developing countries. The lowest coefficients were observed for Population B in the Philippines (0.84), Hong Kong (0.82), Botswana (0.77), and Thailand (0.74), suggesting that the assessment instrument behaved differently in Western than in other cultures.

In the OECD PISA study, the equivalence of item difficulties across national versions (expressed as Rasch difficulty estimates) was explored for the three domains assessed: reading (Grisay & Monseur, 2007) and science and mathematics (Grisay, de Jong, Gebhardt, Berezner, & Halleux-Monseur, 2007). The indicators of equivalence used in these two studies were the commonalities obtained from principal component analyses, in which the item difficulty estimates were used as observations and the various versions were used as variables. The variance in item difficulties explained by the main factor tended to be higher in mathematics (91% of the total variance) than in reading (82%) and science (79%). The commonalities tended to be lower in all three domains for versions translated into non-Indo-European languages (particularly Asian and Middle-East languages) as well as for national versions used in the developing countries.

In a more recent study on the equivalence of item difficulties of the PISA 2006 science assessment across the participating countries, Monseur and Halleux (2009) used the mean absolute deviations of national from international item difficulties as an indicator of the global amount of DIF in each national version. Because the PISA 2006 database contains a relatively large number of countries that used more than one national language in the assessment, the authors were able to use this subset of countries in an analysis of variance (ANOVA) model, in order to disentangle the components of variance of the global indicator into the following: a main effect due to countries' cultural and curricular differences, a main effect due to language differences between the versions used in multilingual countries, a main effect due to possible differences in the functioning of the various test units used in the assessment (stimuli and accompanying questions), and the related interaction effects.

Given the similarities in the results from these different studies, it seemed of interest to expand the analysis by comparing the equivalence of item difficulties in a same domain (reading), but this time using data from students at the primary and secondary levels. The databases from PIRLS 2001 and PISA 2000 were retained. PIRLS 2001 sampled from a population defined as students attending the fourth year of primary education in each participating country, a point at which most students are 9 or 10 years old and are expected to have acquired relatively fluent reading abilities, and so are less dependent on their initial learning of decoding skills. PISA 2000 sampled from an age population, defined as 15-year-old students, in an attempt to measure students' reading proficiency at a time when, in most countries, students are reaching the end of their compulsory schooling.

The two assessments differed somewhat as regards the types of texts used. PIRLS included mainly continuous literary and informative texts, while PISA included both continuous prose (both literary and informative) and non-continuous documents. The processes measured (retrieving information, inferring, interpreting and integrating information, and evaluating the content and the language) were relatively similar, as was the proportion of items presented in multiple-choice and open-ended formats. A total of 43 countries participated in PISA 2000; 35 participated in PIRLS 2001. The two sets of participating countries differed significantly, with a majority of industrialized, high-GDP countries in PISA, and only a minority of developing countries. By contrast, the participation in PIRLS was more equally balanced between industrialized and developing countries.

In this study, two indicators were developed to explore the equivalence of the reading assessment instruments employed respectively in PIRLS 2001 and PISA 2000: an indicator of commonality of item difficulty (i.e., the proportion of variance in national parameters that can be explained by the international dimension in each national version), and an indicator of global magnitude of DIF (i.e., the mean absolute value of the difference between national and international parameters, expressed in logits).[1] Although these two indicators are highly correlated (about 0.90 in both studies), they are not identical. In particular, the indicator of global magnitude of DIF includes information on the dispersion of DIF in each country—information that is not included in the commonality indicator.

---

1 The item response theory (IRT) models used in the PISA and PIRLS international analyses were, respectively, a Rasch model and a three-parameters model. To obtain comparable estimations of the item difficulties in both studies, the PIRLS data were reanalyzed using a Rasch model.

ANALYSES, FINDINGS, AND INTERPRETATIONS

Commonalities and Global Amount of DIF in the National Versions of the PIRLS 2001 and PISA 2000 Reading Tests

These analyses were based on all items that were available for all national versions in all PIRLS or PISA participating countries. Items with missing data at the national level were dropped and the national item parameters were recentered to mean of zero. The PIRLS dataset thus contained 96 items, common to 43 national versions in 35 countries. The PISA dataset contained 121 items, common to 47 versions in 43 countries.[2] The indicators obtained are presented in Figures 1 and 2.[3]

Several similarities can be observed between PIRLS and PISA in Figures 1 and 2, even though the populations used and the sets of countries participating in the two studies[4] differed considerably:

1. In both studies, the mean commonality was about 80% of the total variance in item difficulties (79.4% in PIRLS, 81.9% in PISA). The mean absolute magnitude of DIF was 0.388 logit in PIRLS and 0.334 logit in PISA, suggesting that the average level of equivalence obtained in the studies was rather similar.

2. However, in both studies, there were at least some national versions with clearly concerning values for these two indicators (e.g., commonalities less than 70%, or mean absolute value of DIF greater than 0.500 logit).

3. As can be seen in Table 2, in both studies, the commonalities were lower and the mean absolute magnitude of DIF was higher for versions translated into non-Indo-European languages.[5]

4. In both studies, the commonalities tended to be lower and the mean absolute magnitude of DIF tended to be higher for the versions used in developing countries than for the versions used in industrialized countries. In Table 3, the mean values of the indicators are presented for two groups of countries in each study: the 10 participating countries with the highest GDP, and the 10 countries with the lowest GDP.

---

2 Liechtenstein was dropped from the PISA analyses because the number of students assessed was too low. Similarly, some of the minority versions used in certain PISA countries for a too small number of students (e.g., the German version used in Belgium) were ignored.

3 The names of the national versions appear as abbreviations in Figures 1 and 2 (e.g., CAN.ENG: Canada, English version; CAN.FRE: Canada, French version). A complete list of these abbreviations is provided in Table 1.

4 A total of 24 national versions using the same language in the same country was used in both studies. In Appendix 1, a plot of the mean magnitude of DIF for PISA and PIRLS for those 24 versions has been presented. With the exception of Iceland, where both the commonality and the magnitude of DIF pointed at a much lower level of equivalence in PIRLS than in PISA, the results appeared to be reasonably consistent across the two studies. When excluding Iceland, the correlation of PIRLS and PISA mean magnitudes of DIF was 0.642.

5 Non-Indo-European languages used in PIRLS and PISA include Arabic, Bahasa Indonesian, Chinese, Finnish, Hebrew, Hungarian, Japanese, Korean, and Turkish.

Table 1: Country name abbreviations for PIRLS and PISA

PIRLS			PISA		
Abbreviation	*Country*	*Language*	*Abbreviation*	*Country*	*Language*
ARG.SPA	Argentina	Spanish	ALB.ALB	Albania	Albanian
BGR.BUL	Bulgaria	Bulgar	ARG.SPA	Argentina	Spanish
BLZ.ENG	Belize	English	AUS.ENG	Australia	English
CAN.ENG	Canada	English	AUT.GER	Austria	German
CAN.FRE	Canada	French	BEL.DUT	Belgium	Dutch
COL.SPA	Colombia	Spanish	BEL.FRE	Belgium	French
CYP.GRE	Cyprus	Greek	BGR.BUL	Bulgaria	Bulgar
CZE.CZE	Czech Republic	Czech	BRA.POR	Brazil	Portuguese
DEU.GER	Germany	German	CAN.ENG	Canada	English
ENG.ENG	England	English	CAN.FRE	Canada	French
FRA.FRE	France	French	CHE.FRE	Switzerland	French
GRC.GRE	Greece	Greek	CHE.GER	Switzerland	German
HKG.CHI	Hong Kong SAR	Chinese	CHE.ITA	Switzerland	Italian
HUN.HUN	Hungary	Hungarian	CHL.SPA	Chile	Spanish
IRN.FAR	Iran, Islamic Rep. of	Farsi	CZE.CZE	Czech Republic	Czech
ISL.ICE	Iceland	Icelandic	DEU.GER	Germany	German
ISR.ARA	Israel	Arabic	DNK.DAN	Denmark	Danish
ISR.HEB	Israel	Hebrew	ESP.SPA	Spain	Spanish
ITA.ITA	Italy	Italian	FIN.FIN	Finland	Finnish
KWT.ARA	Kuwait	Arabic	FRA.FRE	France	French
LTU.LIT	Lithuania	Lithuanian	GRC.GRE	Greece	Greek
LVA.LAV	Latvia	Latvian	HKG.CHI	Hong Kong SAR	Chinese
LVA.RUS	Latvia	Russian	HUN.HUN	Hungary	Hungarian
MDA.ROM	Moldova, Rep. of	Romanian	IND.IND	Indonesia	Bahasa Indonesian
MDA.RUS	Moldova, Rep. of	Russian	IRL.ENG	Ireland	English
MKD.ALB	Macedonia, Rep. of	Albanian	ISL.ICE	Iceland	Icelandic
MKD.MAC	Macedonia, Rep. of	Macedonian	ISR.HEB	Israel	Hebrew
MOR.ARA	Morocco	Arabic	ITA.ITA	Italy	Italian
NLD.DUT	Netherlands	Dutch	JPN.JPN	Japan	Japanese
NOR.BOK	Norway	Bokmål	KOR.KOR	Korea	Korean
NOR.NYN	Norway	Nynorsk	LUX.GER	Luxembourg	German
NZL.ENG	New Zealand	English	LVA.LAV	Latvia	Latvian
ROM.HUN	Romania	Hungarian	MEX.SPA	Mexico	Spanish
ROM.ROM	Romania	Romanian	MKD.MAC	Mecdeonia, Rep. of	Macedonian
RUS.RUS	Russian Federation	Russian	NLD.DUT	Netherlands	Dutch
SCO.ENG	Scotland	English	NOR.NOR	Norway	Bokmål
SGP.ENG	Singapore	English	NZL.ENG	New Zealand	English
SVK.HUN	Slovak Republic	Hungarian	PER.SPA	Peru	Spanish
SVK.SVK	Slovak Republic	Slovak	POL.POL	Poland	Polish
SVN.SVN	Slovenia	Slovenian	PRT.POR	Portugal	Portogese
SWE.SWE	Sweden	Swedish	ROM.ROM	Romania	Romanian
TUR.TUR	Turkey	Turkish	RUS.RUS	Russian Fed.	Russian
USA.ENG	United States	English	SCO.ENG	Scotland	English
			SWE.SWE	Sweden	Swedish
			THA.THA	Thailand	Thai
			USA.ENG	United States	English

Figure 1: PIRLS 2001 and PISA 2000 reading: Commonalities of item difficulties across the national versions of the assessment

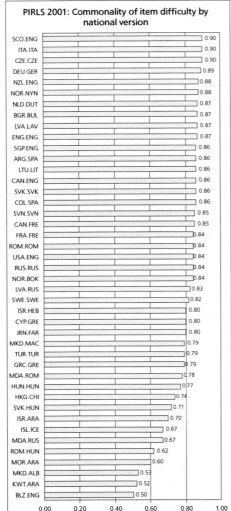

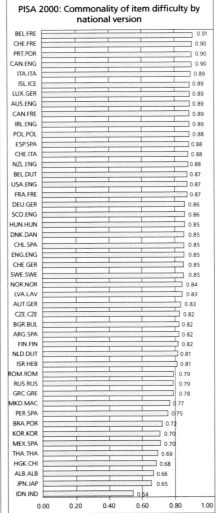

Figure 2: PIRLS 2001 and PISA 2000 reading: Mean absolute magnitude of DIF

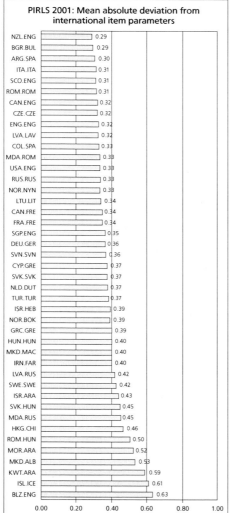

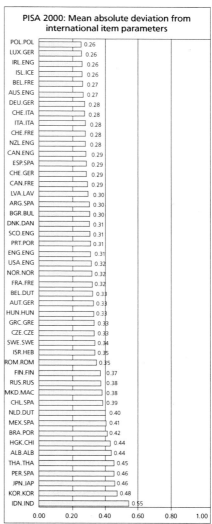

Table 2: Mean commonalities and mean magnitude of DIF in versions using Indo-European and non-Indo-European languages

	Studies	Mean commonality	Mean absolute magnitude of DIF
Indo-European languages	PIRLS (35 versions)	0.81	0.375
	PISA (39 versions)	0.84	0.321
Non-Indo-European languages	PIRLS (8 versions)	0.73	0.454
	PISA (8 versions)	0.72	0.426

Table 3: Mean commonalities and mean magnitude of DIF in groups of countries with the highest and lowest GDP

	Studies	Mean GDP ($US)	Mean commonality	Mean absolute magnitude of DIF
Ten countries with the highest GDP	PIRLS (13 versions)	34,251	0.84	0.376
	PISA (13 versions)	38,368	0.85	0.302
Ten countries with the lowest GDP	PIRLS (13 versions)	7,208	0.73	0.416
	PISA (10 versions)	7,899	0.74	0.414

How can these differences be interpreted, and to what extent is their magnitude a threat for the international comparability of the instruments used in the assessments? The patterns emerging from Tables 2 and 3 suggest at least two potential sources of variation in the equivalence of item difficulties. The first suggested source is linguistic differences, given that the versions translated into languages that are most distant from English and other Indo-European languages tended to have greater amounts of DIF. And the second suspected source is cultural differences because the group of versions used in Western industrialized countries tended to "behave" in more similar ways than those used in other countries.

Some overlap was evident between these two factors: many countries with non-Indo-European languages are also countries with relatively low GDP. Regression analyses using the mean commonalities as a dependent variable were conducted in order to estimate three potential components of variance of the indicator of commonality: the variance explained by the dichotomous variable "language group" (i.e., Indo-

European versus non-Indo-European language) after controlling for GDP; the variance explained by GDP after controlling for language group; and the variance explained jointly by both variables.

In PIRLS, a total of 33% of the variance in commonalities could be explained by the countries' GDP and the dichotomous variable "language group." Of this percentage, about 10% was unique variance explained by GDP, 18% was unique variance explained by "language group," and 5% was variance jointly explained by both predictors. In PISA, the total variance explained was higher (54%), of which 24% was uniquely explained by "language group," 23% was uniquely explained by GDP, and 7% was jointly explained by both predictors. Similar results were obtained when using the mean magnitude of DIF as the dependent variable. These findings confirmed that, despite the overlap, both the language group and the GDP had statistically significant unique effects on the equivalence of item difficulties.

Other possible sources of variation in equivalence could be the following:

1. Differences in the amount of error variance, particularly for versions used to assess linguistic minorities, which were often administered to small sub-samples of students. Because all item parameter estimates used in the analyses were subject to errors (particularly those due to sampling variance), the values presented in Figures 1 and 2 can be considered as estimations of the minimum value of commonalities and of the maximum value of magnitude of DIF. It must be noted, however, that adding the sample size as a predictor in the regressions described above increased the variance explained to a marginal extent only—less than 1.5% in both studies.

2. Differences in the reading curriculum taught to the students.

3. Uneven quality of the translations.

To further explore these issues, some other analyses were conducted.

Commonalities and Global Amount of DIF in the Reading Data Collected in the Various States of a Single Federal Country

In order to appreciate the extent to which the test results were "as comparable across countries as in any standardised test within a single country" (Elley, 1992, p. 97), it seemed of interest to compute the two indicators for each of the sub-samples of students assessed in a monolingual federal country. The PISA 2000 dataset collected in Australia was used for this exercise because English was the language used for the assessment in all six states and two territories in that country. As such, no translation bias would be at play and cultural and curricular differences could be expected to be minimal.

Independent Rasch analyses were conducted for each of the states and territories, and the absolute differences from the item parameters of the country as a whole were computed. Commonalities were obtained from a principal component analysis using the items as observations and the states as variables. The results are presented in Table 4.

Table 4: PISA 2000: Mean commonalities and mean absolute amount of DIF in Australia's states and territories

States and territories	Mean commonality	Mean absolute magnitude of DIF
ST1	0.96	0.160
ST2	0.97	0.142
ST3	0.97	0.139
ST4	0.97	0.149
ST5	0.95	0.177
ST6	0.97	0.142
ST7	0.96	0.165
ST8	0.93	0.212

As expected, the differences were small: most of them were probably due to some technical instability related to the small size of the sub-samples, or to some within-country cultural variation (for example, State 8 had a larger proportion of schools attended by Aboriginal students than did schools in the other states). These results suggest that, in PISA, if all versions used by the participating countries had been as equivalent as was the source version across the various regions in Australia, the average commonality in Figure 1 would probably be around 95% rather than 82% of the variance in item difficulties, and the average magnitude of DIF in Figure 3 would be around 0.15 logit rather than 0.34. In terms of equivalence, these findings give a rough estimation of the "cost" associated with the fact that PISA was not a national but an international assessment, and that it included countries with many different languages and with very diverse cultures and curricula.

Commonalities and Global Amount of DIF in the National Versions of Different Countries Using the Same Language of Instruction

In both PIRLS and PISA, several countries shared the language of instruction. One would therefore expect smaller differences in the item difficulties *within* the groups of versions in a specific language than across different languages, not only because of the common language itself but also because countries using the same language often have historical, cultural, and even curricular similarities. The level of DIF can also be expected to be lower when all countries with a given language use a common version, and somewhat higher when countries use independent translations.

All English-speaking countries participating in the assessments used the source version provided by the PISA International Study Center and by the PIRLS International Study Center, and they included in it some national adaptations. In PISA, a second source version was also provided in French for use by French-speaking countries. As regards other common languages, some countries developed co-operatively a common translation, and then included some national adaptations; others borrowed for their linguistic minorities a version developed by another country; and still others preferred to use their own independent translations.

For each group of languages, the absolute differences between the item difficulties of each national version and the parameters of the whole language group were computed.[6] The results for the English group are presented in Tables 5 (for PIRLS) and 6 (for PISA). In PIRLS, because the English version used in Belize was a clear outlier,[7] two sets of results are presented, first including and then excluding this country.

Table 5: PIRLS 2001: Mean absolute magnitude of DIF within the group of English-speaking countries

National versions	Mean absolute magnitude of DIF (including Belize)	Mean absolute magnitude of DIF (excluding Belize)
BLZ.ENG	0.569	
CAN.ENG	0.214	0.166
ENG.ENG	0.205	0.176
NZL.ENG	0.194	0.163
SCO.ENG	0.198	0.179
SGP.ENG	0.291	0.283
USA.ENG	0.203	0.183
Mean index value across English-speaking countries	**0.268**	**0.192**

Table 6: PISA 2000: Mean absolute magnitude of DIF within the group of English-speaking countries

National versions	Mean absolute magnitude of DIF
AUS.ENG	0.108
CAN.ENG	0.132
ENG.ENG	0.133
IRL.ENG	0.188
NZL.ENG	0.122
SCO.ENG	0.169
USA.ENG	0.196
Mean index value across English-speaking countries	**0.150**

The mean absolute amount of DIF was not much higher in the comparison of the various versions used in English-speaking countries (Tables 5 and 6) than in the former comparison of the Australian states and territories (Table 4). This outcome suggests

6 Because the correlation between commonalities and magnitude of DIF was more than -0.90 in both studies, only the latter indicator was used in the following analyses.

7 The very high magnitude of DIF in Belize was possibly due to the fact that English is not the native language of most students in that country. The situation in Singapore is somewhat similar.

that, in both PIRLS and PISA, neither the national adaptations included in the source version by the English-speaking countries nor their cultural or curricular differences played a major role in terms of equivalence. The picture proved more complex, however, for the other "common" languages, as suggested by the information presented in Table 7.

In PISA, the groups of countries using Dutch, French, German, and Italian developed a common translation into each of these languages, and derived from it their national versions, with a limited number of adaptations. By contrast, each country within the group using Spanish developed its own independent translation. Countries using Portuguese presented an intermediate case: Brazil borrowed the Portuguese translation developed by Portugal, but reworked it quite substantially to take into account the differences between the dialects spoken in the two countries. As expected, the amount of DIF within language groups using the same *common* version was comparable to the DIF observed in Tables 5 and 6 within the English group (usually less than 0.15 logit). By contrast, the differences between the *independent* versions used in the Spanish-speaking countries were substantially larger (mostly between 0.25 to 0.30 logit).

In PIRLS, several countries borrowed the Russian version developed by Russia and adapted it for use in those of their schools attended by Russian-speaking minorities. In the other PIRLS language groups presented in Table 7, each country developed its own independent translation. Compared to the pattern of results for PISA, the pattern of results for PIRLS seemed to be the reverse: the amount of within-language DIF was higher for the common Russian version (about 0.30 logit) and lower for most of the language groups with independent translations (French, Greek, Romanian, and Spanish versions: 0.20 logit or less). Only the three independent Arabic versions showed large within-language DIF, as was the case in PISA for the independent Spanish versions.

Components of Variance in Item Difficulties across the National Versions of Countries Using the Same Language of Instruction

With a view to exploring some of the effects that might contribute to variance in the relative item difficulties, a variance component analysis was conducted on the most common languages in both surveys. Table 8 presents the number of national versions per language included in the analysis (only those languages used for at least three national versions were included).

The variance component analysis is represented graphically in Figure 3. The four effects are (1) the unit, that is, the reading stimulus (usually a text) and the various items related to that stimulus; (2) the item; (3) the language; and (4) the national version. As shown in Figure 3, the effect *national version* is embedded in the *language* effect, and the *item* effect is embedded in the *unit* effect. The dependent variable is the *item by version interaction*. Because the item difficulty estimates are centered by national version, the effect *version* is equal to 0, and the effect *language* is consequently also equal to 0. Also, because the sum of the *item by version interaction* per item is equal

Table 7: Mean absolute amount of DIF within other language groups

PIRLS 2001*

Versions	Mean absolute magnitude of DIF		Mean magnitude across the whole language group
ISR.ARA	0.307	Arabic	0.331
KWT.ARA	0.404		
MOR.ARA	0.280		
CAN.FRE	0.198	French	0.198
FRA.FRE	0.198		
CYP.GRE	0.180	Greek	0.180
GRC.GRE	0.180		
MDA.ROM	0.218	Romanian	0.218
ROM.ROM	0.218		
LVA.RUS	0.273	Russian	0.288
MDA.RUS	0.365		
RUS.RUS	0.226		
ARG.SPA	0.173	Spanish	0.173
COL.SPA	0.173		

PISA 2000

Versions	Mean absolute magnitude of DIF		Mean magnitude across the whole language group
BEL.DUT	0.138	Dutch	0.138
NLD.DUT	0.138		
BEL.FRE	0.124	French	0.151
CAN.FRE	0.198		
CHE.FRE	0.150		
FRA.FRE	0.162		
AUT.GER	0.163	German	0.149
CHE.GER	0.167		
DEU.GER	0.122		
LUX.GER	0.143		
CHE.ITA	0.137	Italian	0.137
ITA.ITA	0.137		
BRA.POR	0.214	Portuguese	0.214
PRT.POR	0.214		
ARG.SPA	0.235	Spanish	0.298
CHL.SPA	0.277		
ESP.SPA	0.295		
MEX.SPA	0.357		
PER.SPA	0.324		

Note: *No results were included in this PIRLS table for the group of Hungarian versions used in Hungary, Romania, and Slovakia, because the sub-samples of students assessed using Hungarian booklets in Romania and Slovakia were too small (fewer than 80 students per booklet in both cases).

to 0, the effect *item* is null, as is the *unit* effect; the areas corresponding to these main effects are shaded in the figure.

Table 8: PIRLS 2001 and PISA 2000: Number of national versions included in the variance components analysis per language

PIRLS		PISA	
Arabic	3	English	7
English	7	French	4
Russian	3	German	4
		Spanish	5

Figure 3: Variance component analysis of item-DIF in national versions using a same language

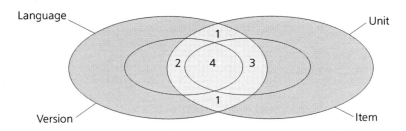

The four non-shaded areas in Figure 3 correspond to the four interaction components that are of interest in this analysis:

1. The area labeled 1 corresponds to the interaction between the *language* and the *unit* effects. A large variance component for this interaction might reflect translation problems in the reading passage used as stimulus for the groups of countries sharing a common version of the materials in a given language. Cultural or curriculum effects could also be at play in this component of variance because students using the same language of instruction in various countries might be more familiar than students elsewhere with certain authors and/or certain types of text.

2. The area labeled 2 represents the interaction between a *national version* and the *unit*. This area might also reflect possible translation errors in the stimulus used for the unit for a particular version. It might furthermore reflect some curriculum specificity in that country.

3. The area labeled 3 represents the interaction between a *language* and an *item*. This component probably reflects a translation error for a particular item in one of the source or shared versions. It might also have occurred because of students using specific languages being more familiar than students using other languages with some item formats or reading processes.

4. Finally, the area labeled 4 represents the interaction between a national version and specific items.

The results of the variance component analyses are presented in Table 9. The PISA variance decomposition was based on 121 items, 35 units, 4 languages, and 18 national versions. The PIRLS variance decomposition was based on 96 items, 8 units, 3 languages, and 13 national versions.

In both studies, Component 4 was the largest component of variance (52% in PISA and 63% in PIRLS), indicating that most of the differences were attributable to the behavior of specific items in specific national versions. Unfortunately, this low-level component was also the least easy to interpret because these idiosyncrasies could be due to any of the potential sources of differences: uneven quality of translation and/ or of national adaptations; printing or layout differences; and cultural or curricular specificities unique to a particular item in a particular version of the instrument. This variance component is also inflated as item difficulty indices are estimated.

Table 9: PIRLS 2001 and PISA 2000: Components of variance of the amount of item-DIF in the groups of countries sharing a same language of instruction

Components	PIRLS 2001		PISA 2000	
	Variance	Percent	Variance	Percent
1. Var(test unit*language)	0.0000	0	0.0180	12
2. Var(version(language)*test unit)	0.0445	17	0.0053	3
3. Var(item(test unit)*language)	0.0526	20	0.0496	33
4. Var(item(test unit)*version(language))	0.1663	63	0.0797	52
Total	0.2634		0.1523	

The second largest component, to which 20% of the variance could be attributed in PIRLS and 33% in PISA, was Component 3, the interaction between items and languages. It indicates the extent to which items tended to behave in a similar way in same-language versions but differently in different-language groups. It would be tempting to consider this component as mainly due to translation, partly because the variance explained was lower in PIRLS (where more of the national versions had independent translations) than in PISA. It must be kept in mind, however, that many cultural and curricular characteristics are often similar among countries sharing the same language, which may have played some role for particular items (e.g., differences in students' familiarity with certain item formats).

The two remaining components (1 and 2) were both related to possible interactions of test units (with languages and with national versions). These components, which differ considerably between PIRLS and PISA, could merit further investigation aimed at identifying the units affected and at finding possible sources of bias, either in the choice of reading passages used in the assessments, or in their translation.

It must be noted, however, that the components related to the test units represented only 15% of the variance in PISA and 17% of the variance in PIRLS. These results were unexpected and interesting. In reading literacy assessments such as PISA and PIRLS, the selection of the reading passages used as stimuli and assurance of their linguistic equivalence are generally considered of prime importance. In fact, the decomposition of the variance indicated that more than 80% of the item by country interaction was related to the *item* effect and *not* to the *unit* effect.

DISCUSSION

The general pattern of results for the two indicators used in this article to assess the equivalence of item difficulties across national versions of the test instruments appeared to be similar in PIRLS and PISA. In particular, there was no evidence in the analyses presented that the younger population assessed in PIRLS was any more sensitive to linguistic differences than the older (and probably more advanced) readers involved in PISA. In both studies, a single factor explained about 80% of the total variance in item difficulties, indicating that the latent dimension measured was substantially common to the various languages and cultures involved in the assessments.

The main objective of these analyses was to explore the residual 20% of variance in item difficulties associated with differences in the behavior of the national language versions of the test instruments used in the participating countries. The results confirmed some of the trends evidenced in previous studies, namely the fact that in both PIRLS and PISA the differences between the national and the international item parameters were larger for developing than for industrialized countries and for countries where the instruments had been translated into non-Indo-European rather than Indo-European languages. This finding suggests that there is still some room for improvement in international studies as regards the cultural targeting of the instruments and the translation procedures used when developing those national versions that are most "linguistically distant" from the source version(s) provided by the international study centers.

Separate analyses of selected countries or groups of countries also turned up interesting results. First, the estimation of the differences between regional and national PISA parameters in a single English-speaking country (Australia) suggested that the value of the indicator of mean absolute magnitude of DIF, although minimal, was not zero. Thus, even in the most favorable case, when no translation issues and very little cultural or curricular differences were at play, a small amount of DIF was still observed (about 0.15 logit, on average, for the 121 items used in the assessment).

Second, in both PISA and PIRLS, comparison of the national parameters of English-speaking countries with the mean parameters of the whole English-language group led to the value of the indicator of mean magnitude of DIF typically sitting between 0.15 and 0.20 logit. This result suggests that, in most cases, neither cultural nor curricular differences among the English-speaking countries, nor the national adaptations that each English-speaking country included in the source version of the instruments had large effects on the equivalence of these national versions. The exceptions were two PIRLS countries—Belize and Singapore—where the values were much higher (possibly because English is a second language for students in these two countries). In other groups of countries sharing the same language of instruction, the average magnitude of within-language DIF varied from less than 0.20 logit (French, German, Dutch, and Italian versions in PISA; French, Greek, and Spanish versions in PIRLS) to more than 0.30 logit (Spanish versions in PISA; Russian and Arabic versions in PIRLS).

A few interesting findings also emerged from a variance component analysis aimed at exploring the effects of potential sources of bias on the magnitude of DIF in the groups of PIRLS and PISA countries sharing the same language. First, in both studies, more than half of the variance of item-DIF was attributable to the behavior of specific items in specific national versions. This was by far the largest component, but since it was associated with the lowest-level interaction, the interpretation was unclear. Any type of bias related to individual items might have contributed to this residual variance, from occasional translation errors or printing flaws to cultural or curricular specificities.

Second, a significant item-by-language interaction was observed (33% of the variance of the DIF indicator in PISA, 20% in PIRLS), indicating that certain items seemed to behave in a deviant way in all or most of the translations into a particular language. This component is probably attributable to the effect of translation factors. However, explanations centered on cultural or curricular similarities between countries sharing the same language of instruction should not be excluded.

Third, a smaller amount of DIF (15% in PISA, 17% in PIRLS) could be attributed to interactions between the test unit and language groups or specific national versions. Given that the stimulus in a reading literacy assessment typically consists of texts or passages (this was especially so in the PIRLS tests, where only continuous prose texts were used as stimuli), curriculum or cultural effects should, in principle, affect the whole unit more than specific items. These results seem to indicate that curriculum or cultural effects related to the selection of reading passages might be less crucial than some critics of international comparative assessments would expect.

Obviously, perfect psychometric equivalence cannot be achieved in multilingual assessments. However, it is important that the technical reports of those studies contain at least some systematic information on the *extent to which* equivalence was achieved for the various versions of the instruments, and, if possible, offer some analysis of the sources of residual bias.

The two indicators proposed in this article are tentative only, primarily because of possible idiosyncrasies due to the relatively small number of countries, versions, and items involved in the analyses and to the small size of some of the sub-samples of students in countries where minority language versions of the assessment were used. Replicating the analyses presented in this article with data from more recent reading assessments could help assess the stability of the results. Both PIRLS 2006 (Mullis, Martin, Kennedy, & Foy, 2007) and PISA 2009 (in progress) include more ample information on curricular aspects than do PIRLS 2001 and PISA 2000, which would probably permit a more precise exploration of the relationships between the magnitude of DIF and cross-country curricular variations.

In addition, new developments in IRT models might provide researchers with a better framework for investigating translation and cultural issues in international surveys. For instance, multi-level IRT models have been recently developed (Fox & Glas, 2001; Kamata & Cheong; 2007; Park and Bolt, 2008; Vermunt, 2007). These models, which can decompose item responses across several levels (item, unit, student, and country), seem particularly promising relative to reading assessments because of their ability to recognize possible item dependencies brought about by the common stimuli on which the test items are based.

References

Elley, W. B. (1992). *How in the world do students read? IEA Study of Reading Literacy*. The Hague: International Association for the Evaluation of Educational Achievement (IEA).

Fox, J.-P., & Glas, C. A. W. (2001). Bayesian estimation of a multilevel IRT model using Gibbs sampling. *Psychometrika, 66*, 269–286.

Grisay, A., de Jong, J. H. A. L., Gebhardt, E., Berezner, A., & Halleux-Monseur, B. (2007). Translation equivalence across PISA countries. *Journal of Applied Measurement, 8*(3), 249–266.

Grisay, A., & Monseur, C. (2007). Measuring the equivalence of item difficulty in the various versions of an international test. *Studies in Educational Evaluation, 33*(1), 69–86.

Kamata, A., & Cheong, F. (2007). Multilevel Rasch model. In M. von Davier & C. H. Carstensen (Eds.), *Multivariate and mixture distribution Rasch models: Extensions and applications* (pp. 217–232). New York: Springer.

Monseur, C., & Halleux, B. (2009). Translation and verification outcomes: National versions quality. In *OECD technical report* (pp. 96–104). Paris: Organisation for Economic Co-operation and Development.

Mullis, I. V. S, Martin, M. O, Kennedy, A. M., & Foy, P. (2007). *PIRLS 2006 international report: IEA's Progress in International Reading Literacy Study in primary schools in 40 countries*. Chestnut Hill, MA: Boston College.

Park, C., & Bolt, D. M. (2008). Application of multi-level IRT to investigate cross-national skill profiles on TIMSS 2003. *IERI monograph series: Issues and methodologies in large-scale assessments* (Vol. 1, pp. 71–96). Hamburg/Princeton NJ: IEA-ETS Research Institute.

Purves, A. C. (1973). *Literature education in ten countries*. Stockholm: Almquist & Wiksell; New York: John Wiley & Sons.

Thorndike, R. L. (1973). *Reading comprehension education in fifteen countries: An empirical study*. Stockholm: Almquist & Wiksell.

Vermunt, J. K. (2007). Multilevel mixture item response theory models: An application in education testing. *Bulletin of the International Statistical Institute* (56th session, Paper #1253, 1–4. ISI 2007). Lisbon: International Statistical Institute.

Appendix 1: Plot of Mean Magnitudes of Item DIF in PIRLS and PISA

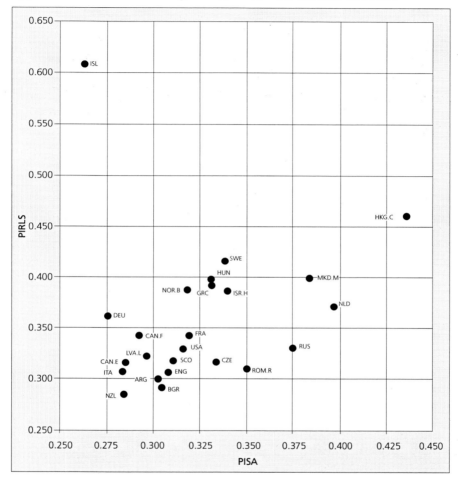

Curriculum coverage and scale correlation on TIMSS 2003

Juliane Hencke, Leslie Rutkowski, and Oliver Neuschmidt
IEA Data Processing and Research Center, Hamburg, Germany

Eugenio Gonzalez
Educational Testing Service, Princeton, New Jersey, United States

TIMSS examines the effectiveness of curriculum and instruction in relation to student achievement, which makes the issue of assessment-curriculum alignment important for test developers and policymakers alike. While TIMSS assessments were developed to represent an agreed-upon framework and were intended to have as much in common across countries as possible, it was inevitable that the match between test and curriculum would not be identical in all countries. This article looks at issues of curriculum coverage and how non-coverage affects scale scores. Using not-covered items identified by the IEA Test–Curriculum Matching Analysis (Mullis, Martin, Gonzalez, & Chrostowksi, 2004), the research team removed from all countries the items listed as not covered for a particular country. The team then rescaled the data using item response theory (IRT) scaling methods, and correlated the resulting scale scores with the reported scale scores. This procedure was repeated using each country's list of not-covered items. The analysis showed that the scale scores for all items correlated very highly with the curriculum-covered items for the country assessed. The results indicate that even if countries did select the items covered in their intended curricula, no statistically significant effects could be found in any country's international standings.

INTRODUCTION

International assessments such as the Trends in International Mathematics and Science Study (TIMSS) provide a reliable means for better understanding the state of education systems in a number of diverse countries. Designed to improve teaching and learning in mathematics and science, TIMSS examines the effectiveness of the intended curriculum and instruction in relation to student achievement and provides opportunity to compare student achievement across countries.

The curricular focus of TIMSS presents a subtle but important difference relative to the focus of other assessments, such as the Programme for International Student Assessment (PISA), which considers workforce knowledge. For TIMSS, the focus on the intended curriculum of many of the participating countries raises a unique range of issues. In particular, test–curriculum alignment is a central consideration for TIMSS validity and for cross-national comparisons. In this article, we seek to gain a deeper understanding of the effect of test–curriculum alignment in a large-scale assessment context.

To ensure that comparisons of student achievement across countries are as fair and equitable as possible, TIMSS developed extensive assessment frameworks and specifications that addressed the important aspects of mathematics and science in countries' curricula and instructional programs. The study also went to great lengths to develop assessment items closely representing those specifications (Mullis, Martin, Gonzalez, & Chrostowksi, 2004).

Using as their referent the frameworks and specifications (Mullis et al., 2003), the TIMSS research consortium proposed a distribution of content and cognitive domains to education system representatives. The consortium used feedback from experts from the participating countries to further refine the assessment framework, and from there to develop assessment specifications. The participating education system representatives then referred to the revised framework and specifications in order to contribute a pool of items, which the consortium subsequently reviewed and field tested prior to conducting the main survey.

During each step of the TIMSS development process, feedback and participation were solicited from representatives of the participating countries, experts in mathematics and science, and testing specialists. Every effort was made to ensure that the tests represented the curricula of the participating countries and that the items showed no bias toward or against a specific country. The final assessments were endorsed by the representatives of the participating countries.

Although the TIMSS assessment is carefully designed to maximize content and cognitive domain coverage as well as curriculum coverage, the nature of working with dozens of diverse countries introduces challenges. As we noted above, TIMSS was developed using an agreed-upon framework; however, some discrepancies between the test and a given education system's intended curriculum persist. Explanations for these discrepancies are offered in the TIMSS 2003 reports. For example, the *TIMSS 2003 International Mathematics Report* (Mullis et al., 2004, p. 397) states:

To restrict test items to just those topics included in the curricula of all participating countries and covered in the same sequence would severely limit test coverage and restrict the research questions that the study is designed to address. The tests, therefore, inevitably have some items measuring topics unfamiliar to some students in some countries.

To understand the degree to which TIMSS 2003 departed from any given curriculum, IEA conducted the Test–Curriculum Matching Analysis (TCMA), based on Beaton's (1998) approach. For each education system, responses were elicited from an individual designated as familiar with that system's curriculum. In particular, respondents indicated whether each TIMSS item was appropriate for more than 50% of students in the assessed grades. Country by country, those items designated as *not covered* were removed from the item set. Simple proportions of items correct were then calculated for all countries based on covered items for a particular country.

Initial findings from the TCMA, which used proportions of items correct, indicate that the noted departures from test–curriculum alignment generally did not affect the relative performance of the education systems (Mullis et al., 2004). Furthermore, removing items considered not covered within one education system consistently increased the proportion of items correct for that system. These results left the overall rankings of countries essentially unchanged, regardless of the items selected for analysis.

Despite findings that indicate trivial effects resulting from various item choices for the TCMA, our experience is that policymakers and researchers continue to voice concern about the possible effects that departures from their respective curricula may have. In response to concerns from TIMSS study participants, we used item response theory (IRT) scaling methods to uncover what, if any, effects test–curriculum mismatch may have on TIMSS achievement. Through use of IRT, we intend to contribute an alternative approach to understanding how item selection affects education system performance on the TIMSS 2003 mathematics assessment. While many of the countries participating in TIMSS have perfect or nearly perfect alignment between their curriculum and the TIMSS assessment, several countries indicated that 85% or fewer TIMSS items were covered in their curriculum. This project draws from and expands on the methods used by Beaton (1998) to understand the extent to which test–curriculum departures affect scale scores for participating countries.

A secondary purpose of this article is to examine the characteristics of not-covered items in terms of item type, content domain, and cognitive domain. This sort of exploratory analysis will allow for a better understanding of the types of items not covered in country curriculums. Additionally, it will allow identification of commonalities across countries in terms of curriculum coverage and item types.

RESEARCH METHODS

Data

TIMSS 2003 was the third in a continuing cycle of curriculum-based international assessments in mathematics and science. The target population of TIMSS 2003 was all students at the end of Grades 4 and 8 in the participating countries. In addition to assessing mathematics and science achievement of fourth and eighth graders internationally, the TIMSS program of studies collects a wealth of background data from students, teachers, and principals or headmasters/mistresses of participating schools. According to the TIMSS assessment framework, the Grade 4 sample is defined as the upper of the two adjacent grades with the most nine-year-olds. The Grade 8 sample includes children aged 13 and 14, and is defined as the upper of the two adjacent grades with the most 13-year-olds (Mullis et al., 2003).

In this study, we used Grade 8 mathematics achievement data along with the TCMA results that indicated whether or not items were covered within the curriculum of each education system. In 2003, 46 education systems and four benchmarking education systems were assessed at the Grade 8 level. To ensure readability of figures and tables, we use country abbreviations throughout this article. Table 1 includes the full country name for each of the abbreviations used.

Table 1: Country abbreviations

Country name	Country abbreviation
ARMENIA	ARM
AUSTRALIA	AUS
BELGIUM FLEMISH	BFL
BULGARIA	BGR
BAHRAIN	BHR
BOTSWANA	BWA
CHILE	CHL
CYPRUS	CYP
EGYPT	EGY
ENGLAND	ENG
ESTONIA	EST
GHANA	GHA
HONG KONG	HKG
HUNGARY	HUN
INDONESIA	IDN
IRAN	IRN
ISRAEL	ISR
ITALY	ITA
JORDAN	JOR
JAPAN	JPN
KOREA	KOR

Country name	Country abbreviation
LEBANON	LBN
LITUANIA	LTU
LATVIA	LVA
MOROCCO	MAR
MOLDOVA	MDA
MACEDONIA	MKD
MALAYSIA	MYS
NETHERLANDS	NLD
NORWAY	NOR
NEW ZEALAND	NZL
PHILIPPINES	PHL
PALESTINE	PSE
ROMANIA	ROM
RUSSIAN FEDERATION	RUS
SAUDI ARABIA	SAU
SERBIA	SCG
SCOTLAND	SCO
SINGAPORE	SGP
SLOVAK REPUBLIC	SVK
SLOVENIA	SVN
SWEDEN	SWE
TUNISIA	TUN
CHINESE TAIPEI	TWN
UNITED STATES	USA
SOUTH AFRICA	ZAF

In the TIMSS 2003 data, the proportion of items reported as covered by a given curriculum varies. In the Grade 8 mathematics assessment, 15 education systems reported that 97% of TIMSS mathematics items were covered in their curricula. In fact, Saudi Arabia and Israel indicated that all items were covered in their curriculum. At the other end of the spectrum, nine countries reported that 85% or fewer of the TIMSS items were covered. Education systems with the lowest coverage included South Africa (62%), Jordan (71%), Scotland (74%), and Ghana (74%). The average proportion of items covered by a given curriculum in this dataset was about 90%. Figure 1 illustrates the distribution of the number of covered and not-covered items across the countries. The black bars indicate the number of covered items for a particular country; the grey bars show the number of not-covered items. The countries are sorted from lowest to highest number of covered items.

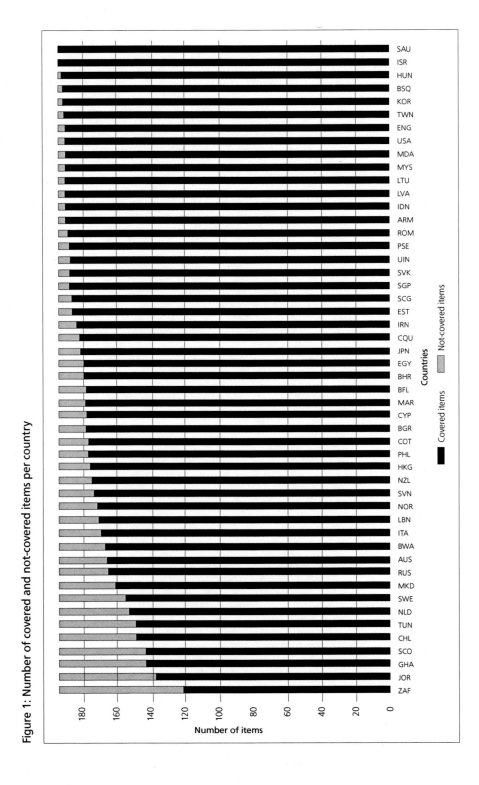

Figure 1: Number of covered and not-covered items per country

Analysis

To answer the research question regarding the possible effects of item selection on education system performance, we completed a number of steps. We first reviewed the TCMA to identify those items indicated as not covered for each country. To gain a further understanding of the types of not-covered items (with respect to content and cognitive domains), we conducted an exploratory analysis of not-covered items. In particular, we compared item difficulties for covered versus not-covered items for each country. We also compared the proportion of covered and not-covered items by content and cognitive domain for each country.

Next, we removed from the entire mathematics achievement database items indicated as not covered in each country to create 46 separate datasets for analysis. Thus, if Country A identified Items 16, 19, and 23 as not covered by their curriculum, we removed those items for all countries, thereby creating the dataset, *Not covered for Country A*. We repeated this process for all countries. The resulting datasets were subsequently scaled with a three-parameter IRT model using PARSCALE (version 4.1), with parameters of the response model estimated by marginal maximum likelihood (MML).

We chose a three-parameter model that would be as consistent as possible with the original scaling of the TIMSS 2003 data. As an initial step in the scaling process, we first calibrated all items with a random selection of one half of the students in the sample. In alignment with the TIMSS 2003 scaling methods and procedures (Martin et al., 2004), we removed student answers coded as not reached during item calibration; however, for scale score estimation, we included these items as incorrect responses. Each scaling analysis resulted in a new set of item parameters for all of the remaining items; the resulting mathematics scores were expected a priori (EAP) estimates.

We standardized the resulting scores to a mean of 500 and a standard deviation of 100, practice consistent with TIMSS 2003 procedures. However, because of slight differences in scaling procedures, our scale scores exhibited trivial differences from those scores included in the international report (Mullis et al., 2004). We expected these differences because we did not use student background information to estimate student achievement distributions (called conditioning) and therefore did not draw plausible values. Because the new scale scores were based on items identified as covered in a specific country, we refer to them as *covered* scale scores.

For all countries, we correlated the 46 sets of new parameters with the item parameters based on all items included in the calibration. We then correlated the new scale scores, standardized to a mean of 500 and a standard deviation of 100, with the scale scores that included all items. We reasoned that, given the problems of explicitly ranking countries, correlating the original scale scores with the *covered* scale scores was a more reasonable approach. High correlations suggest that the original and the *covered* scales are essentially measuring the same thing. Low correlations suggest that the two scales may be measuring two different things, and that this may affect a country's overall performance on the assessment.

RESULTS

This section details results from the exploratory analysis conducted in order to provide information regarding the types of items not covered across countries.

Items by Item Types

We first consider curriculum coverage rates by item type (multiple-choice versus constructed-response). In the TIMSS 2003 assessment, 66% of the administered mathematics items were multiple-choice, while the remaining 33% of the items were constructed-response. Figures 2 and 3 illustrate the rate of coverage for constructed-response and multiple-choice items. The black bars indicate the proportion of covered items for a particular country; the grey bars show the proportion of not-covered items. The dark, heavy line indicates the 85% mark. Black bars above this line indicate that more than 85% of items were covered by the given country's curriculum.

The majority of countries covered 85% or more of the constructed-response items in their respective curricula. However, 10 countries covered less than 85% of the constructed-response items. At the extreme, South Africa covered only half of the constructed-response items. On the other hand, seven countries indicated that all constructed-response items were covered in their curriculum. On average, countries covered about 90% of the constructed-response items.

When the multiple-choice items were compared with the constructed-response items, it was apparent that about the same number of countries reported coverage of 85% or more of the multiple-choice items; however, fewer countries reported coverage of all multiple-choice items. Nine countries reported that fewer than 85% of the multiple-choice mathematics items were covered in their curricula. On average, countries covered about 91% of the multiple-choice items. Scotland and South Africa had the most not-covered multiple-choice items: both countries indicated that about 35% of these items were not covered in their respective curricula. However, it has to be noted that the number of multiple-choice items administered in the TIMSS 2003 assessment was larger than the number of constructed-response items administered.

Items by Difficulty

Here, we examine the difficulty of an item as a specific attribute of that item. We reasoned that items not covered in a country's curriculum would be relatively more difficult than covered items.

To investigate whether not-covered items were generally more difficult than covered items, we compared the average difficulty of covered versus not-covered items in each country. We conducted this analysis using the percentage correct per item in each country as the basis. We took the average percent correct values for each item and country from the data almanacs that are published along with the *TIMSS 2003 User Guide for the International Database* (Martin, 2005). We calculated the percent correct for an item in a country on the basis of the percentage of students answering the item correctly, excluding students who did not reach the item. For multiple-choice items, the percent correct matches the percentage of students choosing the correct

Figure 2: Coverage rates of constructed-response items

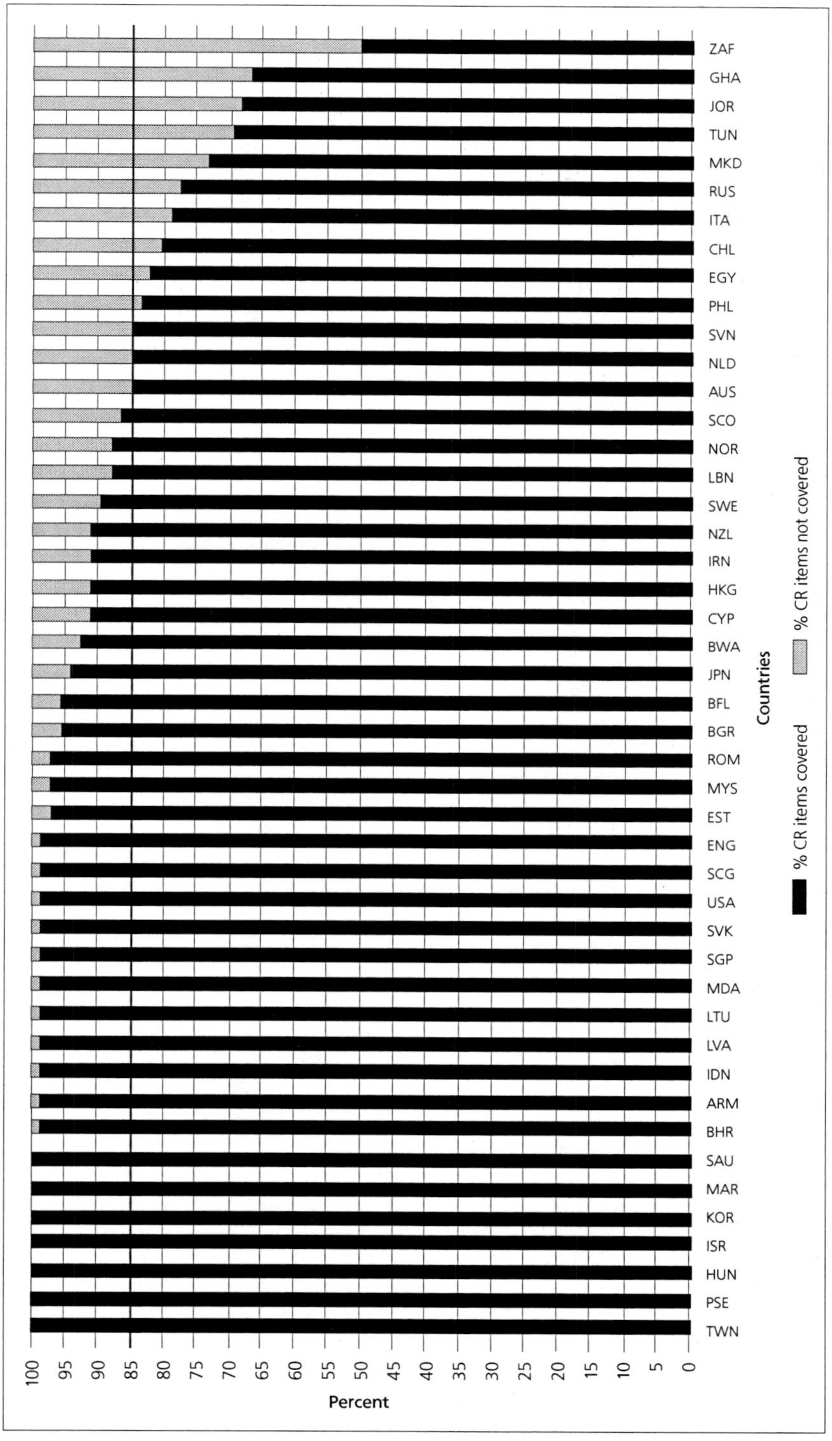

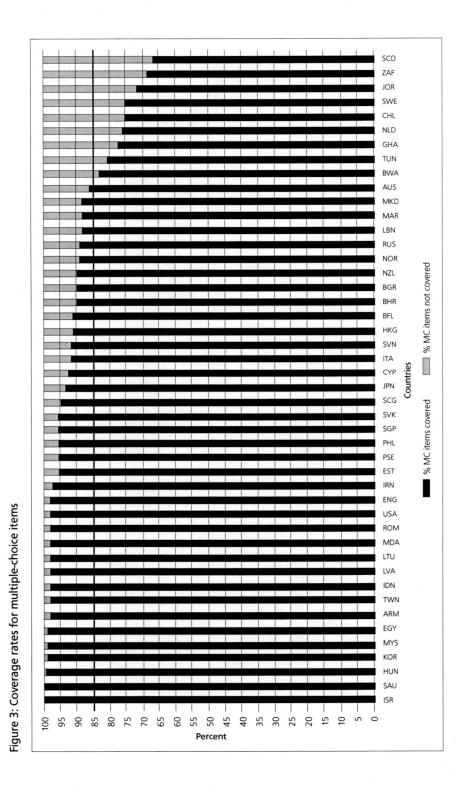

Figure 3: Coverage rates for multiple-choice items

answer category. For constructed-response items worth one score point, the percent correct matches the percentage of students receiving one score point. For constructed-response items worth two score points, we applied a partial credit model. Here, the percent correct is the sum of the percentage of students receiving two score points plus half of the percentage of students receiving one score point.

In order to adjust the difficulty of an item in a country relative to other countries and other items, we calculated the item residuals for each item-by-country according to the following formula based on an ANOVA type model (Beaton & Gonzalez, 1997):

$$\varphi_{res(ic)} = \varphi_{ic} - \bar{\varphi} - (\bar{\varphi}_c - \bar{\varphi}) - (\bar{\varphi}_i - \bar{\varphi}),$$

where $\bar{\varphi}$ = the mean over all countries and all items; φ_{ic} = the overall difficulty for country c on item i; $\bar{\varphi}_c$ = the overall average item difficulty for country c over all items; and $\bar{\varphi}_i$ = the overall item difficulty for item i over all countries. This residual indicates how much better or worse a country performed on an item than would be expected given overall item difficulties, for a particular country, for a particular item in the given country and internationally. We then averaged these residuals for both covered and not-covered items in each country.

Figure 4 shows the item residual average for each country calculated separately for covered and not-covered items. Because Saudi Arabia and Israel had no not-covered items, we did not include them in this analysis. The results are sorted by the differences between the residuals for covered items and those for not-covered items. For countries on the left side of the figure through New Zealand (NZL), the not-covered items were generally less difficult than the covered items. This is illustrated by the positive average residuals for not-covered items (displayed as grey bars), and the negative average residuals for covered items (displayed as black bars). Significant differences in favor of either covered or not-covered items are noted with a country abbreviation placed above the item residual bars. Additionally, the item coverage rates appear in brackets after the country abbreviation to indicate coverage rates in countries where we found significant differences in the covered versus not-covered item difficulties.

While, for the majority of countries, item residuals were not significantly different, 10 countries did significantly better than we would have expected on not-covered items than on covered items. However, for 13 countries, not-covered item performance was significantly worse than we would have expected relative to covered items.

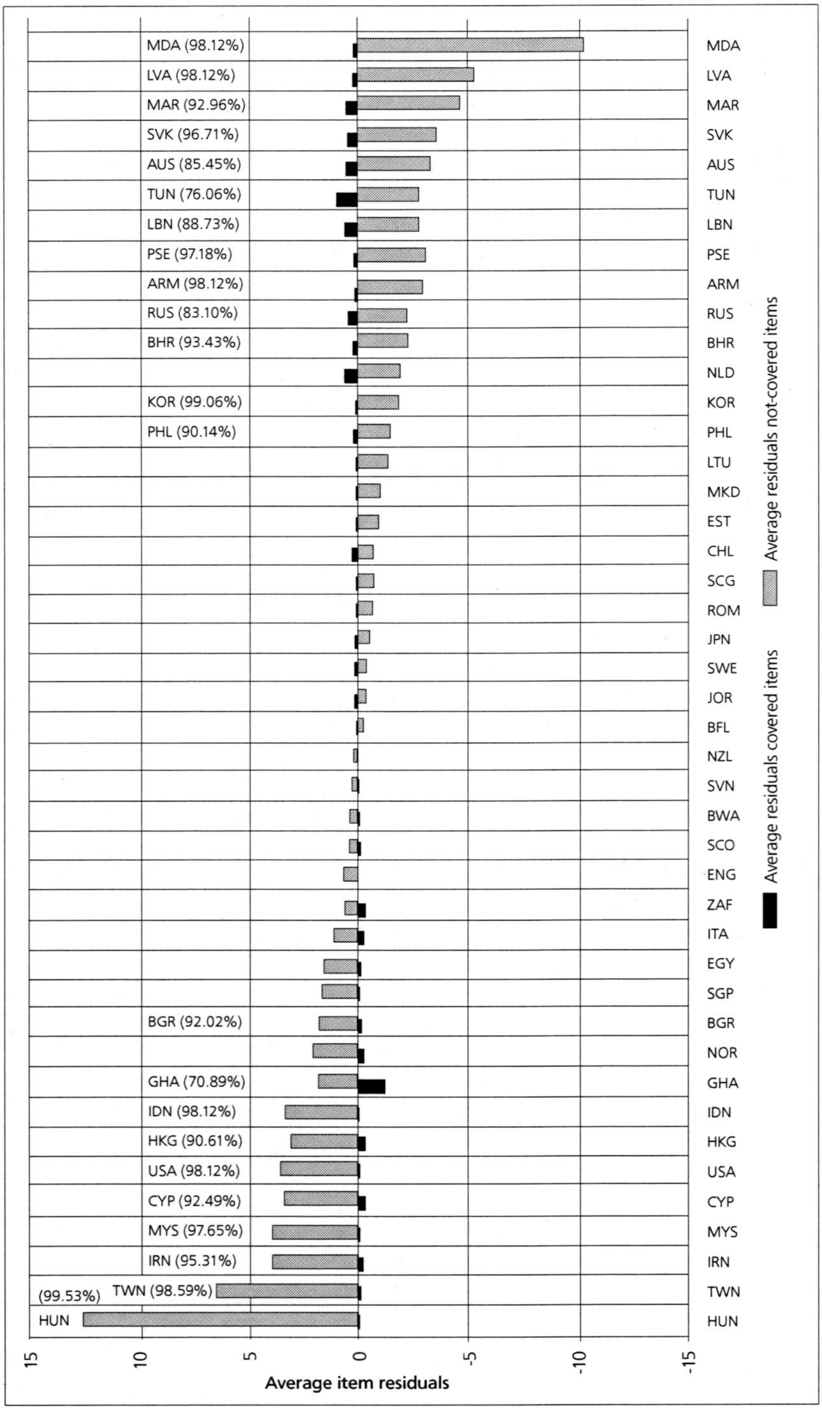

Figure 4: Average item residuals for covered items versus not-covered items

Percentage of Not-Covered Items by Content Domain

We next examined curriculum coverage of the administered items by content domain. Here, content domain refers to the specific mathematics subject matter covered in the TIMSS assessment. Five content domains were used in TIMSS 2003: number, algebra, geometry, measurement, and data. Number was the domain with the most items administered (N = 57), while data was the one with the fewest items assessed (N = 28). The percentages calculated and displayed in Table 2 are based on the number of items not covered in relation to the number of items per reporting category. Results are sorted in each column from lowest to highest percentage of not-covered items.

In the content domain number, 23 out of 46 countries indicated that all number items were covered in their curriculum. Jordan (JOR), with 37%, and Scotland (SCO), with 32%, were the countries with the highest proportion of number items not covered in their respective curriculums.

For the algebra content domain, the highest percentages of not-covered items were found in Chile (CHL), with 47%, followed by Ghana (GHA) and South Africa (ZAF), each with 43%. Eight countries reported that all algebra items were covered in their curriculums.

In the geometry content domain, South Africa (ZAF) and the Netherlands (NLD) had the highest percentage of not-covered geometry items, with 71% and 55%, respectively; nine countries had all geometry items covered. When compared to the other reporting categories, geometry, with 15% not-covered items on average, emerged as the reporting category with the second-highest non-coverage rate.

While the majority of the countries had all measurement items covered (27 out of 46 countries), Jordan (JOR) reported that 32% of the measurement items were not covered in their curriculum. Measurement, compared to the other reporting categories, emerged as the reporting category with the lowest percentage of non-coverage (on average, 3%).

Macedonia (MKD) was the country with the highest percentage of data items not covered (93%), followed by South Africa (ZAF; 86%) and Slovenia (SVN; 54%). However, in 15 countries, all of the data items were covered in the curriculum. On average, 19% of the items in this content domain were reported as not covered. Relative to the other reporting categories, data emerged as the reporting category with the highest, on average, non-coverage rate.

Percentage of Not-Covered Items by Cognitive Domain

We next considered item-curriculum alignment by cognitive domain. The cognitive domains defined the set of behaviors expected of students as they engaged with the mathematics content. The items administered in TIMSS covered four cognitive domains: knowing facts and procedures, using concepts, solving routine problems, and reasoning (Mullis et al., 2003). However, due to some overlap across the four domains, experts felt comfortable in combining the domains into the following three: knowing facts, procedures, and concepts; applying knowledge and understanding; and reasoning (Mullis, Martin, & Foy, 2005).

Table 2: Percentage of items not covered, by content domain

	Country	Number (N=57)	Algebra (N=47)	Geometry (N=31)	Measurement (N=31)	Data (N=28)
1	ARM	0	2	10	0	0
2	AUS	11	26	26	3	4
3	BFL	0	11	19	6	7
4	BGR	0	4	13	0	36
5	BHR	0	9	16	0	18
6	BWA	12	15	26	3	14
7	CHL	2	47	32	13	29
8	CYP	0	6	13	0	32
9	EGY	4	0	0	13	29
10	ENG	4	4	0	0	0
11	EST	2	2	16	3	0
12	GHA	12	43	29	10	43
13	HKG	0	6	16	0	36
14	HUN	0	2	0	0	0
15	IDN	0	2	10	0	0
16	IRN	0	9	0	0	21
17	ISR	0	0	0	0	0
18	ITA	9	17	19	10	11
19	JOR	37	19	19	32	39
20	JPN	2	9	13	10	4
21	KOR	2	0	3	0	0
22	LBN	4	13	13	6	32
23	LTU	0	2	10	0	0
24	LVA	0	2	10	0	0
25	MAR	2	0	26	0	21
26	MDA	0	2	10	0	0
27	MKD	0	13	3	0	93
28	MYS	0	2	3	0	7
29	NLD	12	34	55	3	0
30	NOR	4	23	23	0	7
31	NZL	11	19	10	0	4
32	PHL	2	2	19	3	29
33	PSE	0	2	16	0	0
34	ROM	0	2	13	0	0
35	RUS	0	23	29	3	29
36	SAU	0	0	0	0	0
37	SCG	2	0	0	0	25
38	SCO	32	28	35	3	29
39	SGP	0	2	0	0	21
40	SVK	0	0	0	0	25
41	SVN	4	4	3	3	54
42	SWE	7	36	35	3	21
43	TUN	7	32	32	6	50
44	TWN	0	0	3	0	7
45	USA	0	2	10	0	0
46	ZAF	5	43	71	13	86

Table 3 shows that the highest number of items were those assessing the applying cognitive domain ($N = 93$). Knowing comprised 65 items; reasoning comprised 36 items. The results in each column of the table are sorted from the lowest to the highest percentage of not-covered items.

For knowing, Scotland (SCO) reported the highest proportion (42%) of not-covered knowing items in its curriculum. Ten countries reported that all items in this cognitive domain were covered. With 33% of applying items reported as not covered in its curriculum, South Africa (ZAF) had the highest percentage of not-covered items in the applying cognitive domain. At the other extreme, five countries reported that all applying items were covered by their curriculum. South Africa (ZAF) was again to the fore in reporting the highest proportion of not-covered reasoning items at 69%. This was the highest proportion of not-covered items listed by any country on any of the cognitive domains. However, 14 countries reported that their respective curriculums covered all items on this domain.

Correlations between Countries' Mean Scores and Correlations between Countries' Item Parameters

After removing not-covered mathematics items for each country as indicated by the country curriculum experts and re-scaling the data, we correlated the newly calculated scores with the scores based on all items included. Table 4 displays the results of this analysis. All Pearson correlations were very high (above 0.990), with more than half of the countries (27) showing correlations of 1. The lowest correlations belonged to Jordan (0.992), South Africa (0.992), and Macedonia (0.995), all countries that reported fewer than 85% of items covered by their curriculums.

We also considered the correlation between item parameters (item discrimination, item difficulty, and guessing parameter) based on the original scaling and the modified scaling that included only curriculum-covered items. Rounding the correlations to three decimal places gave correlations that were all 1.000.

Differences between Mean Scores

Because all but two of the selected countries (Israel and Saudi Arabia) indicated that some items were not covered in their intended Grade 8 curriculum, we analyzed the data to determine whether the inclusion of these items had any effect on the international performance comparisons.

The second row of Table 5 represents the maximum number of available score points for the covered items selected by each country. All together, the TIMSS 2003 assessment contained 194 mathematics items. As some of the (constructed-response) items were assigned more than one score point, the number of score points for the entire test was 213. The median number of score points covered across all countries was 199 or 93% of the test. The row shows that the countries varied substantially in their judgments of the number of items that were covered in the Grade 8 curriculum, from Israel and Saudi Arabia having full item coverage to South Africa having 60% of the items included in their intended curriculums.

Table 3: Percentage of items not covered, by cognitive domain

	Country	Knowing (N=65)	Applying (N=93)	Reasoning (N=36)
1	ARM	0	4	0
2	AUS	14	16	11
3	BFL	2	11	11
4	BGR	5	8	17
5	BHR	11	6	3
6	BWA	9	18	11
7	CHL	17	14	14
8	CYP	5	11	8
9	EGY	2	6	19
10	ENG	6	0	0
11	EST	5	3	6
12	GHA	32	18	36
13	HKG	11	6	14
14	HUN	0	1	0
15	IDN	0	4	0
16	IRN	6	6	0
17	ISR	0	0	0
18	ITA	9	10	28
19	JOR	29	32	22
20	JPN	8	4	11
21	KOR	2	0	3
22	LBN	12	11	14
23	LTU	0	4	0
24	LVA	0	4	0
25	MAR	11	6	6
26	MDA	0	4	0
27	MKD	9	19	25
28	MYS	3	1	3
29	NLD	26	16	25
30	NOR	5	14	17
31	NZL	9	10	11
32	PHL	8	5	19
33	PSE	5	1	6
34	ROM	5	0	6
35	RUS	9	11	36
36	SAU	0	0	0
37	SCG	6	4	0
38	SCO	42	18	19
39	SGP	5	4	0
40	SVK	3	5	0
41	SVN	6	11	19
42	SWE	29	17	11
43	TUN	20	20	36
44	TWN	0	2	3
45	USA	0	4	0
46	ZAF	26	33	69

Table 4: Correlation between scores based on all items included and scores based on each country's not-covered items removed (sorted by correlations)

	Coverage pattern	Pearson correlations*
1	JOR	0.992
2	ZAF	0.992
3	MKD	0.995
4	NLD	0.998
5	TUN	0.998
6	SWE	0.998
7	SCO	0.998
8	EGY	0.999
9	PHL	0.999
10	CHL	0.999
11	HKG	0.999
12	SVN	0.999
13	CYP	0.999
14	NZL	0.999
15	NOR	0.999
16	AUS	0.999
17	BWA	0.999
18	IRN	0.999
19	GHA	0.999
20	LBN	1
21	RUS	1
22	BGR	1
23	ITA	1
24	MAR	1
25	ENG	1
26	JPN	1
27	BFL	1
28	SCG	1
29	BHR	1
30	SVK	1
31	SGP	1
32	PSE	1
33	EST	1
34	ROM	1
35	ARM	1
36	IDN	1
37	LTU	1
38	LVA	1
39	MDA	1
40	USA	1
41	MYS	1
42	TWN	1
43	KOR	1
44	HUN	1
45	ISR**	1
46	SAU**	1

Note: * Pearson correlations rounded to three decimal places; **country reported that all items are covered in the curriculum.

Table 5: Average scale score based on subset of items identified by each country as addressing its curriculum

Countries	Average	(se)	SGP	KOR	HKG	TWN	JPN	BFL	NLD	HUN	EST	RUS	LVA	AUS	SVK	USA
	(Number of score points included)															
	213		206	193	211	210	199	198	169	212	204	177	209	206	182	208
SGP	620.64	(3.47)	621.40	620.50	620.21	620.51	619.96	620.08	620.09	620.64	619.97	621.46	621.01	618.19	621.03	621.01
KOR	603.91	(1.71)	603.27	604.31	603.43	603.36	603.64	602.39	597.28	603.85	603.38	601.44	603.67	600.52	602.98	603.67
HKG	603.70	(3.16)	603.92	603.41	603.64	603.44	602.80	602.17	599.92	603.71	602.78	603.60	603.74	601.72	603.62	603.74
TWN	597.78	(4.07)	597.47	597.64	596.87	597.48	596.81	596.55	593.12	597.73	597.43	596.47	597.77	595.39	597.34	597.77
JPN	589.22	(1.95)	589.11	589.77	586.41	589.14	591.49	589.02	586.10	589.21	588.71	586.04	588.99	587.46	588.95	588.99
BFL	561.79	(2.54)	561.16	562.19	558.86	561.51	562.80	562.91	564.15	561.79	562.25	560.95	562.00	564.02	562.00	562.00
NLD	559.63	(3.78)	558.38	559.61	554.06	559.29	560.41	560.57	570.43	559.71	559.75	557.65	560.07	564.92	557.81	560.07
HUN	556.00	(3.10)	556.58	555.86	555.95	556.12	555.41	555.87	555.01	556.02	555.66	555.67	556.17	555.82	556.80	556.17
EST	554.59	(2.94)	554.61	554.92	554.71	554.76	554.73	555.24	554.38	554.59	555.63	554.70	554.09	556.70	554.51	554.09
RUS	536.47	(3.28)	536.90	536.24	538.97	536.48	535.17	535.68	532.05	536.49	536.36	538.14	536.05	533.79	537.10	536.05
LVA	533.34	(3.00)	533.23	533.28	532.46	533.32	533.38	534.18	532.21	533.32	533.34	534.12	533.21	531.66	533.25	533.21
AUS	531.55	(4.27)	530.70	531.66	527.30	531.56	532.41	532.09	537.04	531.59	531.24	528.93	531.95	533.03	530.52	531.95
SVK	530.16	(3.23)	530.46	530.10	531.91	530.57	530.26	531.22	529.15	530.17	530.38	531.02	529.79	531.45	530.55	529.79
USA	529.30	(3.06)	528.43	529.33	525.05	529.20	529.28	529.34	534.39	529.29	529.42	528.70	529.71	528.99	528.36	529.71
MYS	529.20	(3.90)	529.16	529.05	528.63	529.10	529.62	529.15	530.22	529.23	528.32	529.62	529.36	529.23	529.44	529.36
SWE	527.30	(2.48)	525.98	527.74	521.28	527.06	528.07	528.14	535.92	527.35	527.67	524.62	527.74	532.40	525.62	527.74
LTU	526.21	(2.37)	526.21	525.99	523.56	526.16	525.38	526.73	527.76	526.25	526.04	526.36	526.08	526.59	526.06	526.08
SCO	524.97	(3.61)	524.12	525.08	520.12	525.29	526.35	525.82	530.91	524.92	524.97	522.30	525.36	526.54	523.93	525.36
ENG	524.52	(4.42)	523.49	524.62	519.48	524.62	525.47	524.88	530.27	524.53	523.89	521.11	525.01	526.70	523.39	525.01
ISR	522.16	(3.09)	521.53	522.31	522.16	522.46	523.35	522.57	521.21	522.16	522.90	522.57	522.06	520.57	521.90	522.06
NZL	518.89	(4.98)	518.26	519.10	514.08	518.83	519.81	519.36	524.58	518.88	518.51	514.95	519.32	521.00	517.90	519.32
SVN	513.27	(2.19)	513.55	513.45	512.08	513.57	514.11	514.02	516.03	513.32	513.71	512.91	513.40	515.69	513.37	513.40
ITA	511.77	(2.89)	511.60	511.66	511.30	511.60	510.10	512.77	513.97	511.83	511.20	511.74	511.88	513.91	511.16	511.88
ROM	502.99	(4.39)	503.17	502.68	506.41	503.30	501.37	502.30	499.36	502.96	503.18	504.57	502.63	501.25	503.37	502.63
SCG	502.80	(2.31)	502.95	502.67	506.19	502.90	500.95	501.24	498.27	502.77	503.26	504.50	502.71	502.49	503.29	502.71
BGR	500.68	(3.61)	500.67	500.88	502.26	500.98	500.46	501.15	496.92	500.67	501.20	501.68	500.32	499.89	500.69	500.32
ARM	498.30	(2.66)	499.02	498.16	503.91	499.27	496.78	495.55	492.34	498.34	498.58	498.45	497.64	495.20	499.64	497.64
NOR	488.44	(2.35)	487.32	488.66	484.16	488.44	489.44	488.73	494.09	488.46	488.65	486.37	488.52	491.46	487.13	488.52
MDA	487.75	(3.39)	488.85	487.61	492.27	487.80	486.50	487.20	484.35	487.71	488.08	488.32	487.24	487.74	488.70	487.24
CYP	487.38	(1.41)	486.57	487.24	487.74	487.44	486.98	487.67	487.44	487.40	487.37	487.40	487.12	488.29	486.65	487.12
MKD	469.90	(2.86)	469.85	469.81	472.70	469.98	468.74	469.10	468.76	469.89	470.45	470.48	469.55	471.04	470.26	469.55
LBN	463.08	(2.75)	464.14	462.74	467.95	462.83	461.04	463.05	456.40	463.05	463.42	465.13	462.12	460.85	464.49	462.12
JOR	458.34	(3.17)	458.67	458.40	458.93	458.15	458.01	457.37	455.95	458.33	458.11	458.84	458.41	455.88	458.83	458.41
IDN	453.15	(3.20)	453.22	453.08	454.16	453.14	453.34	453.15	452.81	453.15	452.44	453.03	453.06	454.21	453.19	453.06
TUN	447.63	(1.69)	448.63	447.84	450.28	447.93	449.01	449.18	445.8	447.62	448.28	448.93	446.88	447.62	448.39	446.88
IRN	447.12	(1.78)	447.35	447.09	447.50	446.67	447.24	446.65	445.17	447.12	446.32	446.82	446.99	445.92	447.19	446.99
BHR	443.47	(1.09)	444.01	443.44	444.25	443.66	443.89	443.51	442.08	443.47	443.37	444.00	443.30	440.77	444.26	443.30
CHL	442.88	(2.24)	443.04	442.98	439.27	442.96	443.92	444.21	448.23	442.88	443.08	441.22	443.21	445.12	442.42	443.21
EGY	442.16	(2.33)	442.49	442.05	445.05	442.02	442.17	441.60	440.74	442.15	442.28	444.08	442.57	440.87	442.60	442.57
PSE	433.18	(2.09)	433.34	432.96	434.93	433.05	432.76	432.44	431.19	433.18	432.75	433.57	433.04	433.18	433.56	433.04
MAR	431.96	(1.68)	433.03	431.94	432.58	432.12	432.80	433.02	430.24	431.97	432.20	432.53	431.42	431.03	432.98	431.42
PHL	427.99	(3.65)	428.03	428.01	428.44	427.67	427.90	428.11	428.86	427.98	427.94	428.66	428.66	427.88	428.41	428.66
BWA	421.85	(1.70)	422.14	421.83	422.12	421.97	422.69	422.17	424.01	421.83	422.05	422.93	422.20	422.75	422.26	422.20
SAU	399.18	(1.99)	399.84	399.24	401.70	399.54	399.61	399.60	398.03	399.17	399.84	400.78	398.46	399.13	399.77	398.46
GHA	386.85	(1.69)	387.36	386.83	391.73	386.84	387.37	386.52	386.43	386.84	387.33	389.32	387.09	387.43	387.85	387.09
ZAF	382.71	(3.15)	382.81	382.72	384.76	382.71	383.59	383.94	386.84	382.70	383.06	384.71	383.27	385.35	382.95	383.27

MYS	SWE	LTU	SCO	ENG	ISR	NZL	SVN	ITA	ROM	SCG	BGR	ARM	NOR	MDA	CYP	MKD	LBN
209	172	209	158	208	213	191	187	178	207	205	196	209	209	197	188	174	189
620.86	619.38	621.01	618.89	620.08	620.64	619.25	620.61	618.19	620.87	621.16	621.65	621.01	619.29	621.01	620.47	622.84	621.47
603.42	598.04	603.67	597.12	603.02	603.91	600.89	604.41	604.69	603.77	603.29	603.12	603.67	600.36	603.67	604.05	604.62	602.05
603.67	599.76	603.74	600.91	603.38	603.70	601.40	603.95	603.00	603.10	603.69	603.66	603.74	601.77	603.74	603.44	606.38	602.71
597.86	592.66	597.77	593.26	597.23	597.78	594.63	597.83	597.29	597.76	597.41	597.30	597.77	595.33	597.77	597.00	598.84	596.02
588.63	587.30	588.99	587.84	588.57	589.22	588.46	587.48	586.46	588.34	588.89	588.96	588.99	587.29	588.99	587.49	584.78	586.92
561.72	562.73	562.00	562.77	561.65	561.79	564.22	559.79	561.82	561.32	560.98	560.70	562.00	563.66	562.00	559.50	557.31	560.75
559.46	566.99	560.07	565.76	562.06	559.63	564.64	556.11	556.19	559.13	557.92	556.88	560.07	563.90	560.07	554.98	549.66	556.32
556.23	554.87	556.17	554.27	555.11	556.00	556.01	555.36	555.17	555.45	556.62	556.19	556.17	556.94	556.17	554.23	554.66	555.55
554.01	555.20	554.09	554.25	554.89	554.59	555.79	553.12	554.70	554.33	554.46	554.37	554.09	556.46	554.09	554.20	553.12	554.36
536.30	532.68	536.05	532.06	536.08	536.47	534.02	539.67	537.59	536.68	537.01	536.29	536.05	534.16	536.05	537.71	541.65	537.28
533.00	531.38	533.21	529.63	532.30	533.34	533.44	533.54	533.97	533.39	533.14	532.80	533.21	533.16	533.21	532.68	532.37	533.68
531.44	535.93	531.95	535.14	533.47	531.55	534.18	528.21	529.48	531.03	530.45	530.05	531.95	533.75	531.95	527.64	522.68	529.07
529.65	531.47	529.79	527.07	529.39	530.16	530.16	531.31	531.27	530.17	530.38	530.31	529.79	531.44	529.79	532.48	532.48	530.74
529.30	531.45	529.71	530.67	530.12	529.30	530.87	525.68	527.98	529.19	528.33	527.73	529.71	531.16	529.71	525.79	521.16	527.75
529.86	528.85	529.36	528.71	528.77	529.20	529.79	529.43	529.72	528.85	529.44	528.37	529.36	529.06	529.36	528.12	528.29	530.02
527.15	536.02	527.74	534.99	529.76	527.30	532.50	520.22	525.53	526.68	525.74	525.59	527.74	532.54	527.74	523.30	515.54	523.52
526.17	526.49	526.08	525.94	526.28	526.21	526.90	528.28	525.21	526.12	526.02	525.74	526.08	527.45	526.08	524.97	524.71	527.22
525.03	530.61	525.36	531.07	527.24	524.97	528.37	519.85	524.47	524.52	523.83	523.40	525.36	527.32	525.36	520.37	514.57	521.90
524.33	528.60	525.01	529.88	526.85	524.52	527.76	519.23	522.44	523.61	523.16	522.45	525.01	527.03	525.01	519.67	513.75	520.94
522.11	520.69	522.06	520.02	521.80	522.16	520.63	520.64	521.42	522.38	521.58	522.37	522.06	521.68	522.06	521.85	521.49	521.82
518.76	523.63	519.32	523.77	521.10	518.89	522.12	515.52	516.96	517.86	517.92	517.44	519.32	521.95	519.32	514.41	509.27	515.65
512.91	514.63	513.40	514.40	513.08	513.27	514.30	514.30	513.27	512.96	513.20	512.70	513.40	515.16	513.40	512.48	511.19	513.16
511.69	513.06	511.88	511.64	511.56	511.77	513.75	510.39	512.05	511.70	511.42	510.16	511.88	513.04	511.88	512.15	509.18	511.65
502.47	498.38	502.63	498.48	502.09	502.99	499.40	505.90	504.36	503.52	503.22	503.59	502.63	500.66	502.63	506.06	509.39	504.36
502.90	498.06	502.71	497.94	501.78	502.80	500.12	504.61	504.58	503.43	503.25	503.43	502.71	501.27	502.71	505.68	509.57	502.90
500.62	497.71	500.32	498.21	499.76	500.68	499.45	501.60	502.08	500.91	500.66	501.14	500.32	499.87	500.32	503.16	505.52	502.26
498.16	495.15	497.64	493.98	497.55	498.30	494.09	502.81	498.19	499.31	499.43	501.06	497.64	493.73	497.64	504.39	510.49	500.14
488.26	494.71	488.52	494.02	490.33	488.44	491.46	483.73	486.76	488.06	486.92	486.05	488.52	491.53	488.52	485.06	478.88	485.32
487.62	485.63	487.24	487.23	487.45	487.75	485.49	491.40	489.16	488.00	488.88	489.48	487.24	486.48	487.24	490.48	494.81	488.33
487.54	487.21	487.12	486.20	486.90	487.38	486.73	488.00	488.07	487.75	486.51	485.83	487.12	487.14	487.12	489.91	489.62	488.59
469.75	469.96	469.55	469.19	470.44	469.90	469.33	470.07	471.13	470.47	470.14	470.37	469.55	469.74	469.55	472.81	474.16	470.18
462.93	456.52	462.12	457.27	461.11	463.08	460.13	467.03	465.28	463.80	464.53	465.67	462.12	459.28	462.12	464.83	470.62	466.15
458.48	455.82	458.41	457.93	457.36	458.34	456.87	457.41	457.73	458.23	458.98	458.73	458.41	456.29	458.41	459.06	457.45	458.42
453.39	452.06	453.06	452.74	452.85	453.15	453.77	453.42	452.92	452.88	453.38	453.08	453.06	452.90	453.06	452.97	453.34	453.10
447.53	448.96	446.88	449.50	447.14	447.63	447.36	450.56	449.42	448.19	448.69	449.14	446.88	447.81	446.88	450.65	452.99	450.48
446.67	444.67	446.99	447.91	446.88	447.12	447.29	448.75	447.82	447.10	447.30	446.57	446.99	445.73	446.99	448.15	449.92	448.03
443.60	442.82	443.30	445.74	443.44	443.47	442.45	444.27	443.56	443.28	444.18	443.71	443.30	441.57	443.30	442.96	441.95	443.85
442.86	448.42	443.21	445.70	443.73	442.88	444.98	440.30	443.23	442.94	442.57	442.12	443.21	445.77	443.21	440.87	436.57	442.31
442.12	439.54	442.57	440.41	441.30	442.16	440.84	444.23	442.73	442.36	442.61	443.46	442.57	440.17	442.57	443.75	446.68	443.22
433.52	432.84	433.04	432.70	432.95	433.18	432.58	434.66	433.33	433.37	433.55	433.57	433.04	432.50	433.04	435.28	436.08	434.00
432.20	432.28	431.42	432.99	431.88	431.96	431.21	433.36	433.11	432.25	433.04	433.16	431.42	430.89	431.42	432.96	434.64	433.34
428.26	429.43	428.66	429.91	427.81	427.99	429.33	429.51	428.13	428.25	428.39	428.79	428.66	429.07	428.66	427.87	428.41	428.94
422.57	424.79	422.20	424.58	422.09	421.85	423.66	423.38	423.20	421.96	422.26	422.36	422.20	423.75	422.20	420.57	422.02	422.59
398.99	400.40	398.46	402.87	399.72	399.18	398.86	400.59	399.53	399.41	399.74	400.18	398.46	398.57	398.46	400.38	402.34	400.00
387.34	387.41	387.09	389.32	386.66	386.85	386.61	388.56	387.72	387.19	387.83	389.43	387.09	386.30	387.09	390.70	394.47	389.99
383.38	386.40	383.27	387.66	383.14	382.71	384.33	383.65	383.40	382.91	382.96	384.38	383.27	384.87	383.27	384.56	385.8	384.28

103

Table 5: Average scale score based on subset of items identified by each country as addressing its curriculum (contd.)

Countries	Average	(se)	JOR	IDN	TUN	IRN	BHR	CHL	EGY	PSE	MAR	PHL	BWA	SAU	GHA	ZAF
	(Number of score points included)		152	209	162	203	199	192	164	207	198	192	184	213	151	128
SGP	620.64	(3.47)	619.39	621.01	621.08	620.79	621.38	620.58	620.83	620.91	621.32	621.91	618.46	620.64	619.74	619.89
KOR	603.91	(1.71)	604.52	603.67	602.70	604.33	601.87	598.72	608.21	603.71	602.59	604.62	599.69	603.91	602.47	599.28
HKG	603.70	(3.16)	602.22	603.74	602.66	603.72	602.54	601.33	605.82	603.17	603.04	604.79	601.42	603.70	602.49	602.27
TWN	597.78	(4.07)	596.69	597.77	595.39	597.26	596.28	594.08	600.85	597.55	596.62	598.92	593.81	597.78	595.60	594.12
JPN	589.22	(1.95)	586.98	588.99	585.54	588.04	587.88	586.29	587.50	588.47	587.83	586.85	587.61	589.22	584.36	576.31
BFL	561.79	(2.54)	553.53	562.00	560.10	559.98	561.38	564.46	558.82	561.25	560.65	558.35	563.90	561.79	559.48	554.23
NLD	559.63	(3.78)	547.36	560.00	550.43	556.25	560.13	564.14	553.74	558.87	557.02	555.00	563.68	559.63	558.12	546.83
HUN	556.00	(3.10)	550.54	556.17	552.91	554.71	556.06	555.73	552.47	555.50	555.72	553.09	557.76	556.00	552.76	550.99
EST	554.59	(2.94)	552.53	554.09	554.13	554.63	554.84	553.11	551.11	554.30	554.01	552.64	555.86	554.59	553.25	549.81
RUS	536.47	(3.28)	539.94	536.05	537.46	537.37	536.79	530.65	539.18	536.65	536.49	538.97	535.48	536.47	537.89	540.24
LVA	533.34	(3.00)	531.67	533.21	533.08	532.97	533.93	530.46	532.39	533.34	532.60	532.21	532.8	533.34	532.50	530.74
AUS	531.55	(4.27)	517.56	531.95	524.57	528.36	531.01	533.93	527.35	531.01	530.13	526.66	533.53	531.55	528.92	519.14
SVK	530.16	(3.23)	527.28	529.79	532.79	531.93	531.30	532.43	529.91	530.21	531.28	530.45	530.73	530.16	532.76	533.84
USA	529.30	(3.06)	521.57	529.71	523.40	525.77	528.75	528.99	524.29	529.18	528.17	525.43	531.63	529.30	524.66	518.98
MYS	529.20	(3.90)	524.56	529.36	528.29	529.09	529.05	532.56	529.90	528.92	528.52	528.03	528.91	529.20	529.74	531.40
SWE	527.30	(2.48)	509.84	527.74	519.11	523.29	526.91	531.93	518.49	526.79	525.48	519.75	531.61	527.30	526.61	513.13
LTU	526.21	(2.37)	527.03	526.08	524.73	525.31	526.82	524.20	525.57	526.01	525.09	526.94	527.01	526.21	523.30	521.61
SCO	524.97	(3.61)	510.20	525.36	517.65	521.44	524.73	527.29	518.64	524.42	523.66	518.12	527.14	524.97	523.82	509.89
ENG	524.52	(4.42)	508.00	525.01	515.63	520.79	523.37	526.29	518.39	523.45	522.16	517.72	526.75	524.52	521.30	508.94
ISR	522.16	(3.09)	520.33	522.06	521.86	521.83	521.73	520.28	520.86	522.40	522.03	521.73	522.39	522.16	521.25	519.79
NZL	518.89	(4.98)	503.43	519.32	510.85	515.36	518.21	521.54	514.51	517.87	516.82	513.38	521.48	518.89	516.13	503.91
SVN	513.27	(2.19)	508.13	513.40	511.97	512.72	513.40	515.40	512.68	512.99	512.60	513.17	515.14	513.27	511.57	512.18
ITA	511.77	(2.89)	507.83	511.88	511.46	511.67	512.14	513.69	510.23	511.75	511.30	509.67	511.92	511.77	512.49	511.70
ROM	502.99	(4.39)	506.60	502.63	507.04	505.58	503.12	500.38	507.46	503.55	503.98	506.82	501.47	502.99	504.74	511.59
SCG	502.80	(2.31)	505.36	502.71	506.34	504.93	501.96	498.89	506.35	503.25	503.20	505.83	501.25	502.80	504.62	510.71
BGR	500.68	(3.61)	503.11	500.32	505.11	502.90	500.82	498.37	502.53	500.94	500.83	501.45	499.37	500.68	501.68	505.14
ARM	498.30	(2.66)	506.00	497.64	505.67	502.63	499.00	488.88	502.10	499.40	501.68	504.32	497.21	498.30	499.32	511.45
NOR	488.44	(2.35)	473.89	488.52	481.32	485.73	487.36	492.37	482.49	487.91	486.52	483.35	491.28	488.44	489.49	476.11
MDA	487.75	(3.39)	493.72	487.24	491.00	490.13	488.58	485.85	491.59	487.90	488.89	491.89	487.28	487.75	492.24	495.42
CYP	487.38	(1.41)	484.82	487.12	490.68	489.47	486.77	487.58	489.75	487.71	487.46	488.06	486.89	487.38	489.45	491.70
MKD	469.90	(2.86)	472.21	469.55	472.92	471.96	470.10	468.32	471.12	470.34	470.48	470.66	469.93	469.90	471.42	473.99
LBN	463.08	(2.75)	475.11	462.12	467.05	464.40	464.40	459.02	466.35	463.89	464.76	467.75	460.68	463.08	460.05	474.51
JOR	458.34	(3.17)	469.15	458.41	459.59	458.82	457.83	455.91	457.77	458.31	458.60	458.03	456.92	458.34	457.39	456.63
IDN	453.15	(3.20)	455.80	453.06	452.50	453.38	453.40	453.74	453.66	452.88	452.80	452.99	452.96	453.15	452.63	455.50
TUN	447.63	(1.69)	452.59	446.88	455.34	449.99	449.82	452.12	450.41	448.37	450.35	450.81	447.24	447.63	451.57	456.61
IRN	447.12	(1.78)	451.29	446.99	448.60	448.13	446.65	447.36	449.56	447.19	446.01	448.40	444.49	447.12	449.70	450.24
BHR	443.47	(1.09)	451.17	443.30	444.02	443.09	443.86	443.43	443.83	443.50	444.19	444.54	442.34	443.47	443.61	442.05
CHL	442.88	(2.24)	434.23	443.21	440.18	441.27	443.32	447.57	439.88	442.74	442.81	438.70	444.84	442.88	445.68	438.66
EGY	442.16	(2.33)	454.47	442.57	445.89	443.09	441.80	441.94	446.06	442.29	442.82	446.16	440.00	442.16	443.85	451.80
PSE	433.18	(2.09)	442.97	433.04	435.91	434.81	433.10	433.22	434.28	433.19	433.91	434.78	432.78	433.18	435.14	436.33
MAR	431.96	(1.68)	440.76	431.42	435.46	432.95	433.29	432.69	433.63	432.30	433.37	433.24	431.06	431.96	432.87	436.63
PHL	427.99	(3.65)	432.59	428.66	428.31	427.81	428.27	429.74	429.96	428.30	428.60	430.18	428.87	427.99	427.84	434.90
BWA	421.85	(1.70)	424.67	422.20	422.34	420.45	422.34	424.50	423.42	421.94	423.14	424.10	423.95	421.85	421.77	427.49
SAU	399.18	(1.99)	409.01	398.46	403.17	400.76	400.15	401.61	401.38	399.19	399.59	401.60	398.61	399.18	402.42	405.98
GHA	386.85	(1.69)	01.15	387.09	394.62	390.01	387.61	389.51	389.80	387.39	389.41	390.77	385.92	386.85	389.32	402.14
ZAF	382.71	(3.15)	391.17	383.27	386.27	384.06	383.16	387.35	383.76	383.09	383.97	385.10	384.81	382.71	386.99	391.61

The first two grey-shaded columns in Table 5 show the average mathematics scores based on all test items included for each participant and their standard errors in parentheses. All numbers are rounded to two decimal places. The subsequent columns contain the performance of each country based on those items judged appropriate by the participant listed in the header of each column. The table is sorted by performance based on all items, from the highest to the lowest. Singapore received the highest average score (620.64); South Africa had the lowest score (382.71).

An answer to the question of whether or not the selection of items affected average student performance can be obtained by comparing the shaded diagonal cells in Table 5 with the performance of the students on the test as a whole, which is presented in the first shaded column. For example, Singapore reached a score of 621.40 on its own set of items, while it received a score of 620.50 for the items selected by Korea, and a score of 620.21 for the items selected by Hong Kong. The largest effect was found for the Netherlands and Jordan, with both countries gaining 11 score points on their own sets of items. On average, a country gained two score points if its set of not-covered items was removed from the scaling. Two countries, Israel and Saudi Arabia, showed no gain because they declared all items appropriate. Seven countries performed less well on their selected items. The median gain was one score point.

The rows in Table 5 indicate the effect of the different item selections on each country's student performance. The performance of students in Singapore was highest on the items judged as appropriate for Macedonia (622.84) and lowest on the items selected for Italy (618.19). However, the differences between the highest value and the smallest value were small for all countries, on average about 12 score points.

The columns in Table 5 show the relative positions of a country's performance when using the items selected for the other countries. In general, the relative positions of the countries changed very little as a result of the item selection. The high-performing countries consistently remained high-achieving for any item choice, while the low-performing countries consistently achieved at the low end of the distribution. Countries in the middle remained in the middle of the achievement distribution.

For reasons of completeness, Table 6 shows the standard errors associated with the average scale scores (Table 5) by country. The standard error for the score based on the test items included by each of the countries listed in the header row can be read across the row. The columns show the standard error for the score of the country down the left on the items included by the country list in the header row. The standard error for the score for each different country based on its own judgment about the test items included is displayed along the diagonal.

In order to illustrate the findings of Table 5 more clearly, Figure 5 shows the mean country scores calculated with all items included versus mean country scores for covered items only. The mean country scores for both all and covered items are represented by the grey-shaded column titled "Average" and the grey-shaded diagonal cells of Table 5, respectively. We used the jackknife method to estimate the standard errors of these average scores. The black rectangles in the scatterplot

Table 6: Standard errors for average scale scores by country

Countries	Average	(se)	SGP	KOR	HKG	TWN	JPN	BFL	NLD	HUN	EST	RUS	LVA	AUS	SVK	USA
	(Number of score points included)															
	213		206	193	211	210	199	198	169	212	204	177	209	206	182	208
SGP	620.64	(3.47)	3.50	3.46	3.49	3.47	3.44	3.41	3.44	3.47	3.45	3.50	3.49	3.43	3.50	3.49
KOR	603.91	(1.71)	1.71	1.71	1.73	1.71	1.72	1.69	1.63	1.71	1.72	1.72	1.70	1.67	1.710	1.70
HKG	603.70	(3.16)	3.13	3.15	3.12	3.16	3.13	3.12	3.03	3.15	3.14	3.14	3.15	3.06	3.14	3.15
TWN	597.78	(4.07)	4.07	4.06	4.13	4.06	4.01	3.95	3.78	4.07	4.06	4.08	4.05	3.93	4.08	4.05
JPN	589.22	(1.95)	1.94	1.95	1.94	1.95	1.96	1.97	1.92	1.94	1.95	1.95	1.94	1.98	1.94	1.94
BFL	561.79	(2.54)	2.54	2.54	2.57	2.54	2.55	2.53	2.42	2.53	2.53	2.51	2.53	2.51	2.54	2.53
NLD	559.63	(3.78)	3.78	3.78	3.76	3.77	3.76	3.75	3.84	3.78	3.78	3.74	3.77	3.87	3.78	3.77
HUN	556.00	(3.10)	3.11	3.09	3.17	3.10	3.06	3.09	3.03	3.10	3.10	3.17	3.10	3.02	3.13	3.10
EST	554.59	(2.94)	2.94	2.95	2.99	2.94	2.88	2.93	2.93	2.94	2.96	2.98	2.94	2.99	2.94	2.94
RUS	536.47	(3.28)	3.32	3.26	3.50	3.28	3.20	3.22	3.04	3.29	3.26	3.36	3.27	3.14	3.33	3.27
LVA	533.34	(3.00)	2.97	2.98	3.04	2.99	2.94	2.94	2.97	3.00	2.97	2.97	3.02	2.96	2.96	3.02
AUS	531.55	(4.27)	4.28	4.26	4.28	4.25	4.21	4.24	4.19	4.28	4.21	4.25	4.28	4.25	4.28	4.28
SVK	530.16	(3.23)	3.25	3.23	3.32	3.24	3.19	3.24	3.17	3.23	3.21	3.27	3.24	3.14	3.28	3.24
USA	529.30	(3.06)	3.04	3.06	3.06	3.05	3.01	3.04	3.09	3.06	3.04	3.04	3.06	3.07	3.04	3.06
MYS	529.20	(3.90)	3.92	3.89	3.99	3.89	3.84	3.86	3.78	3.90	3.88	3.94	3.87	3.85	3.90	3.87
SWE	527.30	(2.48)	2.47	2.49	2.43	2.49	2.50	2.51	2.56	2.48	2.50	2.46	2.47	2.60	2.47	2.47
LTU	526.21	(2.37)	2.38	2.37	2.43	2.39	2.35	2.38	2.36	2.38	2.37	2.41	2.38	2.44	2.38	2.38
SCO	524.97	(3.61)	3.61	3.61	3.62	3.60	3.57	3.60	3.68	3.61	3.59	3.57	3.61	3.69	3.60	3.61
ENG	524.52	(4.42)	4.41	4.41	4.45	4.39	4.36	4.36	4.44	4.43	4.37	4.4	4.42	4.48	4.40	4.42
ISR	522.16	(3.09)	3.09	3.09	3.08	3.09	3.08	3.04	2.98	3.09	3.09	3.10	3.07	3.04	3.10	3.07
NZL	518.89	(4.98)	4.96	4.99	5.00	4.99	4.95	5.03	4.93	4.98	5.03	4.94	4.95	5.05	4.94	4.95
SVN	513.27	(2.19)	2.20	2.19	2.23	2.19	2.19	2.24	2.21	2.19	2.21	2.18	2.18	2.22	2.19	2.18
ITA	511.77	(2.89)	2.93	2.88	2.96	2.87	2.86	2.86	2.75	2.89	2.89	2.92	2.88	2.84	2.93	2.88
ROM	502.99	(4.39)	4.36	4.39	4.41	4.39	4.36	4.31	4.19	4.39	4.39	4.41	4.37	4.29	4.39	4.37
SCG	502.80	(2.31)	2.32	2.31	2.37	2.31	2.26	2.26	2.22	2.31	2.33	2.37	2.30	2.29	2.32	2.30
BGR	500.68	(3.61)	3.62	3.60	3.67	3.61	3.61	3.50	3.45	3.60	3.64	3.62	3.59	3.59	3.62	3.59
ARM	498.30	(2.66)	2.65	2.65	2.72	2.66	2.68	2.62	2.53	2.66	2.65	2.76	2.65	2.64	2.66	2.65
NOR	488.44	(2.35)	2.36	2.35	2.31	2.36	2.34	2.42	2.45	2.35	2.35	2.35	2.35	2.36	2.36	2.35
MDA	487.75	(3.39)	3.42	3.39	3.48	3.38	3.31	3.31	3.09	3.39	3.39	3.40	3.37	3.31	3.45	3.37
CYP	487.38	(1.41)	1.41	1.41	1.43	1.41	1.41	1.40	1.44	1.41	1.43	1.45	1.39	1.41	1.41	1.39
MKD	469.90	(2.86)	2.85	2.85	2.87	2.84	2.79	2.82	2.82	2.86	2.85	2.85	2.87	2.77	2.85	2.87
LBN	463.08	(2.75)	2.77	2.75	2.80	2.74	2.71	2.76	2.75	2.75	2.75	2.83	2.75	2.74	2.77	2.75
JOR	458.34	(3.17)	3.13	3.17	3.12	3.15	3.12	3.10	3.13	3.17	3.15	3.07	3.16	3.11	3.13	3.16
IDN	453.15	(3.20)	3.17	3.19	3.16	3.20	3.20	3.15	3.09	3.20	3.18	3.14	3.17	3.16	3.18	3.17
TUN	447.63	(1.69)	1.69	1.69	1.65	1.68	1.68	1.66	1.62	1.69	1.70	1.71	1.67	1.59	1.69	1.67
IRN	447.12	(1.78)	1.76	1.78	1.72	1.77	1.77	1.75	1.69	1.78	1.75	1.73	1.78	1.74	1.75	1.78
BHR	443.47	(1.09)	1.08	1.10	1.10	1.09	1.08	1.12	1.11	1.09	1.09	1.12	1.10	1.09	1.09	1.10
CHL	442.88	(2.24)	2.21	2.23	2.19	2.23	2.21	2.23	2.19	2.24	2.23	2.23	2.24	2.22	2.24	2.24
EGY	442.16	(2.33)	2.31	2.32	2.31	2.34	2.29	2.26	2.18	2.33	2.33	2.26	2.31	2.26	2.31	2.31
PSE	433.18	(2.09)	2.10	2.08	2.07	2.09	2.10	2.09	2.01	2.09	2.08	2.07	2.08	1.97	2.10	2.08
MAR	431.96	(1.68)	1.69	1.67	1.65	1.69	1.68	1.67	1.70	1.68	1.70	1.68	1.67	1.58	1.72	1.67
PHL	427.99	(3.65)	3.65	3.65	3.58	3.64	3.62	3.64	3.55	3.65	3.65	3.62	3.65	3.50	3.64	3.65
BWA	421.85	(1.70)	1.68	1.70	1.61	1.70	1.71	1.72	1.70	1.70	1.73	1.68	1.68	1.68	1.67	1.68
SAU	399.18	(1.99)	1.96	1.98	1.94	1.96	1.94	1.90	1.82	1.99	1.96	1.93	1.94	1.95	1.94	1.94
GHA	386.85	(1.69)	1.68	1.70	1.64	1.68	1.67	1.63	1.62	1.69	1.67	1.60	1.70	1.63	1.68	1.70
ZAF	382.71	(3.15)	3.13	3.15	3.00	3.14	3.12	3.12	3.13	3.15	3.15	3.08	3.13	3.09	3.13	3.13

MYS	SWE	LTU	SCO	ENG	ISR	NZL	SVN	ITA	ROM	SCG	BGR	ARM	NOR	MDA	CYP	MKD	LBN
209	**172**	**209**	**158**	**208**	**213**	**191**	**187**	**178**	**207**	**205**	**196**	**209**	**209**	**197**	**188**	**174**	**189**
3.49	3.42	3.49	3.45	3.47	3.47	3.39	3.43	3.39	3.46	3.49	3.50	3.49	3.45	3.49	3.48	3.51	3.48
1.71	1.64	1.70	1.62	1.71	1.71	1.66	1.69	1.72	1.72	1.71	1.72	1.70	1.68	1.70	1.74	1.75	1.72
3.14	3.05	3.15	3.06	3.14	3.16	3.05	3.07	3.05	3.16	3.14	3.14	3.15	3.08	3.15	3.21	3.12	3.18
4.07	3.86	4.05	3.89	4.04	4.07	3.86	4.10	4.00	4.08	4.08	4.09	4.05	3.94	4.05	4.13	4.21	4.09
1.95	1.98	1.94	1.95	1.94	1.95	1.97	1.91	1.84	1.95	1.94	1.97	1.94	1.94	1.94	1.99	1.93	1.97
2.53	2.42	2.53	2.50	2.53	2.54	2.50	2.59	2.56	2.51	2.53	2.56	2.53	2.51	2.53	2.54	2.64	2.57
3.77	3.81	3.77	3.95	3.80	3.78	3.81	3.76	3.57	3.76	3.78	3.84	3.77	3.77	3.77	3.79	3.76	3.78
3.11	3.10	3.10	3.08	3.10	3.10	3.04	3.16	3.05	3.10	3.13	3.16	3.10	3.08	3.10	3.10	3.23	3.18
2.95	2.89	2.94	2.93	2.94	2.94	2.91	2.88	2.94	2.93	2.94	2.95	2.94	2.97	2.94	3.00	3.00	2.95
3.30	3.11	3.27	3.22	3.26	3.28	3.13	3.34	3.35	3.30	3.32	3.31	3.27	3.15	3.27	3.39	3.52	3.36
3.00	2.86	3.02	2.87	2.99	3.00	2.95	2.89	2.96	2.99	2.96	2.94	3.02	2.94	3.02	3.02	2.97	3.00
4.27	4.15	4.28	4.19	4.28	4.27	4.33	4.41	4.16	4.25	4.28	4.24	4.28	4.25	4.28	4.27	4.45	4.31
3.24	3.20	3.24	3.17	3.24	3.23	3.19	3.42	3.31	3.23	3.26	3.27	3.24	3.17	3.24	3.23	3.46	3.30
3.05	3.01	3.06	3.03	3.05	3.06	3.04	3.04	2.98	3.05	3.05	3.04	3.06	3.04	3.06	3.07	3.05	3.02
3.90	3.75	3.87	3.78	3.88	3.90	3.84	3.96	3.94	3.89	3.91	3.93	3.87	3.84	3.87	3.99	4.13	3.95
2.48	2.56	2.47	2.60	2.49	2.48	2.53	2.36	2.34	2.47	2.47	2.51	2.47	2.53	2.47	2.50	2.39	2.43
2.36	2.36	2.38	2.35	2.36	2.37	2.38	2.45	2.36	2.38	2.38	2.42	2.38	2.38	2.38	2.44	2.52	2.43
3.61	3.68	3.61	3.68	3.64	3.61	3.69	3.60	3.47	3.60	3.61	3.62	3.61	3.62	3.61	3.69	3.63	3.61
4.44	4.40	4.42	4.62	4.45	4.42	4.50	4.30	4.35	4.41	4.42	4.40	4.42	4.43	4.42	4.45	4.38	4.38
3.09	3.00	3.07	3.01	3.12	3.09	3.04	3.13	3.06	3.09	3.09	3.10	3.07	3.08	3.07	3.02	3.10	3.05
4.95	5.02	4.95	5.09	5.01	4.98	5.07	4.98	4.94	4.98	4.96	5.02	4.95	5.00	4.95	5.07	5.04	4.98
2.19	2.21	2.18	2.14	2.18	2.19	2.20	2.25	2.18	2.19	2.20	2.20	2.18	2.16	2.18	2.22	2.19	2.20
2.91	2.76	2.88	2.81	2.87	2.89	2.82	2.92	2.94	2.91	2.94	2.93	2.88	2.79	2.88	2.92	2.99	2.89
4.39	4.25	4.37	4.26	4.40	4.39	4.32	4.42	4.36	4.41	4.38	4.36	4.37	4.33	4.37	4.38	4.43	4.36
2.31	2.25	2.30	2.17	2.32	2.31	2.23	2.39	2.37	2.33	2.33	2.32	2.30	2.26	2.30	2.34	2.42	2.33
3.61	3.54	3.59	3.50	3.61	3.61	3.55	3.70	3.65	3.64	3.62	3.63	3.59	3.60	3.59	3.67	3.76	3.62
2.67	2.56	2.65	2.53	2.63	2.66	2.61	2.71	2.65	2.66	2.66	2.63	2.65	2.64	2.65	2.69	2.78	2.69
2.36	2.43	2.35	2.55	2.37	2.35	2.43	2.21	2.30	2.34	2.36	2.35	2.35	2.37	2.35	2.29	2.18	2.31
3.40	3.18	3.37	3.24	3.38	3.39	3.27	3.56	3.48	3.40	3.44	3.40	3.37	3.29	3.37	3.42	3.60	3.44
1.42	1.50	1.39	1.46	1.42	1.41	1.44	1.37	1.45	1.44	1.42	1.41	1.39	1.44	1.39	1.41	1.32	1.41
2.85	2.80	2.87	2.84	2.85	2.86	2.82	2.72	2.83	2.86	2.86	2.82	2.87	2.80	2.87	2.86	2.76	2.88
2.76	2.71	2.75	2.71	2.74	2.75	2.72	2.77	2.84	2.75	2.77	2.70	2.75	2.78	2.75	2.74	2.71	2.80
3.14	3.02	3.16	3.02	3.14	3.17	3.11	3.19	3.13	3.18	3.14	3.11	3.16	3.11	3.16	3.18	3.17	3.11
3.20	3.06	3.17	3.02	3.17	3.20	3.14	3.20	3.20	3.20	3.17	3.13	3.17	3.13	3.17	3.13	3.13	3.15
1.68	1.58	1.67	1.61	1.64	1.69	1.61	1.74	1.69	1.70	1.69	1.67	1.67	1.65	1.67	1.65	1.69	1.69
1.76	1.66	1.78	1.74	1.76	1.78	1.75	1.76	1.80	1.77	1.75	1.73	1.78	1.74	1.78	1.76	1.78	1.76
1.08	1.10	1.10	1.09	1.11	1.09	1.11	1.08	1.11	1.10	1.08	1.09	1.10	1.10	1.10	1.08	1.08	1.11
2.23	2.21	2.24	2.14	2.24	2.24	2.24	2.21	2.22	2.24	2.23	2.16	2.24	2.23	2.24	2.23	2.16	2.26
2.32	2.19	2.31	2.20	2.31	2.33	2.26	2.37	2.32	2.33	2.31	2.31	2.31	2.20	2.31	2.30	2.32	2.26
2.08	1.98	2.08	1.98	2.07	2.09	2.04	2.17	2.10	2.11	2.09	2.09	2.08	2.01	2.08	2.06	2.10	2.07
1.69	1.63	1.67	1.56	1.64	1.68	1.65	1.73	1.75	1.71	1.71	1.68	1.67	1.60	1.67	1.68	1.71	1.72
3.63	3.50	3.65	3.48	3.60	3.65	3.58	3.68	3.62	3.66	3.65	3.58	3.65	3.53	3.65	3.58	3.52	3.58
1.69	1.70	1.68	1.67	1.71	1.70	1.68	1.65	1.72	1.72	1.67	1.67	1.68	1.69	1.68	1.66	1.53	1.67
1.95	1.95	1.94	1.83	1.98	1.99	2.00	1.98	2.04	1.99	1.96	1.86	1.94	1.95	1.94	1.98	1.96	2.00
1.70	1.66	1.70	1.60	1.70	1.69	1.69	1.66	1.62	1.69	1.69	1.61	1.70	1.66	1.70	1.62	1.52	1.64
3.13	3.13	3.13	3.10	3.14	3.15	3.16	3.08	3.11	3.15	3.13	3.06	3.13	3.14	3.13	3.03	2.86	3.09

Table 6: Standard errors for average scale scores by country (contd.)

Countries	Average	(se)	JOR	IDN	TUN	IRN	BHR	CHL	EGY	PSE	MAR	PHL	BWA	SAU	GHA	ZAF
	(Number of score points included)		152	209	162	203	199	192	164	207	198	192	184	213	151	128
SGP	620.64	(3.47)	3.73	3.49	3.45	3.49	3.48	3.42	3.43	3.46	3.47	3.51	3.49	3.47	3.49	3.27
KOR	603.91	(1.71)	1.79	1.70	1.75	1.74	1.70	1.63	1.74	1.72	1.72	1.72	1.69	1.71	1.68	1.68
HKG	603.70	(3.16)	3.31	3.15	3.20	3.19	3.14	3.02	3.10	3.16	3.15	3.16	3.07	3.16	3.03	2.96
TWN	597.78	(4.07)	4.34	4.05	4.17	4.11	4.02	3.83	4.10	4.08	4.09	4.17	3.95	4.07	4.00	4.04
JPN	589.22	(1.95)	2.07	1.94	2.02	2.01	1.96	2.00	1.85	1.96	1.97	1.95	1.96	1.95	1.82	1.92
BFL	561.79	(2.54)	2.74	2.53	2.60	2.59	2.53	2.46	2.56	2.51	2.52	2.57	2.54	2.54	2.49	2.48
NLD	559.63	(3.78)	4.13	3.77	3.69	3.83	3.81	3.83	3.60	3.76	3.77	3.75	3.85	3.78	3.68	3.60
HUN	556.00	(3.1)	3.24	3.10	3.15	3.12	3.14	3.12	3.12	3.11	3.13	3.17	3.07	3.10	3.14	3.15
EST	554.59	(2.94)	2.98	2.94	3.05	2.99	2.90	2.95	2.92	2.94	2.94	2.88	2.94	2.94	2.89	2.90
RUS	536.47	(3.28)	3.46	3.27	3.44	3.39	3.24	3.24	3.43	3.3	3.36	3.31	3.14	3.28	3.39	3.58
LVA	533.34	(3)	3.05	3.02	2.98	3.04	2.93	2.87	2.98	3.00	2.96	2.94	2.88	3.00	2.98	2.97
AUS	531.55	(4.27)	4.46	4.28	4.26	4.29	4.25	4.24	4.40	4.26	4.24	4.40	4.18	4.27	4.07	4.27
SVK	530.16	(3.23)	3.35	3.24	3.33	3.24	3.26	3.15	3.39	3.25	3.28	3.35	3.21	3.23	3.25	3.35
USA	529.30	(3.06)	3.08	3.06	3.02	3.07	3.04	3.01	3.04	3.05	3.05	3.08	3.02	3.06	3.02	2.99
MYS	529.20	(3.9)	4.05	3.87	4.02	3.99	3.88	3.82	4.03	3.89	3.89	3.96	3.79	3.90	3.88	4.06
SWE	527.30	(2.48)	2.62	2.47	2.47	2.52	2.49	2.56	2.27	2.48	2.48	2.39	2.57	2.48	2.37	2.25
LTU	526.21	(2.37)	2.48	2.38	2.49	2.43	2.41	2.36	2.41	2.39	2.40	2.46	2.39	2.37	2.46	2.53
SCO	524.97	(3.61)	3.82	3.61	3.63	3.70	3.62	3.60	3.52	3.60	3.61	3.63	3.60	3.61	3.44	3.57
ENG	524.52	(4.42)	4.58	4.42	4.44	4.46	4.44	4.33	4.22	4.42	4.40	4.38	4.38	4.42	4.27	4.15
ISR	522.16	(3.09)	3.21	3.07	3.01	3.04	3.08	3.05	3.08	3.09	3.10	3.10	3.07	3.09	3.06	2.86
NZL	518.89	(4.98)	5.04	4.95	5.09	5.06	5.02	4.93	4.90	4.98	4.99	5.03	4.96	4.98	4.86	4.98
SVN	513.27	(2.19)	2.34	2.18	2.21	2.21	2.24	2.26	2.26	2.20	2.23	2.22	2.15	2.19	2.17	2.22
ITA	511.77	(2.89)	2.95	2.88	2.92	2.90	2.92	2.82	2.94	2.91	2.94	2.95	2.79	2.89	2.91	3.04
ROM	502.99	(4.39)	4.47	4.37	4.35	4.39	4.33	4.28	4.50	4.40	4.39	4.53	4.32	4.39	4.27	4.37
SCG	502.80	(2.31)	2.36	2.30	2.41	2.32	2.32	2.26	2.37	2.33	2.35	2.38	2.28	2.31	2.36	2.43
BGR	500.68	(3.61)	3.70	3.59	3.72	3.65	3.63	3.53	3.64	3.64	3.65	3.72	3.61	3.61	3.69	3.56
ARM	498.30	(2.66)	2.68	2.65	2.72	2.69	2.64	2.71	2.72	2.66	2.65	2.70	2.63	2.66	2.78	2.81
NOR	488.44	(2.35)	2.29	2.35	2.31	2.31	2.39	2.47	2.16	2.34	2.35	2.20	2.37	2.35	2.30	2.16
MDA	487.75	(3.39)	3.47	3.37	3.45	3.44	3.39	3.20	3.51	3.39	3.40	3.52	3.32	3.39	3.40	3.45
CYP	487.38	(1.41)	1.38	1.39	1.42	1.40	1.44	1.47	1.37	1.43	1.45	1.41	1.44	1.41	1.43	1.43
MKD	469.90	(2.86)	2.79	2.87	2.80	2.83	2.86	2.74	2.73	2.86	2.86	2.72	2.80	2.86	2.82	2.70
LBN	463.08	(2.75)	2.57	2.75	2.80	2.73	2.74	2.79	2.77	2.75	2.75	2.68	2.78	2.75	2.79	2.83
JOR	458.34	(3.17)	3.14	3.16	3.01	3.16	3.12	2.99	3.23	3.18	3.11	3.25	3.10	3.17	2.99	3.12
IDN	453.15	(3.2)	2.98	3.17	3.06	3.16	3.13	3.06	3.22	3.20	3.14	3.18	3.12	3.20	3.08	3.01
TUN	447.63	(1.69)	1.67	1.67	1.68	1.65	1.68	1.65	1.78	1.69	1.68	1.78	1.66	1.69	1.67	1.69
IRN	447.12	(1.78)	1.73	1.78	1.75	1.77	1.74	1.65	1.83	1.77	1.73	1.77	1.71	1.78	1.69	1.69
BHR	443.47	(1.09)	1.12	1.10	1.09	1.09	1.07	1.08	1.08	1.09	1.06	1.07	1.09	1.09	1.10	1.18
CHL	442.88	(2.24)	2.12	2.24	2.22	2.21	2.22	2.24	2.20	2.24	2.24	2.17	2.20	2.24	2.17	2.08
EGY	442.16	(2.33)	2.29	2.31	2.23	2.32	2.28	2.19	2.41	2.33	2.29	2.36	2.29	2.33	2.21	2.16
PSE	433.18	(2.09)	2.07	2.08	2.02	2.07	2.10	1.98	2.16	2.11	2.12	2.18	2.04	2.09	2.05	2.07
MAR	431.96	(1.68)	1.74	1.67	1.83	1.69	1.73	1.66	1.67	1.70	1.77	1.67	1.61	1.68	1.68	1.75
PHL	427.99	(3.65)	3.52	3.65	3.47	3.58	3.65	3.43	3.69	3.66	3.64	3.67	3.61	3.65	3.46	3.47
BWA	421.85	(1.7)	1.60	1.68	1.60	1.63	1.68	1.62	1.65	1.72	1.71	1.66	1.73	1.7.00	1.58	1.50
SAU	399.18	(1.99)	1.74	1.94	1.90	1.96	1.98	1.86	2.02	1.99	1.92	2.01	1.92	1.99	1.95	2.02
GHA	386.85	(1.69)	1.44	1.70	1.50	1.63	1.67	1.68	1.66	1.68	1.66	1.63	1.61	1.69	1.62	1.41
ZAF	382.71	(3.15)	2.80	3.13	2.98	3.05	3.11	3.12	3.03	3.14	3.12	3.04	3.11	3.15	2.98	2.76

illustrate the mean country score when all items were included regardless of whether or not the country covered the item. The grey circles indicate the position of the mean country score when we removed those items not covered in a country during scaling. The confidence intervals show if the differences were significant or not. As in most countries, the mean country scores based on covered and not-covered items were about the same; the black rectangles in the scatter plot are often not visible.

Figure 5: Differences between score based on all items and score based on covered items

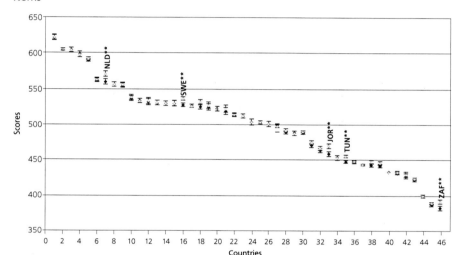

Figure 5 clearly shows that, for the great majority of the countries, no significant differences existed between mean country scores based on all items included and those based on covered items only. However, the mean country score was significantly higher in a few countries—Jordan, the Netherlands, South Africa, Sweden, and Tunisia— when not-covered items were removed before scaling. Each of these countries is highlighted in the figure via the appropriate country abbreviation and ** above its score. The largest differences evident in the figure are those for the Netherlands and Jordan, with both gaining 11 score points. Sweden and South Africa gained about nine score points, and Tunisia would have increased its score points by about eight if its covered items had been considered in the scaling. However, because we used EAP scores, the standard errors generated from this analysis were generally underestimated.

Influence on Rank Positions

We also considered the effect of curriculum coverage on country rankings. As was the case for most other countries, no rank changes were noted for Jordan and South Africa when not-covered items were removed from the scaling. The Netherlands would have increased its relative rank position by one position, and thereby exchanged its rank position with Belgium Flemish, if its not-covered items had been removed. However, the difference between the score from the Netherlands and the score from Belgium Flemish was not statistically significant. Tunisia also would have increased its position by one, and thereby exchanged rank position with Indonesia. Again, the difference between the scores was not significant. The largest increase was that for Sweden, where we would have observed a rank increase of six positions from 16 to 10 if its not-covered items had been removed. However, if we look at the countries included on rank positions 10 to 16 and then look at their scores based on Sweden's curriculum, we can see that the differences between the scores of these countries are very small and not significant.

DISCUSSION AND CONCLUSION

During the study described in this article, we used TIMSS 2003 Grade 8 mathematics data to examine the effect of curriculum coverage on scale scores. We also conducted an exploratory analysis to gain a better understanding of the types of items that given countries reported as not covered in their respective intended curriculums. We used an IRT scaling approach to understand the effect of curriculum coverage on scale scores and simple descriptive statistics for the exploratory analysis.

Our exploratory analysis uncovered a number of interesting findings. In terms of constructed-response versus multiple-choice items, we found a majority of the participating countries reported full coverage of constructed-response items but not of multiple-choice items. We also found that, for 13 countries, performance on the not-covered items compared to performance on the covered items was significantly worse than we had expected. Our expectation here was reasonable, because we would expect that students would be more likely to correctly answer covered items than not-covered items. However, our results also showed that, in 10 countries, students did significantly better than we had expected on not-covered items than on covered items. Interestingly, these countries were distributed throughout the achievement range and did not seem to exhibit any immediately obvious patterns.

When we considered items by content domain, the data domain had, on average, the highest rates of not-covered items. In fact, for 17 countries, 25% or more of the data items were not covered by their curriculums. Nonetheless, 15 countries reported that all data items were covered by their curriculum. It is interesting to note that while many of the countries reporting full coverage in the data domain were Eastern European (Armenia, Estonia, Hungary, Latvia, Lithuania, Moldova, and Romania), a number of geographically similar countries reported high rates of non-coverage (Bulgaria, Macedonia, Russia, Slovakia, and Slovenia). Finally, Ghana, Jordan, and South Africa consistently reported low rates of curriculum coverage across all content domains, which is in line with low rates of general coverage. Across the three cognitive domains assessed in the TIMSS 2003 mathematics items, we found a wide distribution of curriculum coverage. In general, the low rates of curriculum coverage in the cognitive domains were consistent with the rates of coverage overall.

The findings from our analysis of the effect of item–curriculum coverage on scale scores for TIMSS 2003 suggested that scale scores for all items correlated very highly with curriculum-covered items for each country assessed. The same was true for correlations between the item parameters when those items were scaled with all items and only those items covered in a country.

The results of the differences in the mean scores and the countries' rank positions accord with Beaton's (1998) findings and the findings of the TCMA reported in the *TIMSS 2003 International Mathematics Report* (Mullis et al., 2004). Our results indicate that even if countries had selected the items covered in their intended curriculums, we would have found no statistically significant effects across the countries' international standings. Although there were small increases in some of the countries' performances on their own subsets of items, this situation did not substantially affect the overall picture. Similar to the findings of the TCMA (Mullis et al., 2004), countries with high or low performance on the full set of mathematics items exhibited relatively high or low performance regardless of the set of items used for comparison. Given that the TIMSS 2003 research consortium conducted an extensive process during test development to ensure that the study's assessment was as fair as possible, our results are not unexpected and support earlier findings. Because the majority of countries indicated that they covered most items in their intended curriculums, the calculated scale scores were based on a highly similar set of items.

Implications and Areas for Further Research

Our findings suggest that a high degree of confidence can be placed in the estimated scale scores for all countries assessed during TIMSS 2003 regardless of item selection. Our results also should help validate earlier findings regarding assessment performance and departures from test–curriculum alignment.

Further studies designed to investigate the effect of curriculum coverage on science scores or conducted with the Grade 4 sample may be useful for validating the current findings. Additionally, scaling items reported as not covered may provide valuable information regarding the characteristics of items not covered by a particular country's curriculum.

References

Beaton, A. (1998). Comparing cross-national student performance on TIMSS using different test items. *International Journal of Educational Research, 29*(6), 529–542.

Beaton, A., & Gonzalez, E. (1997). Reporting achievement in mathematics and science content areas. In M. Martin & D. Kelly (Eds.), *Third International Mathematics and Science Study technical report: Vol. II. Implementation and analysis* (pp. 175–185). Chestnut Hill, MA: Center for the Study of Testing, Evaluation, and Educational Policy, Boston College.

Martin, M. (2005). *TIMSS 2003 user guide for the international database.* Chestnut

Hill, MA: TIMSS & PIRLS International Study Center, Lynch School of Education, Boston College.

Martin, M., Mullis, I., & Chrostowksi, S. (2004). *TIMSS 2003 technical report*. Chestnut Hill, MA: TIMSS & PIRLS International Study Center, Lynch School of Education, Boston College.

Mullis, I., Martin, M., & Foy, P. (2005). *IEA's TIMSS 2003 report on achievement in the mathematics cognitive domains*. Chestnut Hill, MA: TIMSS & PIRLS International Study Center, Lynch School of Education, Boston College.

Mullis, I., Martin, M., Gonzalez, E., & Chrostowksi, S. (2004). *TIMSS 2003 international mathematics report*. Chestnut Hill, MA: TIMSS & PIRLS International Study Center, Lynch School of Education, Boston College.

Mullis, I., Martin, M., Smith, T., Garden, R., Gregory, K., Gonzalez, E., Chrostowksi, S., & O'Connor, K. (2003). *TIMSS assessment frameworks and specification 2003* (2nd ed.). Chestnut Hill, MA: TIMSS & PIRLS International Study Center, Lynch School of Education, Boston College.

Questionnaire construct validation in the International Civic and Citizenship Education Study

Wolfram Schulz

Australian Council for Educational Research, Camberwell, Victoria, Australia

International studies tend to use student, teacher, and/or school questionnaires to collect contextual data on student and teacher characteristics, background, and activities, and the school's learning environment. Student measures of values, attitudes, and behavioral intentions are also often viewed as important learning outcomes, in particular within the context of studies of civic and citizenship education. The scaling of questionnaire items to obtain measures of students', teachers', and principals' perceptions and attitudes should therefore ideally be subject to a thorough cross-country validation of the underlying constructs. However, whereas those conducting international studies spend considerable effort ensuring measurement equivalence for international test instruments, the issue of equivalency of questionnaire data does not always receive the same attention. Using a set of student questionnaire items as an example, this article describes different methodological approaches to assess cross-national construct validation. With reference to an example from the field trial analyses for the IEA International Civic and Citizenship Education Study (ICCS), the article also shows the extent to which classical item statistics, factor analysis, and item response modeling help to assess the construct validity of questionnaire data obtained from international studies.

INTRODUCTION

The International Civic and Citizenship Education Study (ICCS) is the third international IEA study designed to measure the context and outcomes of civic and citizenship education, and it is explicitly linked through common questions to the IEA Civic Education Study (CIVED), which was undertaken in 1999 and 2000 (Amadeo, Torney-Purta, Lehman, Husfeldt, & Nikolova, 2002; Torney-Purta, Lehmann, Oswald, & Schulz, 2001; Schulz & Sibberns, 2004). The study, which builds on CIVED and is being conducted during 2008 and 2009, surveys 13- to 14-year-old students in 38 countries and will report on student achievement and perceptions related to civic and citizenship education.[1] Outcome data are being obtained from representative samples of students in their eighth year of schooling; context data are being collected from the students, their schools, and their teachers as well as through the study's national centers.

The aim of ICCS is to gather data on (a) student knowledge, conceptual understanding, and competencies in civic and citizenship education; (b) student background characteristics and participation in active citizenship; and (c) student perceptions of aspects of civics and citizenship. Instruments used in ICCS include an online national context survey completed by the national centers, a student test, a student questionnaire, a teacher questionnaire, and a school questionnaire. The ICCS assessment framework (Schulz, Fraillon, Ainley, Losito, & Kerr, 2008) outlines the aspects addressed in the cognitive test and the student perceptions questionnaire and provides a mapping of factors that might influence outcome variables and explain their variation.

It is recognized that there is substantial diversity in the field of civic and citizenship education within and across countries. Consequently, maximizing the involvement of researchers from participating countries in this international comparative study has been of particular importance for the success not only of this study in general but also for the process of developing an assessment framework and instruments. Input from national research centers has been sought throughout the study, and strategies were developed to maximize country contributions from the time of the early piloting activities through to selection of the final main survey instruments in June 2009. The main data collection was carried out between October and December 2008 in the Southern Hemisphere and between February and May 2009 in the Northern Hemisphere.

The students surveyed at these times were students enrolled in the grade that represents eight years of schooling, counting from the first year of primary school,

---

1 ICCS is managed by a consortium of three partner institutions (the Australian Council for Educational Research, the National Foundation for Educational Research in the United Kingdom, and the Laboratorio di Pedagogia Sperimentale at the Roma Tre University). The three institutions work in close co-operation with the IEA Secretariat, The IEA Data Processing and Research Center, and the national research coordinators (NRCs) of the participating countries. Further information about ICCS can be found at http://iccs.acer.edu.au/.

provided that their mean age at the time of testing was at least 13.5 years. According to this definition, for most countries the target grade was the eighth grade, or its national equivalent. The rationale for this definition was to have cross-nationally comparable student populations that are of the same age but also have similar levels of schooling.

One important feature of the ICCS data collection was measurement of value beliefs, attitudes, and behavioral intentions. This was typically done by administering questionnaires that included sets of four-point Likert-type items scaled to derive measures of latent constructs. Consequently, the comparability of these constructs became an important requirement for the ICCS data collection.

Language differences can have a powerful effect on equivalence (or non-equivalence). As with most international studies (see, for example, Chrostowski & Malak, 2004; Grisay, 2002), ICCS implements reviews of national adaptations and rigorous translation verifications to achieve a maximum of "linguistic equivalence." However, even slight deviations in wording (sometimes due to linguistic differences between source and target language) can lead to differences in item responses (see Harkness, Pennell, & Schoua-Glusberg, 2004; Mohler, Smith, & Harkness, 1998).

Non-equivalence in international studies can also be caused by cultural differences among the participating countries. Cultural habits can influence the degree to which respondents endorse certain item statements. In addition, differences between education systems (with different instructional practices and policies) and curricula can influence how respondents understand and interpret questionnaire items. For example, student responses indicating unfavorable learning conditions (such as disruptions at the beginning of each lesson) can be interpreted differently depending on what is commonly experienced in the national context (for an example, see Schulz, 2003).

According to van de Vijver and Tanzer (1997), while instruments might work properly, the cultural characteristics of groups of respondents can introduce bias in measurement. Byrne (2003) distinguishes three types of bias in cross-national research:

1. *Construct bias* refers to cases where a construct may be meaningful in one country, but not in another country;

2. *Method bias* refers to cases where data are biased by differences in responses to the instruments caused by cultural traits; and

3. *Item bias*, which refers to bias occurring at the level of the individual item. Constructs might be well measured in general, but some items may exhibit differential item functioning due to cultural differences.

Confirmatory factor analysis (CFA), which is based on the analyses of variances and covariances, provides an important tool for reviewing the cross-cultural validity of questionnaire constructs (see Kaplan, 2000). Little (1997) proposed extending the use of CFA to multiple-group analysis of mean and covariance structures (MACS) in order to test the comparability of measurement equivalence of psychological constructs and thereby detect possible socio-cultural variation of factor loadings and intercept parameters. Item response modeling (ref. item response theory or IRT; see Hambleton, Swaminathan, & Rogers, 1991) has also been used to detect non-equivalence of questionnaire constructs across countries (see, for example, Schulz, 2006; Wilson, 1994). IRT has furthermore been used to review the existence of different response patterns across cultural contexts in studies employing data collection instruments containing Likert-type items (Walker, 2007).

This article documents how both analyses of variances and covariances as well as item response modeling were used to address questionnaire construct validity and measurement equivalence during analysis of the ICCS field trial data. The analysis included reviews of item dimensionality, item/scale characteristics, and the measurement equivalence of model parameters across the participating countries.

DATA AND METHODS

The international field trial for ICCS was carried out in 32 participating countries between October 2007 and January 2008. On average, about 25 schools with about 600 students in the target grade in intact classrooms were selected. The following international instruments were used in the field trial:

- *The international student test:* This comprised 98 items in six different clusters administered in a completely rotated design with six randomly allocated booklets, each consisting of three 20-minute clusters;

- *The international student questionnaire:* Containing 71 background and 201 perceptions items, this was administered in three randomly allocated questionnaire forms;

- *The international teacher questionnaire:* This contained around 32 questions that took about 30 minutes to answer; and

- *The international school questionnaire:* This contained 22 questions that took 20 to 30 minutes to answer.

In addition, regional field trial instruments were administered in Europe and Latin America. These instruments consisted of short knowledge tests and questionnaire material designed to capture region-specific knowledge and perceptions.

The following verification procedures were implemented before the international field trial to ensure the highest possible level of instrument comparability:

- *Review of national adaptation:* During the first stage, the national centers submitted national adaptation forms (NAFs) for all instruments to the international study center (ISC) for review. ISC staff members reviewed the adaptations and sent the forms back with recommendations for further improvement, where appropriate. These forms were particularly useful as references during further instrument verification steps and data processing.

- *Translation verification:* After implementing suggestions from the adaptation review, the national centers submitted all instruments to be verified by professional language experts. The IEA Secretariat coordinated this activity. The verification outcomes were sent back to the national centers with (where appropriate) suggestions for improving the translations.

- *Layout verification:* After implementing suggestions from translation verification, the national centers assembled the final field trial instruments and submitted them for final layout verification by the ISC. The results of this final check were sent back to the countries.

The ICCS field trial analyses were based on a data collection in 718 schools in 31 countries and comprised questionnaire data from 19,369 students, 9,383 teachers, and 681 school principals. The analyses presented in this article focus on a set of items included in the student questionnaire and measuring students' expected civic participation in the future. This set of items is used to illustrate the following approaches, scope, and interpretation.

- *Exploratory factor analysis (EFA):* This was used at the preliminary analyses stage in order to review expected dimensionality of questionnaire items and to make preliminary decisions regarding the allocation to scales.

- *"Classical" item and scale statistics (such as reliabilities and item-total correlations):* These were computed to provide information on scaling characteristics and to permit a country-by-country review of item and scale performance.

- *Confirmatory factor analysis (CFA):* This was estimated for the pooled sample and separately for country sub-samples. These analyses were used not only to review the measurement model but also to review its fit as well as correlations between the latent variables across countries.

- *Multiple-group CFA:* This was estimated with different constraints to test measurement invariance more systematically across countries. However, multiple-group modeling was not systematically implemented in the analyses of ICCS field trial data.

- *Rasch modeling:* This provided information on item fit as well as estimates of item-by-country interaction with regard to the item location parameters.

This article discusses the results of these different analysis steps with regard to their usefulness for reviewing scale/item characteristics and validating constructs in international studies. To gain full benefit from this discussion, it is important to distinguish the following criteria:

- *Item performance:* Single items can be judged with regard to their appropriateness for measuring a construct both internationally and for individual education systems.

- *Construct measurement:* Scales can be scrutinized with regard to the extent to which it is possible to measure a certain construct reliably using a set of indicators.

- *Cross-country validation:* Constructs may be measured reliably in one country but not in another, which raises the question of whether, and to what extent, it is possible to measure the same construct with an internationally defined measurement model.

Each of the analysis approaches provides different pieces of information helpful to readers wanting to determine if items and scales used in an international study comply with their national criteria.

ICCS Field Trial Data Analysis

Exploratory Factor Analysis

In this article, the procedures for the ICCS questionnaire constructs are illustrated through analysis of a set of items measuring students' expectations about their future participation in political activities as an adult or as adolescent. Because of missing data, not all country datasets could be included in the analyses of these items. Table 1 shows the wording of the items used in the analyses. Expected participation in political life as an adult (Question I03) was measured with a set of seven items. Two dimensions were expected: expected electoral participation (scale name: VOTEPART, items I03a to I03c) and expected active political participation (scale name: POLPART, items I03d to I03g). Expected participation as an adolescent in the near future (Question I04) was measured with seven items expected to form a scale measuring expected informal civic participation (INFPART).

Table 1: Items measuring students' expected civic participation

Item	Question/item wording	Expected scale
Question I03	Listed below are different ways adults can take an active part in political life. **When you are an adult, what do you think you will do?**	
I03A	Vote in <local elections>	VOTEPART
I03B	Vote in <national elections>	VOTEPART
I03C	Get information about candidates before voting in an election	VOTEPART
I03D	Help a candidate or party during an election campaign	POLPART
I03E	Join a political party	POLPART
I03F	Join a trade union	POLPART
I03G	Stand as a candidate for a local or city office	POLPART
Question I04	Listed below are different actions that you as a young person could take during the next few years. **What do you expect that you will do?**	
I04A	Volunteer time to help people in the <local community>	INFPART
I04B	Collect money for a social cause	INFPART
I04C	Talk to others about your views on political and social issues	INFPART
I04D	Try to get friends to agree with your political opinions	INFPART
I04E	Write to a newspaper about political and social issues	INFPART
I04F	Contribute to an on-line discussion forum about social and political issues	INFPART
I04G	Join an organization for a political or social cause	INFPART

Note: Response categories were (1) I will certainly do this, (2) I will probably do this, (3) I will probably not do this, and (4) I will certainly *not* do this.

During the first stage of the ICCS field trial analysis, exploratory factor analyses were undertaken to review the expected dimensionality of questionnaire items following a review of item frequencies for valid and missing categories. The pooled international sample was used for these preliminary analyses, and the first decisions were made about the mapping of items to constructs for further analyses. Items were analyzed using principal component analyses with PROMAX rotation, which allows factors to be correlated. The software package MPLUS was used to estimate the results (Muthén & Muthén, 2001).[2]

Table 2 shows the results of the EFA for the items measuring students' expected political participation. The expected three-factor solution had an unsatisfactory model fit. The results for a four-factor solution clearly show that items I04A (volunteering time) and I04B (collecting money) loaded on a different factor than informal participation. As there were only two items measuring a fourth construct, "expected community

Table 2: EFA results for expected civic participation items (factor loadings for four-factor solution and factor correlations)

Item		Factors			
		1	2	3	4
I03A	Vote in <local elections>	**0.85**	0.01	- 0.03	0.01
I03B	Vote in <national elections>	**0.95**	- 0.06	- 0.02	- 0.05
I03C	Get information about candidates before voting	**0.56**	0.08	0.06	0.05
I03D	Help a candidate or party during campaign	0.16	0.06	0.09	**0.46**
I03E	Join a political party	- 0.03	- 0.05	- 0.02	**0.90**
I03F	Join a trade union	- 0.01	- 0.02	0.05	**0.72**
I03G	Stand as a candidate for a local or city office	- 0.04	0.04	0.07	**0.69**
I04A	Volunteer time to help people	- 0.03	**0.79**	0.00	0.02
I04B	Collect money for a social cause	- 0.03	**0.80**	0.01	- 0.06
I04C	Talk to others about your views	0.10	0.18	**0.52**	0.01
I04D	Try to get friends to agree with your opinions	0.01	0.04	**0.61**	0.04
I04E	Write to a newspaper	- 0.04	- 0.02	**0.81**	0.01
I04F	Contribute to an on-line discussion forum	- 0.01	- 0.10	**0.85**	- 0.04
I04G	Join an organization for a political or social cause	- 0.06	0.09	**0.61**	0.14
Correlations between factors					
	Factor 1	**1.00**			
	Factor 2	**0.42**	**1.00**		
	Factor 3	**0.41**	**0.61**	**1.00**	
	Factor 4	**0.44**	**0.46**	**0.64**	**1.00**

Note: PROMAX rotation with maximum likelihood estimation based on pooled international field trial sample; RMSEA = 0.051, RMR = 0.018. Factor loadings > 0.4 in **bold**.

---

2 In general, maximum likelihood estimation was used for the majority of items with four categories in the ICCS field trial analyses. A mean- and variance-adjusted weighted least square (WLS) estimator was used for items with fewer categories.

participation," these two items were not viewed as sufficient for construct measurement and were discarded from the subsequent scaling analyses. The results also show quite strong positive correlations across the four factors. However, the size of these correlations still indicates that this item-set measures four clearly distinguishable factors.

Using EFA as a first analysis step is useful for confirming whether expectations about item dimensionality and scaling are reasonable. For the ICCS field trial analysis, EFA was used only with the pooled international sample because comparing results for each country dataset could have become complex. Also, CFA analysis was viewed as more appropriate for determining whether expectations regarding item dimensionality held for individual country data.

Classical Item and Scale Analysis

Once the preliminary analysis of dimensionality had been undertaken, the expected mapping of items to scales was revised according to the results of the exploratory factor analyses. Based on the revised item classification of scaled items, the following classical item statistics were computed for the pooled dataset and separately for each country.

- *Item-total correlations:* Pearson correlation coefficients between each item and the (corrected) overall raw score are a particularly useful means of reviewing translation errors. For example, a negative correlation with the overall score may indicate that a negatively phrased item ("Students of my age are too young to have a say in school matters") was translated as a positive one ("Students of my age have a say in school matters").

- *Scale reliabilities (Cronbach's alpha):* This coefficient gives an estimate of the internal consistency of each scale. For scales that are not used for individual test scores, but rather for group-level comparisons, we may refer to values over 0.7 as a satisfactory reliability and values over 0.8 as a high reliability. However, it is important to note that the coefficient is influenced by the number of items included in the scale.

Table 3 shows an example of classical item statistics for three items measuring students' expected participation in activities related to elections in each of the participating countries that had sufficient data. The table also shows the median statistics across the countries. In the table, each participating country has printed beside it the scale reliability (Cronbach's alpha), the number of items, the corrected item-score correlations, the number of cases, the percentage of missing responses, the mean of the raw scale (taking the average of all items), and the correlation of the raw score with the student performance in the test of civic knowledge.

Both the scale reliabilities and the item-total correlations indicated a high degree of consistency across countries. For all three items in most of the countries, the percentage of missing values did not exceed two. Only one country appeared to have a considerable proportion of students with no response. In most countries, there was a positive correlation between expected electoral participation and civic knowledge and understanding as measured by the international cognitive test.

Table 3: Classical item statistics for items measuring expected electoral participation (VOTEPART)

Country	Alpha coefficient	Items	Items ISR103A	Items ISR103B	Items ISR103C	Valid numbers of cases	% missing responses	Scale mean	Correlation with test performance
CNT1	.727	3	.671	.654	.352	351	.85	1.82	.319
CNT2	.790	3	.687	.688	.529	418	1.65	2.10	.241
CNT3	.849	3	.736	.784	.639	339	2.87	2.17	.323
CNT4	.893	3	.800	.850	.724	482	1.43	2.00	.096
CNT5	.763	3	.611	.651	.524	516	3.37	2.40	.183
CNT6	.853	3	.776	.768	.641	158	2.47	2.18	.459
CNT7	.704	3	.576	.594	.409	301	22.62	2.14	-.016
CNT8	.861	3	.779	.798	.638	121	.82	1.91	.230
CNT9	.862	3	.776	.824	.625	406	1.69	2.11	.208
CNT10	.764	3	.652	.685	.466	335	.30	2.04	.281
CNT11	.804	3	.658	.726	.573	415	.48	2.16	.237
CNT12	.771	3	.685	.674	.479	402	.50	2.29	.390
CNT13	.779	3	.673	.689	.505	361	1.63	2.18	.410
CNT14	.792	3	.672	.679	.567	395	.75	2.38	.479
CNT15	.774	3	.719	.673	.461	351	.85	2.20	.120
CNT16	.817	3	.697	.712	.601	542	4.58	1.78	.279
CNT17	.827	3	.708	.719	.629	369	1.34	2.13	.291
CNT18	.755	3	.632	.648	.482	574	5.12	2.36	.263
CNT19	.725	3	.597	.676	.399	190	2.06	1.89	.318
CNT20	.870	3	.773	.796	.687	589	2.97	1.89	.357
CNT21	.879	3	.814	.866	.633	182	3.19	2.31	.340
CNT22	.858	3	.776	.798	.633	448	2.40	1.97	.397
CNT23	.788	3	.690	.730	.486	369	.27	2.15	.272
CNT24	.809	3	.695	.695	.590	352	5.88	2.37	.192
CNT25	.768	3	.644	.651	.529	380	1.55	2.26	.239
CNT26	.788	3	.677	.693	.526	417	.48	1.89	.370
CNT27	.842	3	.745	.780	.602	403	1.47	2.16	.337
CNT28	.874	3	.776	.829	.676	405	1.46	2.08	.486
CNT29	.849	3	.779	.769	.618	563	.71	2.41	N/A
CNT30	.873	3	.832	.793	.654	553	.90	2.05	.343
Median	**.806**	**3**	**.696**	**.715**	**.581**		**1.511**	**2.15**	**.291**

Note: Items were coded to values 0 (I will certainly *not* do this), 1 (I will probably *not* do this), 2 (I will probably do this), and 3 (I will certainly do this). N/A = not available.

For the scale derived from the items measuring expected political participation, VOTEPART showed good internal consistencies across participating countries, with a median Cronbach's alpha coefficient of 0.81. Similar results were obtained for POLPART and INFPART. The median reliabilities across countries were 0.81 and 0.83 respectively.

Tables featuring classical item statistics are useful for reviewing the performance of items and scales for each individual country dataset. The national centers of the participating countries were given guidelines on interpretation and were asked to review their own national item statistics. In cases of low reliabilities, inverted item-by-total correlations, and any other unusual findings for a particular country, the ISC asked the national center staff of the country concerned if translation problems or any specific aspects of the country's context could explain these deviations.[3]

Confirmatory Factor Analysis

The classical item tables used in ICCS are particularly useful for assessing the internal consistency of scales and the extent to which items in individual countries have similar correlations with the raw score. However, the review of classical item statistics does not allow a test of how well the expected model fits the observed data. To achieve this purpose, CFA can be carried out through the use of structural equation modeling (SEM) techniques (see Kaplan, 2000).

Within the SEM framework, latent variables are linked to observable variables via measurement equations. An observed variable x is modeled as

(1) $x = \Lambda_x \xi + \delta$,

where Λ_x is a $q \times k$ matrix of factor loadings, ξ denotes the latent variable(s), and δ is a $q \times 1$ vector of unique error variables. The expected covariance matrix is fitted according to the theoretical factor structure. With continuous variables, maximum likelihood (ML) estimation provides model estimates that try to minimize the differences between the expected (Σ) and the observed covariance matrix (S).

For CFA, an expected covariance matrix is fitted according to the theoretical factor structure. Model estimates can be obtained by minimizing the differences between the expected (*) and the observed covariance matrix (S). Measures for the overall fit of a model are then obtained by comparing the expected * matrix with the observed S matrix. If the differences between both matrices are close to zero, then the model "fits the data." If the differences are somewhat larger, the model "does not fit the data."[4]

---

3 Classical item statistics are usually also provided by most standard software (including ACER ConQuest) for item response modeling. SPSS macros were used to collate this information for the ICCS field trial analyses.

4 However, it needs to be noted that ML estimation assumes a normal distribution and continuous variables. Jöreskog and Sörbom (1993) therefore recommend for non-normal ordinal variables the use of WLS with polychoric correlation matrices and corresponding asymptotic covariance weight matrices. To simplify procedures for the ICCS field trial analyses, four-point Likert-type items were treated as continuous variables. This approach meant that standard software (such as the SAS CALIS procedure) could be used to estimate the results separately for each country in an efficient manner.

The following fit indices were used to assess the model fit of the CFA.

- The *root mean square error of approximation* (RMSEA): This measures the "discrepancy per degree of freedom for the model" (Browne & Cudeck, 1993, p. 144). A value of 0.05 and below indicates a close fit; values greater than 0.1 indicate a poor model fit.

- The *root mean square residual* (RMR): This has a similar interpretation, as the RMSEA with values below 0.05 indicate a close model fit.

- *Comparative fit index* (CFI) and the *non-normed fit index* (NNFI) (also known as the Tucker-Lewis Index, TLI): Like the RMSEA, these indices are less dependent than many other indices on sample size and are generally viewed as the most appropriate indices because they are less influenced by model complexity (see Bollen & Long, 1993). High values for CFI and TLI (over 0.9) indicate a satisfactory model fit.

Multi-dimensional CFAs were estimated in order to assess the relationships between the related latent dimensions measured in ICCS. CFA results for multi-dimensional models provide information about the appropriateness of the measurement models as well as about the correlation across the latent factors. A very high estimated latent correlation between two factors may indicate that the items measure reasonably similar dimensions and that a solution with fewer dimensions could be considered as an alternative model. If, for example, in a three-dimensional model, two of the dimensions are highly correlated, it might be more appropriate to assume a two-factor solution in which the items loading on the two highly correlated factors are used to measure only one combined factor.

Figure 1 shows a CFA for a three-factor model of ICCS items measuring students' expected participation. It shows a good model fit and positive correlations between the three latent dimensions. Although the correlation between POLPART and INFPART is very high (0.70), it indicates that both sets of items still reflect separate dimensions. Inspection of factor loadings reveals that some of the items measure the latent dimensions better than others: items I03C (VOTEPART) and I03D (POLPART) in particular have relatively lower factor loadings.

Figure 1: CFA results for items reflecting expected participation

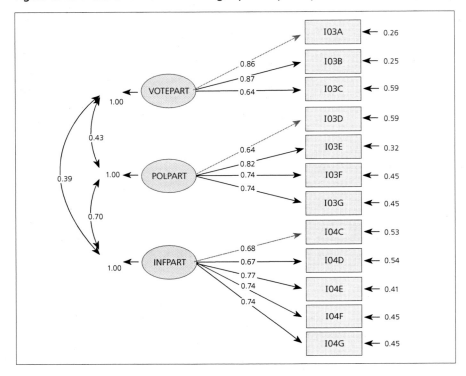

Note: LISREL estimates with maximum likelihood estimation for pooled international sample. Items were coded to values 0 (I will certainly *not* do this), 1 (I will probably *not* do this), 2 (I will probably do this), and 3 (I will certainly do this). RMSEA = 0.070; RMR = 0.044; NNFI = 0.94; CFI = 0.95.

With international studies, it may not be appropriate to assume the same factor structure for each population. One way of looking at the consistency of factor structures is to use separate CFA for each country and to review model fit within each population in a comparative perspective. For the ICCS field trial analyses, separate models were estimated using the SAS CALIS procedure (see Hatcher, 1994). Table 4 presents the CFA results for expected participation items for each of the 30 country sub-samples. It also sets out the median values across the participating countries. The three-dimensional solution shows a satisfactory model fit in most countries, and the correlations between latent dimensions tend to be similar across countries.

Table 4: Comparison of model fit and latent correlation for items reflecting expected participation

Country	Model fit				Latent correlations		
	RMSEA	RMR	CFI	NNFI	VOTEPART/ POLPART	VOTEPART/ INFPART	POLPART/ INFPART
CNT 1	0.12	0.08	0.88	0.88	0.33	0.28	0.63
CNT 2	0.08	0.06	0.94	0.94	0.42	0.41	0.65
CNT 3	0.10	0.05	0.90	0.90	0.45	0.45	0.60
CNT 4	0.08	0.06	0.95	0.95	0.49	0.39	0.68
CNT 5	0.06	0.04	0.96	0.96	0.46	0.23	0.69
CNT 6	0.08	0.05	0.93	0.93	0.45	0.41	0.74
CNT 7	0.07	0.07	0.95	0.95	0.61	0.49	0.81
CNT 8	0.10	0.06	0.92	0.93	0.50	0.52	0.63
CNT 9	0.08	0.06	0.95	0.95	0.48	0.43	0.78
CNT10	0.08	0.04	0.91	0.92	0.37	0.21	0.49
CNT11	0.08	0.03	0.94	0.94	0.41	0.32	0.53
CNT12	0.07	0.06	0.93	0.93	0.30	0.28	0.55
CNT13	0.10	0.07	0.92	0.92	0.34	0.51	0.73
CNT14	0.08	0.05	0.92	0.92	0.39	0.39	0.69
CNT15	0.08	0.06	0.93	0.93	0.29	0.24	0.64
CNT16	0.07	0.04	0.96	0.96	0.71	0.50	0.74
CNT17	0.06	0.04	0.95	0.95	0.40	0.30	0.69
CNT18	0.05	0.04	0.97	0.97	0.29	0.32	0.72
CNT19	0.09	0.07	0.90	0.90	0.28	0.21	0.64
CNT20	0.10	0.06	0.90	0.90	0.40	0.40	0.62
CNT21	0.11	0.07	0.93	0.93	0.23	0.29	0.80
CNT22	0.11	0.05	0.91	0.91	0.41	0.47	0.55
CNT23	0.09	0.07	0.91	0.91	0.41	0.25	0.57
CNT24	0.06	0.05	0.96	0.96	0.54	0.26	0.72
CNT25	0.08	0.05	0.94	0.94	0.35	0.38	0.79
CNT26	0.07	0.04	0.94	0.94	0.33	0.36	0.64
CNT27	0.09	0.06	0.91	0.92	0.30	0.36	0.53
CNT28	0.09	0.04	0.94	0.94	0.48	0.41	0.68
CNT29	0.09	0.04	0.93	0.93	0.23	0.42	0.64
CNT30	0.08	0.04	0.95	0.95	0.40	0.41	0.63
Median	0.08	0.05	0.93	0.93	0.40	0.38	0.65

Note: SAS CALIS estimates with maximum likelihood estimation. Items were coded to values 0 (I will certainly *not* do this), 1 (I will probably *not* do this), 2 (I will probably do this) and 3 (I will certainly do this).

Multiple-Group Analysis

A comparison of CFA results across countries shows the extent to which the measurement model fits the data for the pooled sample and in each dataset. In the case of multi-dimensional models, it also shows whether similar correlations between latent variables can be observed. However, it does not provide information about measurement invariance as such because country-specific models may fit the data but have different parameters.

To test parameter invariance, it is possible to use multiple-group modeling, which is an extension of standard SEM. If one considers a model where respondents belong to different groups indexed as g = 1, 2, ..., G, the multiple-group factor model becomes

(2) $x_g = \Lambda_{xg}\xi_g + \delta_g,$

A test of factorial invariance (H_Λ), where factor loadings are defined as being equal, can be written as

(3) $H_\Lambda : \Lambda_1 = \Lambda_1 = \Lambda_2 ... = \Lambda_g$

Hypothesis testing using tests of significance tends to be problematic, in particular with data from large samples, where even smaller differences appear to be significant. Therefore, a modeling approach that looks at relative changes in model fit is preferable. This can be done by placing different equality constraints on parameters in multiple-group models and then comparing model-fit indices across different multiple-group models, each having an increasing degree of constraint, with the first having no constraints whatsoever. Different types of constraints can be used in order to review the invariance of model parameters. Once the invariance of factor structure and factor loadings has been confirmed, further constraints can be placed on the intercepts and factor covariances.

In the multiple-group analyses presented in this article, four different models were tested, with latent variables within each country having a mean of 0.[5] Because chi-square-based tests of statistical significance tend to be problematic with larger sample size, the results should be judged according to "relative model fit" of models with different degrees of constraints. The four models compared during the analysis of the ICCS field-trial data on expected civic participation were:

A. An unconstrained model with all parameters treated as country-specific;

B. A model with constrained factor loadings across countries;

C. A model with constraints on factor loadings and intercepts; and

D. A model with constraints on factor loadings, intercepts, and factor variances and covariances.

Table 5 shows the fit indices for the different multiple-group models for expected participation items RMSEA, NNFI, and CFI (for the overall model) as well as the median of RMR across individual country samples.

---

5 Because of the short timeline for analyzing the ICCS field-trial data, multiple-group analyses could not be fully implemented.

As is evident from the table, the differences in model fit between Model A (unconstrained) and Model B, with its constrained factor loadings, were minor, indicating that the assumption of constrained factor loadings is reasonable for the three-factor solution. With Model C, where the item intercepts were also constrained, the median RMR indicates that the indices fit is still satisfactory in a majority of countries but that the overall model fit is no longer satisfactory. The completely constrained Model D, where the factor variances and covariances were also assumed to be equal across countries, clearly does not fit the data. However, different factor variances and covariances can be viewed as a plausible finding, and it might therefore be unrealistic to expect that constructs related to expected participation have the same correlations regardless of the differences in political and civic culture between countries.

Table 5: Multiple-group models for expected participation items

	Model A	Model B	Model C	Model D
	Unconstrained	Constrained loadings	Constrained loadings and intercepts	Completely constrained model
RMSEA	0.08	0.08	**0.11**	**0.13**
NNFI	0.91	0.92	0.86	0.82
CFI	0.93	0.93	0.85	0.76
Median RMR across countries	0.05	0.06	0.07	**0.12**

Note: LISREL estimates with maximum likelihood estimation. RMR statistics indicate the fit for each individual country dataset; RMSEA, NNFI, and CFI indicate the fit for the overall model. RMR or RMSEA indices > 0.1 in bold.

Information from this type of analysis provides information about the extent of similarity for measurement models with different constraints across countries. When scaling data across countries, the assumption is made that items measure a given construct in the same, or at least in a very similar, way. Multiple-group modeling can be used to test this assumption in a more systematic way.

Item Response Modeling

Item response theory (IRT) (Hambleton et al., 1991) is often used in national or international large-scale studies for deriving individual scale scores for cognitive tests. Using IRT provides a large number of advantages for item analysis and allows the equating of different tests as well as the description of scales with test items. Increasingly, IRT is also used for deriving scale scores from questionnaire items (see Organisation for Economic Co-operation and Development, 2005; Schulz & Sibberns, 2004).

One example of how probabilities of responses to categorical items (e.g., Likert-type items) can be modeled is the *Partial Credit Model* (Masters & Wright, 1997), which is defined as

$$(4)\ P_{x_i}(\theta) = \frac{\exp \sum_{j=0}^{x_i} (\theta_n - (\delta_i + \tau_{ij}))}{\sum_{h=0}^{m_i} \exp \sum_{j=0}^{h} (\theta_n - (\delta_i + \tau_{ij}))} \qquad x_i = 0,1,2,\ldots,m_i ,$$

where $P_{x_i}(\theta)$ is the probability of person n to score x on item i. θ_n denotes the person's latent trait, the item parameter δ_i gives the location of the item on the latent continuum, and τ_{ij} is an additional step parameter for each step j.

One common measure of item fit is the weighted mean-square statistic (*infit*), a residual-based fit statistic. Weighted *infit* statistics can be computed for both item and step parameters; values close to 1 indicate good item fit. Values above 1 show an item discrimination that is lower than expected, given the model, whereas values below 1 indicate that the item discrimination is higher than expected. Reviewing this residual-based item fit indicates the extent to which each item fits the item response model. However, there are no clear rules for acceptable item fit, and it is generally recommended that analysts and researchers interpret residual-based statistics with caution (see Rost & von Davier, 1994).

Equation (5) below shows that the part of the model related to the item consists of the item parameter δ_i for item i and the step parameter τ_{ij} for step j of item t. In the context of a cross-national study, item parameters are assumed to be the same, similar to the assumption made in relation to a (one-dimensional) multiple-group model with constrained parameters. Tests of parameter invariance across countries can be reviewed by calibrating items separately within countries and then comparing model parameters and item fit. But it is also possible to estimate group effects directly by including further parameters in the scaling model. A partial credit model that includes estimates of item-by-country interactions can be described with this equation:

$$(5)\ P_{x_i}(\theta) = \frac{\exp \sum_{j=0}^{x_i} (\theta_n (\delta_i - \eta_c + \lambda_{ic} + \tau_{ij}))}{\sum_{h=0}^{m_i} \exp \sum_{j=0}^{h} (\theta_n - (\delta_i - \eta_c + \lambda_{ic} + \tau_{ij}))} \qquad x_i = 0,1,2,\ldots m_i$$

For the purpose of measuring parameter equivalence across a group of countries c, an additional parameter for country effects λ_{ic} is added to the (constrained) model. However, to obtain proper estimates, it is also necessary to include the overall country effect (η_c) in the model.[6] Both item-by-country interaction estimates (λ_{ic}) and overall country effects (η_c) are constrained to having a sum of 0.

---

6 The minus sign ensures that higher values of the country group effect parameters indicate higher levels of item endorsement in a country. An even less constrained model could go one step further by adding a country interaction and replacing the term τ_{ij} with an interaction between country and step parameters τ_{ijc}. This would allow an estimation of separate step parameters for each country. However, reviewing and interpreting the results of such an analysis becomes rather difficult, which is why only the item-by-country interaction effect was analyzed.

Models with country interaction effects provide estimates of the degree of parameter invariance across countries or groups of countries. The degree of parameter variation across countries can be summarized to provide information about the degree of measurement equivalence. In the ICCS field trial analysis, the median of absolute values for item-by-country interaction effect was taken as an indicator of parameter invariance for each item. In addition, the minimum and maximum effects were displayed to demonstrate the range of deviations across countries.[7]

For the analysis of ICCS field trial data, the scaling software *ACER ConQuest* (Wu, Adams, Wilson, & Haldane, 2007) was used for parameter estimation. Table 6 presents the results of the IRT analyses for the three ICCS scales reflecting expected participation. The first and second columns show the scale and item names. The third and fourth columns show the overall (international) item parameter and its fit for the pooled field trial sample. The fifth column shows the median of absolute values of item-by-country estimates across countries, and the sixth and seventh columns show the minimum and maximum values of item-by-country estimates. Because the estimation of parameter estimates and fit indices is less reliable for short scales, the low number of items in each scale (three, four, and five in the VOTEPART, POLPART, and INFPART scales, respectively) has to be taken into account when interpreting these analyses.

Table 6: IRT results for items reflecting expected participation

		International calibration results		Item-by-country interaction (λ_{ic})		
Scale	Item	Parameter (δ_i)	Item fit (infit)	Median of absolute values	Minimum value across countries	Maximum value across countries
VOTEPART	I03A	- 0.183	0.92	0.16	- 0.600	0.562
VOTEPART	I03B	- 0.073	0.89	0.17	- 0.674	0.341
VOTEPART	I03C	0.257	1.21	0.19	- 0.719	0.840
POLPART	I03D	- 0.503	1.18	0.23	- 0.673	0.698
POLPART	I03E	0.235	0.86	0.14	- 0.581	0.398
POLPART	I03F	0.137	0.99	0.16	-1.050	0.521
POLPART	I03G	0.131	1.00	0.17	- 0.433	0.497
INFPART	I04C	- 0.601	1.05	0.16	- 0.581	0.478
INFPART	I04D	- 0.179	1.08	0.16	- 0.494	0.991
INFPART	I04E	0.280	0.93	0.12	- 0.356	0.321
INFPART	I04F	0.234	0.99	0.15	- 0.345	0.324
INFPART	I04G	0.265	1.02	0.19	- 0.778	0.470

Note: ACER ConQuest estimates. Items were coded to values 0 ("I will certainly *not* do this"), 1 ("I will probably *not* do this"), 2 ("I will probably do this"), and 3 ("I will certainly do this").

---

7 More detailed lists of effects by country were included in appendices to the field trial analysis report sent to the participating countries.

Overall, Table 6 shows that the items in the scales appear to fit well. Only Item I03C ("Get information about candidates before voting") in the VOTEPART scale and Item I03D ("Help a candidate or party during campaign") in the POLPART scale show some evidence of less than ideal fit. These results correspond to the findings that these items also have relatively lower item-score correlations (see Table 3) and factor loadings in the CFA (see Figure 1).

When looking at the individual item-by-country interactions, we see that only Item I03D stands out as having slightly higher median cross-country variation of item location parameters when compared to other items. The minimum and maximum values show that, for most items, there are (at least some) countries whose estimated (national) parameters deviate considerably (more than 0.3 logits) from the international ones.

As with multiple-group model analyses, IRT modeling also allows us to compare overall model fit with and without taking the item-by-country interactions into account. The differences between deviances (a statistic indicating how well the item response model fits the data) are displayed in Table 7. The comparison shows that, for all three comparisons of (uni-dimensional) scaling models with and without item-by-country interaction effects, there is a statistically significant difference, which means that the model with country-specific parameters fits better.[8] Furthermore, the overall improvement of model fit is relatively small for each of the three model comparisons (about 2% less deviance).

Table 7: Deviance statistics for IRT models with and without item-by-country interaction effects

	VOTEPART	POLPART	INFPART
Model with interaction	72930 (100)	107227 (137)	133252 (171)
Model without interaction	74656 (10)	109415 (13)	135659 (16)
Difference in deviance	1726	2188	2407
Difference in degrees of freedom	90	124	155
χ^2	0.000	0.000	0.000

Note: ACER ConQuest estimates.

Estimating the item-by-country interaction of item location parameters provides researchers with an indication of the extent to which they can reasonably assume that student responses can be scaled with international item parameters. Given the relatively large sample sizes used in international studies, tests of the statistical significance of item-by-country estimates would inevitably lead to rejection of the hypothesis of measurement invariance. Another aspect to consider is that there are no clear criteria regarding the amount of item-by-country effects that is still tolerable. However, inclusion of this information during screening of the field trial material

---

8 The difference in deviance follows a chi-square distribution in which the degrees of freedom are equal to the difference between the parameters used in both models.

means that item selection preference can be given to those items and scales that show less item-by-country interaction.

CONCLUSION AND IMPLICATIONS

The analyses presented in this article drew on ICCS field trial data to show how different analysis methods can be used for construct validation purposes in international studies. Combining different approaches such as "classical" item analyses, factor analyses, and item response modeling has the potential to provide a comprehensive means of reviewing the extent to which one may assume measurement equivalence for questionnaire constructs in international studies.

In the case of the ICCS items regarding students' expected civic participation in the future, it was possible to derive three reliable scales measuring *expected electoral participation, expected active political participation, and expected informal civic participation*, with all reflecting highly similar dimensions across participating countries. Exploratory factor analysis showed two items clearly related to a fourth dimension, which was not included in subsequent analysis. Confirmatory factor analysis (CFA) illustrated that the three latent dimensions measured with the remaining 12 items, although positively correlated, reflected three distinct constructs. And while the three-dimensional model was shown as appropriate across the participating countries, the results from the multiple-group models and the item response modeling of item-by-country interaction effects provided evidence for a noticeable amount of between-country variation.

The results of each of the analysis steps illustrated in this article are complementary, and many of the findings about item or scale performance give similar information. For example, item-total correlations, factor loadings, and IRT item fit tend to coincide with the extent to which items measure a given construct. Likewise, there are numerous indices of scale reliability: within the context of classical item analysis, Cronbach's alpha is probably the most widely used index. But indices of scale reliability could also be derived from factor loadings in a CFA, and there are different IRT-based measures of scale reliabilities.

The results of the exploratory and confirmatory factor analyses also tended to be highly similar with regard to the analysis of item dimensionality. However, although exploratory factor analysis (EFA) already gives sufficient information about the dimensionality of items, CFA provides a way of modeling data under the assumption of items loading on only one factor, thereby allowing analysts to correctly estimate the correlation between latent factors.

Item response models can be conceptualized and are mathematically equivalent to logistic confirmatory factor analyses (see Glöckner-Rist & Hoijtink, 2003). But whereas estimating CFA for questionnaire items assesses primarily the overall fit of the expected dimensional model for sets of items, using item response modeling focuses on the performance of individual items under a logistic item response model.

Both multiple-group models and IRT models of item-by-country effects provide information about the differences between international and/or country-specific item parameters. They also give an indication of the extent to which one can reasonably impose a "one size fits all" approach to the measurement model. In both cases, stringent tests of measurement invariance are difficult to implement, and there are no clear rules about "tolerable" levels regarding the lack of measurement invariance. Researchers accordingly have to rely on "rules of thumb" and reviews of comparative rather than hypothesis testing.

The sequence of analysis of the ICCS field trial data allowed the collection of useful information at each step, with each step serving a different purpose. At the initial stage, the EFA results gave preliminary results regarding the expected item dimensionality that informed the allocation of items to scales for subsequent analyses. Tables with classical item statistics then provided information about how scales and individual items worked in each of the participating countries and enabled the international study center (ISC) to flag problematic items at both the international and the country level. Classical item statistics had the advantage of being easily understood by national center staff.

The use of multi-dimensional CFA for the pooled international sample made it possible to construct a general description of the general measurement model for a given set of items and procurement of estimates of the correlations between latent variables. Estimating these models separately for each country set enabled assessment of the appropriateness of the dimensional model in comparative terms. Using multiple-group model CFA can be seen as an alternative to comparing separate CFA with a more advanced tool that provides a test of measurement invariance for models with different parameter constraints. Because of its greater complexity and general timeline constraints, this step was not systematically implemented in the ICCS field trial analysis.

Item response modeling gives a different perspective because it focuses on the appropriateness of modeling item responses via use of a logistic model instead of analyses of covariances. Given that items in many international studies are scaled using IRT, it is important to assess the appropriateness of the assumption of using the scaling model with internationally determined item parameters across countries.

Using a stepwise approach made it possible to achieve a high level of scrutiny with regard to the validity of measuring constructs with questionnaire items across countries. Each step provided some additional information regarding the performance of individual items, the scalability of items, and the measurement of constructs and their cross-country validity. The combination of these different sources of information provided a good basis for item selection for the ICCS main survey.

It needs to be acknowledged that some aspects regarding cross-national comparability raised in the literature could not be addressed within the scope of the ICCS field trial analyses presented in this article. For example, concerns exist regarding the general viability of using Likert-type items for construct measurement in cross-cultural studies because of differences in response patterns across countries (see, for example, Heine, Lehman, Peng, & Greenholtz, 2002).

As already observed in other international studies, the analysis of ICCS field trial data generally shows a noticeable extent of parameter variance across countries. Indeed, it would be somewhat ingenuous to assume that questionnaire items translated into different languages and administered in different cultures and education systems could ever be responded to in exactly the same way. The crucial question, however, is at what level parameter variation really becomes a problem and leads to biased results in comparative studies. Answers to questions such as this require further methodological research (using, for example, simulation studies) directed at comparing the impact of different levels of construct measurement equivalence on analysis results.

References

Amadeo, J., Torney-Purta, J., Lehmann, R., Husfeldt, V., & Nikolova, R. (2002). *Civic knowledge and engagement: An IEA study of upper secondary students in sixteen countries*. Amsterdam: International Association for the Evaluation of Educational Achievement (IEA).

Bollen, K. A., & Long, S. J. (1993). (Eds.). *Testing structural equation models*. Newbury Park, CA: Sage.

Browne, M. W., & Cudeck, R. (1993). Alternative ways of assessing model fit. In K. A. Bollen & S. J. Long (Eds.), *Testing structural equation models* (pp. 136–162). Newbury Park, CA: Sage.

Byrne, B. M. (2003). Testing for equivalent self-concept measurement across culture. In H. W. Marsh, R. G. Craven, & D. M. McInerney (Eds.), *International advances in self-research: Speaking to the future* (pp. 291–314). Greenwich: Information Age Publishing.

Chrostowski, S. J., & Malak, B. (2004). Translation and cultural adaptation of the TIMSS 2003 instruments. In M. O. Martin, I. V. S. Mullis, & S. J. Chrostowski (Eds.), *TIMSS 2003 technical report* (pp. 93–108). Amsterdam: International Association for the Evaluation of Educational Achievement (IEA).

Glöckner-Rist, A., & Hoijtink, H. (2003). The best of both worlds: Factor analysis of dichotomous data using item response theory and structural equation modeling. *Structural Equation Modeling: A Multidisciplinary Journal, 10*(4), 544–565.

Grisay, A. (2002). Translation and cultural appropriateness of the test and survey material. In R. J. Adams & M. Wu (Eds.), *PISA 2000 technical report* (pp. 57–70). Paris: OECD Publications.

Hambleton, R. K., Swaminathan, H., & Rogers, H. J. (1991). *Fundamentals of item response theory*. Newbury Park, CA: Sage.

Harkness, J., Pennell, B., & Schoua-Glusberg, A. (2004). Survey questionnaire translation and assessment. In J. Presser, M. Rothgeb, J. Couper, E. Lessler, E. Martin, & E. Singer (Eds.), *Questionnaire development evaluation and testing methods* (pp. 453–473). Hoboken, NJ: Wiley.

Hatcher, L. (1994). *A step by step approach to using the SAS system for factor analysis and structural equation modeling*. Cary, NC: SAS Institute.

Heine, S. J, Lehman, D. R., Peng, K., & Greenholtz, J. (2002). What's wrong with cross-cultural comparisons of subjective Likert scales? The reference group effect. *Journal of Personality and Social Psychology, 82*(6), 903–918.

Jöreskog, K. G., & Sörbom, D. (1993). *LISREL 8 user's reference guide*. Chicago: Scientific Software International, Inc.

Kaplan, D. (2000). *Structural equation modeling: Foundation and extensions*. Thousand Oaks, CA: Sage.

Little, T. D. (1997). Mean and covariances structures (MACS) analyses of cross-cultural data: Practical and theoretical issues. *Multivariate Behavioural Research, 32*(1), 53–76.

Masters, G. N., & Wright, B. D. (1997). The partial credit model. In W. J. van der Linden & R. K. Hambleton (Eds.), *Handbook of modern item response theory* (pp. 101–122). New York: Springer.

Mohler, P. P., Smith, T. W., & Harkness, J. A. (1998). Respondent's ratings of expressions from response scales: A two-country, two-language investigation on equivalence and translation. In J. A. Harkness (Ed.), ZUMA-*Nachrichten spezial No.3: Cross-cultural survey equivalence* (pp. 159–184). Mannheim: ZUMA.

Muthén, L. K., & Muthén, B. O. (2001). *Mplus: Statistical analysis with latent variables*. Los Angeles: Author.

Organisation for Economic Co-operation and Development (OECD). (2005). *Technical report for the OECD Programme for International Student Assessment*. Paris: OECD Publications.

Rost, J., & von Davier, M. (1994). A conditional item-fit index for Rasch models. *Applied Psychological Measurement, 18*(2), 171–182.

Schulz, W. (2003). *Validating questionnaire constructs in international studies: Two examples from PISA 2000*. Paper presented at the annual meeting of the American Educational Research Association (AERA), Chicago, April 21–25, 2003.

Schulz, W. (2006). *Testing parameter invariance for questionnaire indices using confirmatory factor analysis and item response theory*. Paper presented at the annual meeting of the American Educational Research Association (AERA), San Francisco, April 7–11, 2006.

Schulz, W., Fraillon, J., Ainley, J., Losito, B., & Kerr, D. (2008). *International Civic and Citizenship Education Study assessment framework*. Amsterdam: International Association for the Evaluation of Educational Achievement (IEA).

Schulz, W., & Sibberns H. (Eds.). (2004). *IEA Civic Education Study technical report*. Amsterdam: International Association for the Evaluation of Educational Achievement (IEA).

Torney-Purta, J., Lehmann, R., Oswald, H., & Schulz, W. (2001). *Citizenship and education in twenty-eight countries*. Amsterdam: International Association for the Evaluation of Educational Achievement (IEA).

van de Vijver, F. J. R., & Tanzer, N. K. (1997). Bias and equivalence in cross-cultural assessment: An overview. *European Review of Applied Psychology, 47*, 263–279.

Walker, M. (2007). Ameliorating culturally based extreme item tendencies to attitude items. *Journal of Applied Measurement, 8*(3), 267–278.

Wilson, M. (1994). Comparing attitudes across different cultures: Two quantitative approaches to construct validity. In M. Wilson (Ed.), *Objective measurement II: Theory into practice* (pp. 271–292). Norwood, NJ: Ablex.

Wu, M. L., Adams, R. J., Wilson, M. R., & Haldane, S. (2007). ACER ConQuest 2.0: *General item response modelling software* [computer program manual]. Camberwell, VIC: ACER Press.

Cluster analysis for cognitive diagnosis: An application to the 2001 PIRLS reading assessment

Chia-Yi Chiu
Department of Educational Psychology, Rutgers University, New Brunswick, New Jersey, United States of America

Minhee Seo
Department of Educational Research Methodology, University of North Carolina at Greensboro, Greensboro NC, United States of America

Demand for large-scale assessments that report more diagnostically informative results about examinees' cognitive profiles is increasing. Traditionally, classification based on examinees' attribute patterns has been carried out by fitting data with cognitive diagnosis models. A recently proposed method of reaching the same classification goal uses classical cluster analysis without utilizing an item response model. The only requirements are a valid sample statistic, usually obtained by summarizing data, and the assumed item-by-attribute matrix used in most cognitive diagnosis modeling. After constructing a particular vector of sum-scores, *K*-means cluster analysis or hierarchical agglomerative cluster analysis can be applied with the purpose of clustering subjects who possess the same skills. An application to the 2001 Progress in International Reading and Literacy Study (PIRLS) (Gonzalez & Kennedy, 2001) reading data is conducted to illustrate how the methods can be implemented in practice.

INTRODUCTION

The significance of large-scale assessments in public education has grown tremendously in recent years. Along with the increasing demand for this type of assessment, there is increasing pressure to make the assessments more diagnostically informative about students' cognitive strengths and weaknesses (Leighton & Gierl, 2007). However, most existing large-scale assessments, including PIRLS, report only students' overall performances on the test, a practice that provides limited diagnostic information about students' cognitive capacities. One factor limiting application of cognitive diagnosis analysis to large-scale data is that these assessments are usually not designed for the purpose of diagnosis. To adequately extract information on examinees' cognitive abilities, items have to be written in a way that ensures the item responses identify if the examinee possesses the required skills for answering a particular item correctly. Issues such as these associated with test construction and diagnostic testing have been widely discussed. Gorin (2007), for example, having assembled several popular methods of diagnostic testing, provides a thorough discussion on how to develop and construct and evaluate them.

Among the various types of analysis in the cognitive diagnosis context, classification based on students' mastery or non-mastery of each attribute in a set of attributes is considered necessary because it can lead to more efficient remediation for examinees' learning. Progress in International Reading and Literacy Study (PIRLS) data have been analyzed using Item Response Theory (IRT)-based models, in which continuous latent traits are assumed. However, most models developed for the purpose of cognitive diagnosis are from the family of latent class models. Models with continuous latent variables may achieve the goal of classifying examinees by partially ordering them according to their general latent traits, but those with discrete latent variables classify examinees by directly assigning them to the most likely group. By modeling many ordered latent classes, we can see that the IRT model can be approximated by the latent class model.

However, several questions arise during exploration of differences between the conclusions that might be reached from these models. Certainly, there is some convenience in sorting examinees into a few small bins, but we must question whether this level of classification is too coarse. Also, if the item response probabilities across the latent classes cannot be ordered, we must question if there is also some sort of multidimensionality when the latent variable is seen as continuous. This consideration raises issues about the definition of dimensionality and its dependence on whether the viewpoint taken is a latent trait or latent class one. We prefer these latent class models in applications in which the number of latent classes is not too large. Therefore, with the purpose of identifying examinees' cognitive profiles, the latent variable is assumed to be discrete, and the underlying model is taken from the cognitive diagnosis context.

When a cognitive diagnostic model is specified, classification can be done by fitting the model and by estimating parameters through likelihood functions. However, applying complex cognitive diagnostic models requires sophisticated software along with the expectation–maximization (EM) algorithm, or Markov chain Monte Carlo (MCMC). However, most software for estimating cognitive diagnostic models is not available in the public domain, and the implementation of either EM or MCMC requires advanced computational skills.

As an alternative, Chiu, Douglas, and Li (in press), propose a new classification method for achieving the same goal of classifying examinees based on their attribute profiles—a method that utilizes exploratory cluster analysis. The classification requires clustering on a properly chosen summary score of the data, which may be constructed by incorporating the pre-determined item-by-skill information; no further model assumptions are needed. Unlike the model-based method, users can run familiar and widely available software to conduct classifications; depending on the method being used, computer running time can be very short. We elaborate details of the new method in a later section.

As mentioned, most large-scale assessments are not designed to measure students' cognitive capacities. Another concern additional to the issue of test construction is that of missing the pre-established Q-matrix (Tatsuoka, 1985) during classification. A Q-matrix is an array of entries of either 1 or 0 indicating the item-by-skill information, and is usually established according to experts' opinions. Through the Q-matrix, information about whether an examinee possesses particular cognitive attributes can be assessed by analyzing his or her responses to items requiring those skills. The Q-matrix for the data of interest to us, PIRLS 2001, is not yet available. However, the fact that the items in PIRLS were written with reference to specific reading purposes and procedures provides a possible framework from which to relate items to their potential required skills.

It is this feature that made this assessment stand out for us over the other large-scale assessments and gave us an opportunity to conduct this preliminary classification study. Despite the possibility of extra noise in the data due to rough Q-matrix specifications and instability of the classification results, this item-by-skill structure provided us with the information that we needed not only to make use of the new classification method but also to inform future research based on more elaborate Q-matrix specifications. Our primary interest therefore in conducting the study was to investigate if the way the PIRLS items are written provides an applicable means of obtaining information about examinees' skill profiles. We also wanted to examine the effect of utilizing cluster analysis to classify PIRLS data based on the method developed by Chiu and colleagues (in press).

RESTRICTED LATENT CLASS MODELS FOR COGNITIVE DIAGNOSIS

Most specialized latent class models for cognitive diagnosis are formulated under the assumption of a pre-determined Q-matrix. A Q-matrix is a $J \times K$ array **Q**, in which the (j, k) entry q_{jk} denotes whether or not the jth item requires the kth attribute. The latent ability variable is assumed to be discrete and multidimensional, meaning that, for each examinee, his or her profile is a composite of multiple discrete attributes. An attribute could refer to a skill required to solve items or an unobservable psychological construct. More specifically, let $\boldsymbol{\alpha}$ be a K-dimensional vector for which the kth component, α_k, indicates whether or not an examinee possesses the kth attribute or skill, for $k = 1,2,...,K$. The vector $\boldsymbol{\alpha}$ can take 2^K distinct values, each indicating one of the 2^K latent classes in the model. The feature that distinguishes the models from one another is the assumptions that dictate how attributes are utilized to construct responses. In this study, we used DINA (deterministic input, noisy output "AND" gate) (Junker & Sijtsma, 2001) as a model for comparison to cluster analysis. (For more information about cognitive diagnostic models, see Rupp & Templin, 2007.)

The DINA Model

The DINA model is a member of restricted latent class models. Its item response function is expressed as,

$$P(Y_{ij} = 1 \mid \alpha_i) = (1 - s_j)^{\eta_{ij}} g_j^{(1-\eta_{ij})},$$

where for all i, $s_j = P(Y_{ij} = 0 \mid \eta_{ij} = 1)$ and $g_j = P(Y_{ij} = 1 \mid \eta_{ij} = 0)$ are the probabilities of slipping and guessing, respectively, for the jth item, and $\eta_{ij} = \prod_{k=1}^{K} \alpha_{ik}^{q_{jk}}$

is the ideal response equaling 1 if the ith examinee possesses all skill(s) required for answering the jth item correctly, and 0 if any required skill(s) is missing. As we can see, the η_{ij} maps the examinee's skill possession and the item requirements into the set $\{0,1\}$.

The DINA model is characterized by its conjunctive structure, where the probability of answering an item correctly will substantially drop if any of the required attributes are not mastered or possessed. The estimation of the DINA model has been successfully carried out by employing the EM algorithm (Haertel, 1989) or MCMC (de la Torre & Douglas, 2004; Tatsuoka, 2002).

Cluster Analysis

The DINA model and other latent variable models for cognitive diagnosis all require sophisticated software for fitting, either with the EM algorithm or by MCMC. Cluster analysis can serve as an alternative method of classifying examinees despite not having complete knowledge of the underlying cognitive diagnostic model. This section briefly describes two commonly used cluster analysis methods—K-means and hierarchical agglomerative cluster analysis (HACA). The rationale for using cluster analysis in the cognitive diagnosis setting is outlined in the next section.

K-means

K-means cluster analysis is a widely used partitional clustering technique for clustering subjects based on a vector of data. The K-means algorithm requires estimating the cluster centers, with the number of clusters being pre-determined. Once the centers are decided, data are sent to the closest cluster. Specifically, consider a data matrix with N subjects and K observed variables, where the row entries are $\boldsymbol{w}_1, \boldsymbol{w}_2, ..., \boldsymbol{w}_N$, and the goal is to cluster the N subjects into M clusters, where $M=2^K$. Then, taking Euclidean distance, for instance, the K-means assigns data point $\boldsymbol{w}_1$ to the $\boldsymbol{m^{th}}$ cluster if $\| w_1 - \hat{c}_m \|^2$ is minimal over all $\mathbf{m}$. Here, $\hat{c}_m$ is the estimated center of the $\boldsymbol{m^{th}}$ cluster, and is simply the average of the data in the cluster. The iteration to carry out the final solution is as follows:

1. Choose M initial K-dimensional cluster centers;

2. Assign data points to the closest cluster;

3. Obtain the updated cluster center by averaging the assigned observations;

4. Repeat 2 and 3 until the assignment is not changed.

It is known that the K-means outcome is affected by the initial values. Convergence to local optima may occur if poor starting values are used. Many methods of initializing starting values for the K-means algorithm have been proposed (Bradley & Fayyad, 1998; Forgy, 1965; Kaufman & Rousseeuw, 1990; MacQueen, 1967; Steinley, 2006). Random selection is a commonly used criterion, but in order to make it more efficient and adequate, several variations are available. For example, a variation proposed by Forgy (1965) begins with the analyst randomly selecting a set of data points as seeds of cluster centers, assigning the rest of the data to the closest cluster, updating the centers of the clusters by averaging the data within the clusters, and then taking these averages as starting values for the K-means algorithm. In addition to the series of random selection methods, Kaufman and Rousseeuw (1990) proposed a sophisticated method that determines one center at a time by maximizing a criterion index.

To learn which of the initialization methods worked more adequately than others, Pena, Lozano, and Larranaga (1999) conducted an empirical comparison study for a variety of methods, and suggested that the random method and the Kaufman and Rousseeuw (1990) methods outperformed the others in terms of some criteria. However, it is worth noting that while one method may be more appropriate than the other under certain conditions, there is no global solution for this issue. In our study, we used the software R to carry out the analysis. If the user specifies only the number of desired clusters—2^K in our case—but not a starting point, R selects a random set of 2^K distinct rows as the initial center. The function for multiple sampling is also available by furthermore specifying the number of such random sets being used in the algorithm to create a better initial point.

Hierarchical agglomerative cluster analysis (HACA)

HACA differs from K-means in a few respects. First, with K-means, data are partitioned into exclusive clusters; with HACA, hierarchical clustering forms a dynamic tree structure. Second, HACA is much simpler than K-means in computational terms, and does not require the selection of initial values. There are different variations of HACA's clustering algorithm, depending on how we define the distance between data points and the distance between clusters. Once the distance measures are decided, the HACA algorithm starts by defining one cluster for each subject. The next step is to cluster the two subjects for whom the distance between them is smallest. (Note that the distance of two clusters is basically the distance of the two data points in the clusters.) At each step thereafter, a new cluster is formed by fusing the two closest clusters, and the distance between clusters here is a function of the distances between their data points. Defining these distances between clusters is what distinguishes the different linkage methods for HACA. Clusters are combined by using one of the following linkages to minimize the distance between the clusters that are fused in each step until the process is stopped at a fixed number of clusters or until only one cluster, containing all of the objects, remains. In our application, the process is stopped at the point where there are $2K$ clusters.

Following are some common linkages for HACA. The first is complete linkage, in which the distance between clusters is the maximum distance between two data points from the two target clusters. The two clusters that have the smallest such maximum distance are merged to form a new cluster. Specification of this linkage means that the data in each cluster at each stage are enclosed within a certain known range; complete linkage clustering therefore tends to produce homogeneous, but not necessarily separate, clusters. Single linkage, on the other hand, defines distance according to the minimum distance resulting from taking a point from each cluster. Single linkage tends to produce long, stringy clusters and non-convex shapes, a tendency that is known as the chaining effect. Findings (Chiu & Douglas, 2008; Chiu et al., in press) show that this method performs poorly in similar applications, so we did not employ this linkage in our study.

In contrast to the two extreme distance measures, average linkage clustering defines the mean of distances between data points in two different clusters as the distance between the two clusters. Average linkage tends to produce ball-shaped clusters and is a quite robust method. Considering cluster homogeneity from the within-cluster variability point of view, Ward (1963) proposed a hierarchical clustering method in which clusters are chosen to merge so that the updated within-cluster sum of squared errors is minimized. The classification rationale behind this linkage is similar to that of K-means. Therefore, Ward's (1963) linkage possesses properties similar to those of K-means because it tends to produce nearly equal-sized clusters that are convex and compact. However, it suffers from sensitivity to outliers (Milligan, 1980).

RATIONALE BEHIND THE STUDY METHOD

In this section we introduce the classification method developed by Chiu and colleagues (in press). We do this by presenting a description of how to construct an appropriate sample statistic as an input for the clustering technique selected to classify examinees into the correct latent classes based on their cognitive patterns.

The Selected Sample Statistic

The first step in this method is to construct a sum-score vector, with entries indicating the sub-sum scores corresponding to the required skills. Begin by defining the vector as $\boldsymbol{W}_i$ for the ith examinee; the kth entry of $\boldsymbol{W}_i=(W_{i1}, W_{i2},...,W_{iK})'$ is then expressed as

$$W_{ik} = \sum_{j=1}^{j} Y_{ij}\ q_{jk}\ ,$$

where Y_{ij} is the response of the ith examinee on the jth item, and q_{jk} is the Q-matrix entry corresponding to the jth item and k^{th} skill. As we can see, each element in $\boldsymbol{W}$ corresponds to a sum score on a certain skill. In the next step, the vector $\boldsymbol{W}$ is taken as the input to a user-chosen method of cluster analysis, with a fixed number of 2^K clusters. The methods of cluster analysis we have investigated for this application are K-means and HACA with a variety of linkages. Supported by the asymptotic classification theory, which we introduce later, HACA with complete linkage and other linkages can classify data accurately and consistently to correct groups under some convergence assumptions.

In their study, Chiu and colleagues (in press) state three lemmas and develop a formal theory that justifies the application of cluster analysis with the system-scores as input. For details of the proofs, please refer to Chiu et al. (in press).

ANALYSIS OF PIRLS DATA

Data

We used the PIRLS 2001 reading assessment data for our empirical application. The PIRLS reading assessment aimed to measure the progress of 9- to 10-year-old children on reading literacy. The reading comprehension test consisted of eight sets of blocks, based on different reading passages (Table 1). Each block included 11 to 14 items, and a booklet was formed by including two blocks. In each booklet, two item formats, multiple-choice and constructed-response, were used, and each format contained both dichotomous and polytomous responses. Because the classification theory focused on analyzing dichotomous responses, our analysis included only items of dichotomous responses. Table 1 summarizes the booklet contents and item characteristics.

Table 1: Characteristics of PIRLS 2001 data by test booklet

Booklet	Topic	Required skill	Number of items			
			MC [a]	CR [b]	Dichotomous[c]	Total
1	Antarctica	Acquire and use information	4	7	7	11
2	Leonardo	Acquire and use information	6	6	8	12
3	Pufflings	Acquire and use information	8	5	10	13
4	River	Acquire and use information	3	8	6	11
		Subtotal	21	26	31	47
5	Clay	Literary experience	6	7	10	13
6	Flower	Literary experience	7	6	10	13
7	Hare	Literary experience	5	6	7	11
8	Mice	Literary experience	7	7	12	14
		Subtotal	25	26	39	51
		Total	46	52	70	98

Note: [a] MC = multiple-choice items, [b] CR = constructed-response items; [c] dichotomous: dichotomously scored items included both multiple-choice and constructed-response items.

In 2001, a total of 146,490 students from 35 countries took the test; each booklet was administered to about 25% of the examinees. To apply the classification method, examinees had to take common items. Therefore, examinees were grouped according to which booklets they took, and were classified within the group. Table 2 presents the distribution of examinees based on blocks/booklets.

Table 2: Distribution of examinees according to blocks taken

Group ID	Size	Block								Total (Items used)	Total (Items)
		1 (*L1)	2 (L2)	3 (L4)	4 (L3)	5 (**I2)	6 (I1)	7 (I4)	8 (I3)		
A	10,697	x	x							15	23
***B	11,090	x					x			17	24
***C	11,446	x							x	19	25
D	10,943		x		x					14	23
***E	10,787		x			x				18	25
***F	29,551			x				x		17	24
***G	11,343				x		x			16	24
***H	11,409				x				x	18	25
I	10,561					x	x			20	26
J	10,875					x			x	22	27
Total	128,702	33,233	32,427	29,551	32,379	32,223	32,994	29,551	33,730		

Note: * L = the skill of literary experience, ** = the skill of acquire and use information, *** = the groups taking booklets where combined items required both skills (i.e., acquire and use information and literary experience).

We can see from Table 2 that there were about 10,000 examinees from across the 35 countries in each group, with the exception of Group F, where about 30,000 examinees were identified. We acknowledge that examinees of different backgrounds may interpret or answer items differently. If item bias does not exist, the above differentiations can be seen as due solely to the differences in examinees' cognitive capability based on the assumption of local independence.

Although differential item functioning (DIF) studies on PIRLS data are currently unavailable, we looked at the effect of two possible factors of item bias evident in the literature of large-scale assessments, namely gender and language. As Mullis, Martin, Gonzalez, and Kennedy (2003) and Twist, Sainsbury, Woodthorpe, and Whetton (2003) record, girls outperformed boys in all participating countries in PIRLS. However, in terms of item response functions, we can again consider this as a difference in cognitive ability that will not produce influential noise in the clustering algorithm. In reporting their study on test equality, Whetton and Twist (2003) specifically pointed out that English is regarded as a deep orthography, more inconsistent and complex than some other European languages. Although we were still uncertain as to whether the differences would cause item bias, we decided to eliminate the possibility by conducting our analysis on data from the English- and European-speaking countries so that the samples would be more homogeneous in terms of language spoken by the examinees.

Because every student took items from only one booklet, the dataset was very sparse. At the current developmental stage of our new classification method, we do not yet have a fully available mechanism for dealing with missing data due to administration design. But because these missing data are not missing at random, imputation techniques are inappropriate for filling up the incomplete spots. Suspecting that responses were missing due to reasons other than administration method, we excluded the affected cases from subsequent analysis. Table 3 indicates the number of cases that we used for our analysis and the deletion rate for each dataset.

Table 3: Sample sizes of datasets used for analysis, and missing data deletion rates

		Sample size		
Group	Language	Before deletion	After deletion	Deletion rate (%)
Group B	English	2,569	2,419	5.8
	European	6,434	6,091	5.3
Group C	English	2,546	2,420	4.9
	European	6,549	6,286	4.0
Group E	English	2,552	2,400	6.0
	European	6,489	5,770	11.1
Group F	English	7,060	6,638	6.0
	European	18,749	16,734 (6,000 were used)	10.7
Group G	English	2,602	2,475	4.9
	European	6,518	6,220	4.6
Group H	English	2,544	2,423	4.8
	European	6,509	6,262	3.8

Preparation of the Q-matrices

The items of the PIRLS assessment were written on the basis of two purposes for reading, across four processes of comprehension. Although this specific structure can be used to construct the Q-matrices by taking the two purposes, the four processes, or (possibly) the eight crossed blocks composed by the two purposes and the four processes as required skills, there are limitations on Q-matrix construction for the PIRLS data. Let us take an assessment of four skills as an example.

A test comprising four required skills means $2^4 = 16$ possible examinees' attribute patterns in the data. Although some clusters are likely to be empty, a more reasonable assumption to maintain when dealing with large-scale data of large sample size is that all possible clusters are non-empty so that the number of misclassified examinees can be minimized. However, under the PIRLS' design, every examinee took, on average, 24.6 items, as shown in Table 2. Of these items, only 17.6 items were dichotomous. If we form 16 clusters with 17.6 items, using cluster analysis, it is likely that we will obtain unreliable and inconsistent results (Chiu et al., in press). Furthermore, as shown in the study by Chiu and colleagues, if we want to identify all possible examinees' attribute patterns, the test needs to include all possible single-skill items. In other words, items of patterns (1 0 0 0), (0 1 0 0), (0 0 1 0), and (0 0 0 1) are needed. Because, on average, there were only 17.6 items in a booklet, it is possible that the single-skill items for particular skills would be missing. As a result, the test would not be able to identify examinees of certain attribute patterns, and it is likely that these examinees would be misclassified to a wrong cluster. This is an especially likely occurrence with reading assessments because more than one skill is usually required to answer an item correctly. Given this situation, we decided, when applying the new classification method to the PIRLS data, to take only the "purpose" information to form two skills. The reading purpose of each block was indicated in Table 1 above; the Q-matrix for the dataset with examinees taking Blocks 1 and 6 is listed in Table 4.

Taking as our basis the booklets that the examinees took, we divided the data into 10 groups, as shown in Table 2 above. However, as we mentioned in the previous section, if a test is to identify all possible examinees' attribute patterns, all possible single-skill items have to be included. Only six sets of items covered both required skills of *literary experience* and *acquire and use information*, and these, as indicated in Table 2, were the ones we accordingly used in our analysis.

Table 4: The Q-matrix for the dataset containing examinees taking items in Blocks 1 and 6, by assessment purpose

Block	Item	Purpose	Q-matrix	
1	1	Acquire and use information	1	0
1	2	Acquire and use information	1	0
1	3	Acquire and use information	1	0
1	5	Acquire and use information	1	0
1	6	Acquire and use information	1	0
1	10	Acquire and use information	1	0
1	11	Acquire and use information	1	0
6	61	Acquire and use information	0	1
6	62	Literary experience	0	1
6	63	Literary experience	0	1
6	64	Literary experience	0	1
6	65	Literary experience	0	1
6	66	Literary experience	0	1
6	68	Literary experience	0	1
6	70	Literary experience	0	1
6	71	Literary experience	0	1
6	73	Literary experience	0	1

Procedures

We carried out the classification analysis according to the following procedures. First, we constructed sum-scores vectors, W, from the data and used these as an input to the clustering algorithms. Next, we used K-means and HACA with complete, average, and Ward's linkages to classify examinees. We then fitted the DINA model using EM algorithm for parameter estimation. Note that we did not take the DINA model as the true underlying model of the data in the analyses, but rather used it to compare the outcomes of the cluster analysis and model-based method.

Evaluation

Cluster size, within-cluster mean of W, and within-cluster sum of squares (WCSS) of W were the indices we used to evaluate the quality of classification for each method. The within-cluster mean of W indicates how well the examinees' patterns within a cluster have been identified, in the sense that the means, when taken as vectors, should be quite distinct across the possible clusters. If examinees in a particular cluster have the same attribute pattern, mean W should have a pattern of relatively large value(s) on the dimension(s) of 1's, and much smaller value(s) on 0's. If there are misclassified examinees in a cluster, the expected pattern of W is likely to become unclear, thus allowing examination of the classification quality. WCSS provides us with a sense of the extent to which grouping the data in a certain way explains the variability in the dataset. An adequate classification should yield separate clusters, each of which is formed compactly. This requirement implies that WCSS should be small for a well-classified cluster.

In order to study the interrelationships between methods, we applied the adjusted Rand index (ARI) to indicate the agreement between classifications. Let $\{g_i\}_{i=1}^G$ and $\{h_j\}_{j=1}^H$ be two partitions of N objects. Denote $N_{i\cdot}$ and N_j as the numbers of objects classified into clusters g_i and h_j, respectively, and N_{ij} as the number of objects classified into both cluster g_i and cluster h_j. The ARI is then defined as

$$ARI = \frac{\sum_{i=1}^G \sum_{j=1}^H C_2^{N_{ij}} - \sum_{i=1}^G C_2^{N_{i\cdot}} \cdot \sum_{j=1}^H C_2^{N_{\cdot j}} / C_2^N}{\frac{1}{2}[\sum_{i=1}^G C_2^{N_{i\cdot}} + \sum_{j=1}^H C_2^{N_{\cdot j}}] - \sum_{i=1}^G C_2^{N_{i\cdot}} + \sum_{j=1}^H C_2^{N_{\cdot j}} / C_2^N}.$$

Note that the *ARI* ranges from 0 to 1 and does not require equal numbers of clusters. We conducted, for each group, the analysis with full data. The only exception was the group taking Blocks L4 and I4. Data-mining left 16,734 examinees across the European countries, but this process ran out of the memory limit set up by R (the software we used for analyses). We thus reduced the sample size by randomly drawing 6,000 examinees out of the total 16,734 so that the sample size was about the same as the sample sizes of the other groups. In regard to the organization of the outputs, we labeled clusters formed by running DINA-EM with the attribute pattern that maximized the posterior likelihood. Although *K*-means and HACA algorithms did not directly provide labels for clusters, we sorted the results along with the sum of the raw scores, taking advantage of the feature whereby patterns were partially ordered among the four attribute patterns.

RESULTS

The data were stratified into English-speaking countries, including Belize, Canada (Ontario and Quebec), England, New Zealand, Scotland, Singapore, and the United States, and European-speaking countries, including Bulgaria, Cyprus, the Czech Republic, France, Germany, Greece, Hungary, Iceland, Italy, Latvia, Lithuania, Macedonia, the Netherlands, Norway, Romania, the Russian Federation, the Slovak Republic, Slovenia, Sweden, and Turkey. Both language sets were fitted by the DINA model and analyzed by HACA with various linkages and *K*-means through the statistics **W**. In this design, we did not take DINA as the assumed model, but as a contrast in order to show what results we could obtain, and whether it is beneficial to analyze the data using cluster analysis, in a situation where we have little information about the true model and where we choose DINA as the fitted model.

Table 5 displays the classification results for the data from Group B, which took items from Blocks 1 and 6. In this set of items, seven items required the skill of acquiring and using information, and the other 10 items required the skill of literacy experience. According to the results under the mean **W** category, HACA with complete and average linkages provided clear and interpretable patterns for both languages. DINA-EM, however, produced larger mean **W** values for the cluster of pattern (0 0) than did the other clustering methods, a finding which demonstrates that DINA tended

Table 5: Classification results for Group B (took Blocks 1 and 6)

(A) Cluster analysis									
English-speaking					European-speaking				
Size	Mean W		WCSS (total)	MSum Y	Size	Mean W		WCSS (total)	MSumY
HACA with complete linkage					HACA with complete linkage				
286	2.00	3.00	1,089.00	5.00	149	1.23	2.15	207.69	3.38
223	4.75	4.23	387.27	8.98	201	1.56	5.44	309.18	7.00
481	3.99	8.20	1,220.42	12.20	1641	4.59	5.14	5650.57	9.72
1,429	6.28	8.50	2,922.59	14.78	4100	5.90	8.60	8,979.12	14.49
			(5,619.28)					(15,146.56)	
HACA with average linkage					HACA with average linkage				
136	1.46	1.68	239.50	3.13	393	2.34	3.15	1,388.94	5.49
540	3.69	4.96	2,034.61	8.65	25	5.04	1.60	20.96	6.64
2	2.00	9.50	0.50	11.5	1,353	4.58	5.51	4,672.18	10.09
1,741	5.94	8.60	4,259.74	14.53	4,220	5.86	8.54	9,363.41	14.40
			(6,534.35)					(15,445.49)	
HACA with Ward linkage					HACA with Ward linkage				
564	3.08	3.91	2777.29	6.99	621	3.17	3.02	2169.31	6.19
615	5.11	6.99	1576.03	12.09	1654	4.23	6.24	6076.90	10.47
545	5.37	9.42	529.27	14.79	2148	5.72	7.99	3266.31	13.71
695	6.81	9.00	579.78	15.81	1668	6.56	9.44	820.89	16.00
			(5,462.37)					(12,333.41)	
K-means					K-means				
Size	Mean W		WCSS (total)	MSum Y	Size	Mean W		WCSS (total)	MSumY
354	2.40	3.00	1,297.63	5.40	830	3.13	3.53	2,962.96	6.66
508	5.50	6.04	948.36	11.53	905	3.36	7.34	1,737.15	10.70
408	3.87	7.89	732.84	11.76	1284	5.87	6.26	1,742.01	12.13
1,149	6.36	9.18	1,189.44	15.54	3072	6.19	8.95	3,794.63	15.14
			(4,168.27)					(10,236.75)	

(B) DINA-EM									
English-speaking					European-speaking				
Pattern	Size	Mean W		WCSS (total)	Pattern	Size	Mean W		WCSS (total)
(0 0)	583	2.97	4.07	3,014.90	(0 0)	1,521	3.36	4.83	6,985.22
(1 0)	46	6.26	4.50	26.37	(1 0)	198	6.23	4.55	218.40
(0 1)	47	2.70	8.45	45.45	(0 1)	161	2.94	8.53	125.44
(1 1)	1,743	5.96	8.56	4,214.29	(1 1)	4,211	6.03	8.42	9,268.02
				(7,301.01)					(16,597.1)

(C) ARI across all selected methods										
English-speaking						European-speaking				
	DINA	Comp	Ave	Ward	K-means	DINA	Comp	Ave	Ward	K-means
DINA	1	0.27	0.81	0.28	0.37	1	0.67	0.64	0.31	0.47
Comp	*	1	0.59	0.24	0.41	*	1	0.82	0.38	0.46
Ave	*	*	1	0.22	0.36	*	*	1	0.37	0.45
Ward	*	*	*	1	0.48	*	*	*	1	0.39
K-means	*	*	*	*	1	*	*	*	*	1

to misclassify data to the lowest cluster, for both languages. This finding implies that cluster analysis is more robust than the model-based method, even with such a short test. However, HACA with Ward linkage and K-means do not yield recognizable W patterns for some clusters, a happenstance which signals that examinees of a certain attribute pattern were misclassified to a wrong cluster.

In terms of within-cluster variability, DINA-EM produced clusters of larger variability than did the other methods for both the English and the European data, indicating that the clusters formed by using DINA-EM were not as homongenous as those formed through use of the other methods. Note that the WCSS should be interpreted with caution. As mentioned, HACA with Ward linkage and K-means tend to minimize the sum of within-cluster variances, and therefore tend to produce tight clusters of small WCSS.

The ARI portion of Table 5 indicates that HACA with complete and average linkages were in high agreement for both datasets. However, HACA with complete linkage had a high agreement with DINA-EM for the European data but a low agreement for the English data. Note that a large ARI does not necessarily imply good classification quality. Good quality can only be assumed when one of the compared partitions is known to perform well. A large ARI may simply reflect that both compared partitions behave similarly with some particular data structure.

Table 6 concludes the results for Group C, which took Blocks 1 and 8. Seven of the items required the skill of acquiring and using information; 12 required the skill of literacy experience. For the English data, HACA with average linkage performed better than the other methods. For the European data, HACA with complete and average linkages both performed well, based on their mean W patterns. DINA not only again clustered most examinees to the two ends of the classes with large mean W values for the lowest class, but also yielded much larger WCSSs than the other methods. The ARI portion of the table shows that, for the European data, HACA with average and complete linkages classified data in high agreement. What is evident, in addition to these two methods generating a well-recognized mean W pattern (see the information provided above), is that these two methods can produce consistent classifications with this group of European data.

Table 7 shows the results for Group E, which took Blocks 2 and 5, where eight of the 18 items required the skill of acquiring and using information and 10 required the skill of literacy experience. For both the English and the European data, DINA-EM performed well, producing recognizable mean W patterns. HACA with average linkage and K-means also performed quite well. However, DINA-EM still had the problem of large WCSS. The ARI portion of the table does not show any method providing high agreement.

Table 8 displays the results for Group F, which took Blocks 3 and 7. Ten of the items required the skill of acquiring and using information, and seven required the skill of literacy experience. As discussed, only 6,000 European data were randomly drawn and analyzed. In this case, HACA with complete linkage performed better than

Table 6: Classification results for Group C (took Blocks 1 and 8)

(A) Cluster analysis								
English-speaking				European-speaking				
Size	Mean W		WCSS (total)	MSum Y	Size	Mean W		WCSS (total)	MSumY
HACA with complete linkage					HACA with complete linkage				
208	1.60	3.11	677.75	4.07	365	1.90	3.56	960.43	5.46
93	3.60	1.96	206.11	5.56	558	2.87	7.10	1,089.68	9.97
574	5.28	6.60	1,438.75	11.88	1248	5.17	5.62	4,162.54	15.68
1,545	5.59	10.05	6,050.10	15.64	4115	5.93	9.75	10,420.02	10.79
			(8,372.71)					(16,632.67)	
HACA with average linkage					HACA with average linkage				
235	2.15	2.19	818.17	4.34	470	2.17	3.33	1,373.60	5.51
542	4.29	5.87	1,527.84	10.15	228	2.34	8.45	555.48	10.79
11	1.82	9.36	6.18	11.18	1516	4.83	6.09	4,236.05	10.91
1,632	5.81	10.01	4,769.02	15.83	4072	5.97	9.74	9,976.01	15.71
			(7,121.21)					(16,141.14)	
HACA with Ward linkage					HACA with Ward linkage				
229	1.93	2.29	701.41	4.23	1,077	3.06	4.42	5,083.81	7.49
700	4.64	6.25	2,515.52	10.89	1,312	2.87	7.07	2,120.32	11.95
985	5.41	9.61	2,377.17	15.02	1,955	5.60	8.92	4,337.04	14.52
506	6.55	11.42	248.44	17.97	1,947	6.45	10.76	1,814.54	17.21
			(5,842.54)					(13,355.71)	
K-means					K-means				
Size	Mean W		WCSS (total)	MSum Y	Size	Mean W		WCSS (total)	MSumY
275	2.16	2.53	1,031.45	4.69	810	2.75	3.98	3,276.68	6.73
510	4.41	6.00	1,325.34	10.41	1,260	4.04	8.33	2,251.59	12.37
738	5.24	8.85	1,439.00	14.09	1,358	5.76	6.79	2,505.92	12.56
897	6.27	10.99	1,079.63	17.25	2,858	6.30	10.30	4,232.76	16.61
			(4,875.42)					(12,266.95)	

(B) DINA-EM									
English-speaking					European-speaking				
Pattern	Size	Mean W		WCSS (total)	Pattern	Size	Mean W		WCSS (total)
(0 0)	635	3.03	4.49	4,009.23	(0 0)	1,712	3.46	5.47	9,039.31
(1 0)	51	6.14	5.14	54.08	(1 0)	148	6.26	5.22	213.80
(0 1)	24	2.54	9.58	25.79	(0 1)	96	2.70	9.61	82.98
(1 1)	1710	5.87	9.82	5,484.36	(1 1)	4330	6.02	9.55	1,2215.95
				(9,573.46)					(21,552.04)

(C) ARI across all selected methods										
English-speaking						European-speaking				
	DINA	Comp	Ave	Ward	K-means	DINA	Comp	Ave	Ward	K-means
DINA	1	0.40	0.69	0.24	0.34	1	0.65	0.67	0.31	0.35
Comp	*	1	0.60	0.45	0.38	*	1	0.92	0.32	0.46
Ave	*	*	1	0.43	0.52	*	*	1	0.33	0.45
Ward	*	*	*	1	0.47	*	*	*	1	0.43
K-means	*	*	*	*	1	*	*	*	*	1

Table 7: Classification results for Group E (took Blocks 2 and 5)

(A) Cluster analysis									
English-speaking					European-speaking				
Size	Mean W		WCSS (total)	MSum Y	Size	Mean W		WCSS (total)	MSumY
HACA with complete linkage					HACA with complete linkage				
351	1.83	1.93	820.76	3.76	882	2.73	2.73	2,211.83	5.47
390	4.48	2.89	938.41	7.37	1,624	4.98	4.80	6,706.74	9.77
744	4.66	7.28	2,537.81	11.94	1,100	3.88	7.74	3,647.03	11.62
915	7.01	7.94	2,994.28	17.94	2,164	6.70	8.12	4,402.68	14.82
			(7,291.26)					(16,968.28)	
HACA with average linkage					HACA with average linkage				
609	2.77	2.20	2,004.71	4.97	610	2.54	1.81	1593.25	4.35
372	4.04	5.97	690.15	10.01	4	0.75	8.50	1.75	9.25
214	6.01	4.01	334.94	10.02	2,496	4.59	5.08	9,490.90	9.67
1,205	6.47	8.36	3,385.94	14.82	2,660	6.11	8.45	6,571.69	14.56
			(6,415.74)					(17,657.59)	
HACA with Ward linkage					HACA with Ward linkage				
506	2.42	2.02	1,641.36	4.45	1789	3.93	3.15	7,625.00	7.08
555	5.05	4.45	1,466.67	9.50	1290	3.85	6.79	2,958.54	10.64
737	5.56	7.32	2,105.11	12.88	706	6.55	6.43	548.29	12.98
602	6.88	9.30	805.08	16.18	1985	6.38	8.74	3202.37	15.11
			(6,018.22)					(14,334.2)	
K-means					K-means				
Size	Mean W		WCSS (total)	MSum Y	Size	Mean W		WCSS (total)	MSumY
585	2.58	2.20	1,890.62	4.79	1317	3.19	2.74	4,449.50	5.93
536	5.53	4.76	1,455.84	10.30	1114	5.64	5.11	2,064.73	10.75
436	4.49	7.47	903.53	11.96	1210	4.01	7.32	2,245.62	11.33
843	6.92	8.76	1,327.98	15.68	2129	6.54	8.51	3,700.89	15.05
			(5,577.97)					(12,460.74)	

(B) DINA-EM								
English-speaking					European-speaking			
Pattern	Size	Mean W		WCSS (total)	Pattern	Size	Mean W		WCSS (total)
(0 0)	855	3.17	2.90	3,957.36	(0 0)	1,905	3.57	3.42	8,349.24
(1 0)	44	6.70	3.09	88.80	(1 0)	48	7.13	3.33	45.92
(0 1)	33	2.61	7.64	31.52	(0 1)	192	2.69	7.52	255.17
(1 1)	1468	6.25	7.91	5,341.40	(1 1)	3,625	5.96	7.77	11,899.17
				(9,419.08)					(20,549.5)

(C) ARI across all selected methods										
English-speaking						European-speaking				
	DINA	Comp	Ave	Ward	K-means	DINA	Comp	Ave	Ward	K-means
DINA	1	0.39	0.59	0.33	0.38	1	0.30	0.35	0.37	0.37
Comp	*	1	0.47	0.29	0.36	*	1	0.41	0.41	0.54
Ave	*	*	1	0.41	0.55	*	*	1	0.42	0.48
Ward	*	*	*	1	0.58	*	*	*	1	0.56
K-means	*	*	*	*	1	*	*	*	*	1

Table 8: Classification results for Group F (took Blocks 3 and 7)

(A) Cluster analysis									
English-speaking					European-speaking				
Size	Mean W		WCSS (total)	MSum Y	Size	Mean W		WCSS (total)	MSumY
HACA with complete linkage					HACA with complete linkage				
496	2.07	1.89	1,116.48	3.95	471	2.70	2.61	1,064.28	5.31
732	2.27	5.22	1,246.84	7.49	462	2.20	5.24	989.04	7.44
2,163	4.81	5.85	5,267.41	10.66	203	6.47	3.17	415.51	9.64
3,247	7.81	6.35	6,926.22	14.15	4864	6.74	6.14	18,995.98	12.88
			(14,556.95)					(21,464.81)	
HACA with average linkage					HACA with average linkage				
481	1.96	1.92	927.40	3.89	281	1.63	2.43	1,052.52	4.05
230	5.39	2.70	578.68	8.10	1	7.00	0.00	0.00	7.00
1,325	3.17	5.13	3,402.09	8.30	2,931	4.59	5.47	9,648.06	10.05
4,602	6.97	6.45	15,136.72	13.41	2,787	8.07	6.26	4,864.93	14.33
			(20,044.89)					(15,565.51)	
HACA with Ward linkage					HACA with Ward linkage				
933	2.37	2.78	3,143.42	5.15	1,122	2.84	3.80	4,912.55	6.65
1,973	4.05	5.91	3,908.66	9.95	2,096	5.13	5.94	3,371.26	11.07
1,931	6.52	6.14	2,673.32	12.66	1,901	7.50	6.16	2,169.12	13.65
1,801	8.70	6.61	1,660.29	15.31	881	9.31	6.51	551.48	15.81
			(11,385.69)					(11,004.41)	
K-means					K-means				
Size	Mean W		WCSS (total)	MSum Y	Size	Mean W		WCSS (total)	MSumY
855	2.47	2.54	2,731.26	5.02	824	3.27	2.95	2,860.88	6.22
1,222	3.23	5.83	2,127.72	9.06	895	3.25	5.90	1,230.97	9.15
2,741	6.04	6.11	4,394.48	12.15	2,474	6.13	6.06	3,560.68	12.19
1,820	8.70	6.58	1,838.26	15.28	1,807	8.65	6.33	2,213.76	17.98
			(11,091.72)					(9,866.29)	

(B) DINA-EM									
English-speaking					European-speaking				
Pattern	Size	Mean W		WCSS (total)	Pattern	Size	Mean W		WCSS (total)
(0 0)	1602	3.26	3.49	7,128.80	(0 0)	1401	3.69	3.72	5,722.63
(1 0)	7	8.57	2.86	2.57	(1 0)	12	8.25	2.83	3.92
(0 1)	976	3.55	6.44	1,507.73	(0 1)	842	3.81	6.39	1,167.00
(1 1)	4,053	7.33	6.44	10,513.01	(1 1)	3745	7.45	6.28	9,124.10
				(19,152.11)					(16,017.65)

(C) ARI across all selected methods									
English-speaking					European-speaking				
	DINA	Comp	Ave	Ward	K-means	DINA	Comp	Ave	Ward	K-means
DINA	1	0.48	0.61	0.34	0.38	1	0.37	0.32	0.24	0.37
Comp	*	1	0.43	0.44	0.35	*	1	0.13	0.21	0.23
Ave	*	*	1	0.24	0.31	*	*	1	0.57	0.30
Ward	*	*	*	1	0.68	*	*	*	1	0.37
K-means	*	*	*	*	1	*	*	*	*	1

the other cluster methods for the European data, and HACA with average linkage performed best for the English data. The above notion was based on whether the mean *W* patterns were more recognizable than the other mean *W* patterns. However, the clusters formed by these methods contained large WCSSs, implying that misclassification occurs with the two methods when clustering data. If we take a closer look, it is not hard to find that the mean *W* values of the highest class produced by the two methods were smaller than those produced by the other methods. This outcome means that many data with patterns different from (1 1) were classified into the (1 1) cluster. Although the mean *W* values provided useful information for identifying the underlying pattern for each cluster, that information was not sufficient to allow us to determine if a particular method outperformed the others.

Table 9 shows the results of Group G, which took Blocks 4 and 6. In this set, the first six items required the skill of acquiring and using information, and the last 10 items required the skill of literacy experience. The results imply that, for both datasets, DINA-EM is a better choice than the others. HACA with average linkage produced acceptable classifications, although the mean *W* patterns were not very clear. An interesting finding is that HACA with average linkage formed clusters with unusually large WCSSs for both datasets, implying that HACA with average linkage was unable to classify examinees into the correct cluster with this particular data structure, rendering the results untrustworthy. As the ARI portion of the table shows, DINA-EM had good agreement with HACA, with average linkage for the English data, and a good agreement with HACA, but with complete linkage for the European data.

In Table 10, examinees took Blocks 4 and 8. Here, six items required acquiring and using information, while the last 12 items required literacy experience. Among the cluster analysis methods, HACA with complete linkage produced tighter and better separated means of *W* than the other methods for the European data. DINA-EM produced recognizable mean *W* patterns, but the issue of misclassification remained. In addition, HACA with average and complete linkages behaved similarly with both the English and the European data, based on the ARI index.

CONCLUSIONS AND IMPLICATIONS

Given that PIRLS was not designed to detect examinees' cognitive capacity, use of the retrofitting approach to analyze data is usually a great concern. As Gierl (2007) points out, using retrofitting procedures to pursue cognitive analysis for existing testing invariably produces weak fit between the cognitive model and the data. The main reason why is that the assessments were not designed for the cognitive diagnostic purpose and so could not provide much useful information. This area of research is an important and developing one because, at the current stage, applying retrofitting procedures to analyze large-scale data seems unavoidable. Under this circumstance, where the parametric approach encounters the issue of model fit, a useful direction for overcoming the limitation is to develop robust non-parametric or quasi-parametric approaches as alternatives to minimize the bias due to model misfit. Motivated by this

Table 9: Classification results for Group G (took Booklets 4 and 6)

(A) Cluster analysis									
English-speaking					European-speaking				
Size	Mean W		WCSS (total)	MSum Y	Size	Mean W		WCSS (total)	MSumY
HACA with complete linkage					HACA with complete linkage				
366	1.68	2.87	1,198.20	4.55	338	1.33	2.30	688.04	3.63
281	4.56	5.14	425.00	9.71	1,120	3.13	4.88	2,486.86	8.02
731	3.32	7.78	1,844.10	11.09	407	1.97	8.40	1,289.37	10.37
1,097	5.49	8.91	1,336.61	14.40	4,355	4.81	8.32	11,455.33	13.12
			(4,803.91)					(15,919.6)	
HACA with average linkage					HACA with average linkage				
192	1.38	1.72	380.29	3.10	12	3.83	0.58	6.58	4.42
1	6.00	2.00	0.00	8.00	827	2.23	3.34	2,683.04	5.57
644	3.21	5.24	2,356.18	8.44	155	0.77	6.85	197.92	7.61
1,638	4.89	8.70	3,409.21	13.59	5,226	4.53	8.05	18,651.39	12.58
			(6,145.68)					(21,538.93)	
HACA with Ward linkage					HACA with Ward linkage				
243	1.24	2.29	7,18.51	3.53	2,194	2.87	5.04	11,230.79	7.91
504	3.59	4.96	1,078.27	8.55	1,146	3.53	8.82	1,170.44	12.34
766	4.30	7.56	1,628.35	11.86	1,270	5.10	7.50	929.40	12.60
962	5.14	9.47	1,017.02	14.61	1,610	5.52	9.44	797.52	14.96
			(4,442.15)					(14,128.15)	
K-means					K-means				
Size	Mean W		WCSS (total)	MSum Y	Size	Mean W		WCSS (total)	MSumY
301	1.53	2.48	914.12	4.01	926	2.24	3.48	3,024.07	5.72
471	3.77	5.23	951.38	9.00	1354	2.74	7.49	2,615.41	10.23
621	3.58	7.88	1,061.11	11.46	1200	4.74	6.30	3,226.02	11.04
1,082	5.44	9.11	1,202.74	14.55	2740	5.19	9.11	1,533.00	14.30
			(4,129.35)					(10,398.5)	

(B) DINA-EM									
English-speaking					European-speaking				
Pattern	Size	Mean W		WCSS (total)	Pattern	Size	Mean W		WCSS (total)
(0 0)	616	2.26	3.87	2,904.95	(0 0)	1665	2.46	4.73	7,244.48
(1 0)	40	5.18	4.40	33.38	(1 0)	121	5.30	4.30	140.58
(0 1)	53	1.70	8.13	41.25	(0 1)	255	2.11	8.57	288.55
(1 1)	1,766	4.90	8.48	4451.05	(1 1)	4,179	4.89	8.45	9,539.33
				(7,430.63)					(17,212.94)

(C) ARI across all selected methods										
English-speaking						European-speaking				
	DINA	Comp	Ave	Ward	K-means	DINA	Comp	Ave	Ward	K-means
DINA	1	0.34	0.70	0.33	0.37	1	0.64	0.42	0.27	0.37
Comp	*	1	0.44	0.35	0.71	*	1	0.53	0.13	0.31
Ave	*	*	1	0.48	0.52	*	*	1	0.02	0.23
Ward	*	*	*	1	0.53	*	*	*	1	0.33
K-means	*	*	*	*	1	*	*	*	*	1

155

Table 10: Classification results for Group H (took Booklets 4 and 8)

(A) Cluster analysis								
English-speaking				European-speaking				
Size	Mean W		WCSS (total)	MSum Y	Size	Mean W		WCSS (total)	MSumY
HACA with complete linkage					HACA with complete linkage				
250	1.16	2.11	576.46	3.27	331	1.64	1.99	745.89	3.63
73	3.70	2.63	86.38	6.33	479	0.32	5.69	1,346.04	7.01
642	4.00	6.38	2,232.49	10.38	643	4.03	5.17	1,232.44	9.20
1,458	4.68	10.16	4,647.09	14.84	4809	4.60	9.27	17,133.88	13.87
			(7,542.42)					(20,458.25)	
HACA with average linkage					HACA with average linkage				
275	1.73	1.90	654.89	3.63	331	1.64	1.99	745.89	3.63
1	0.00	10.00	0.00	10.00	1,236	2.14	6.62	3,587.10	8.76
820	3.66	6.41	3,230.45	10.08	474	4.40	5.02	905.90	9.41
1,327	4.87	10.43	2,948.49	15.31	4,221	4.88	9.49	12,231.15	14.37
			(6,833.83)					(17,470.04)	
HACA with Ward linkage					HACA with Ward linkage				
454	1.91	2.96	1887.13	4.86	1679	2.60	4.95	8791.82	7.55
372	4.04	6.22	552.67	10.26	1619	3.32	9.13	2982.47	12.46
1,068	4.39	9.28	2,625.44	13.68	775	5.34	7.32	644.98	12.66
529	5.47	11.46	339.03	16.93	2189	5.48	10.28	2,775.63	15.76
			(5,404.27)					(15,194.90)	
K-means					K-means				
Size	Mean W		WCSS (total)	MSum Y	Size	Mean W		WCSS (total)	MSumY
329	1.65	2.26	909.35	3.91	849	2.25	3.42	3,258.60	5.67
512	3.52	5.90	1,299.72	9.42	1,103	2.35	7.61	2,106.76	9.96
731	4.27	8.86	1,401.50	13.13	2,184	4.87	7.93	3,846.41	12.79
851	5.27	11.03	1,045.37	16.30	2,126	5.06	10.66	3,043.66	15.72
			(4,655.94)					(12,255.43)	

(B) DINA-EM								
English-speaking				European-speaking				
Pattern	Size	Mean W		WCSS (total)	Pattern	Size	Mean W		WCSS (total)
(0 0)	628	2.20	3.86	3,452.19	(0 0)	1,484	2.30	4.87	7,557.61
(1 0)	38	5.16	4.50	56.55	(1 0)	120	5.25	4.73	234.43
(0 1)	33	1.70	9.39	48.85	(0 1)	317	2.06	8.98	465.82
(1 1)	1,723	4.83	9.70	6,221.05	(1 1)	4,341	4.88	9.36	13,464.06
			(9,778.64)					(21,721.92)	

(C) ARI across all selected methods										
English-speaking						European-speaking				
	DINA	Comp	Ave	Ward	K-means	DINA	Comp	Ave	Ward	K-means
DINA	1	0.44	0.42	0.34	0.32	1	0.60	0.74	0.32	0.34
Comp	*	1	0.78	0.35	0.41	*	1	0.69	0.16	0.22
Ave	*	*	1	0.35	0.48	*	*	1	0.24	0.38
Ward	*	*	*	1	0.55	*	*	*	1	0.30
K-means	*	*	*	*	1	*	*	*	*	1

idea, we would like to learn whether the new classification method is reliable with large-scale assessment, and whether its robustness over the model-based method provides valuable benefit to remedy the weaknesses with retrofitting procedures.

The classification theory developed by Chiu and colleagues (in press) is built on the assumption of long tests. Application of this theory to the PIRLS data has provided a good opportunity for understanding how reliable the method is for short tests. This empirical application revealed that DINA-EM tends to classify data to the clusters at the two extreme ends. However, the cluster analysis seemed to have difficulty correctly assigning examinees to middle clusters. One possible explanation for the unreliable classifications is that the two procedures for reading and the four skills of comprehension were designed to nest within each other. Although we took only the two purposes as the required skills, we remain unclear as to whether examinees' wrong answers are caused purely by absence of a certain skill with respect to a purpose or by the absence of some more specific skills nested within the purpose. If the cause relates to missing skills of procedures, and not simply to missing the specific skill of the purpose, then we could assume that some measurement error is contributing to and thus inflating the systematic noise, and that the true absence or presence of the skill being measured will be difficult to detect. This consideration again reflects the importance of writing items appropriate to the cognitive diagnosis aim.

Previous studies concerning use of this cluster analysis method to classify examinees under the cognitive diagnosis setting indicate that this method, depending on the type of structure of the dataset, is more robust than is fitting a wrong model (see, for example, Chiu & Douglas, 2008). This finding is consistent with the results in the current study. When DINA-EM fits the data well (e.g., Group E or Group G), we have in place a cluster analysis that performs as well as the DINA-EM. When the DINA does not appear to be the true model (e.g., Group C and Group F), it is possible to find a cluster analysis that is more reliable. While more work is needed on labeling, given that this is critical and important for the K-means and HACA, the feature of easy access and the convincing results from simulations and real applications make the theory, at this point, an appreciable alternative for classification.

References

Bradley, P., & Fayyad, U. (1998). Refining initial points for K-means clustering. In J. Shavlik, (Ed.), *Proceedings of the fifteenth international conference on machine learning* (pp. 91–99). Burlington, MA: Morgan Kaufmann.

Chiu, C., & Douglas, J. (2008). *Cluster analysis for cognitive diagnosis: A robustness study in relation to model misspecification*. Paper presented at the annual meeting of the Psychometric Society, Durham, NH.

Chiu, C., Douglas, J., & Li, X. (in press). Cluster analysis for cognitive diagnosis: Theory and applications. *Psychometrika*.

de la Torre, J., & Douglas, J. A. (2004). Higher order latent trait models for cognitive diagnosis. *Psychometrika, 69*, 333–353.

Forgy, E. W. (1965). Cluster analysis of multivariate data: Efficiency versus interpretability of classifications. *Biometrics, 21*, 768–769.

Gierl, M. (2007). Making diagnostic inferences about cognitive attributes using the rule-space model and attribute hierarchy method. *Journal of Educational Measurement, 44*, 325–340.

Gonzalez, E. I., & Kennedy, A. M. (2001). *PIRLS 2001 user guide for the international database.* Retrieved January 2007, from http://isc.bc.edu/pirls2001i/PIRLS2001_Pubs_UG.html.

Gorin, J. (2007). Test construction and diagnostic testing. In J. P. Leighton & M. J. Gierl (Eds.), *Cognitive diagnostic assessment for education* (pp. 173–201), Cambridge: Cambridge University Press.

Haertel, E. H. (1989). Using restricted latent class models to map the skill structure of achievement items. *Journal of Educational Measurement, 26*, 333–352.

Junker, B. W., & Sijtsma, K. (2001). Cognitive assessment models with few assumptions, and connections with nonparametric item response theory. *Applied Psychological Measurement, 25*, 258–272.

Kaufman, J., & Rousseuw, P. (1990). *Finding groups in data: An introduction to cluster analysis.* New York: Wiley.

Leighton, J., & Gierl, M. (2007). Why cognitive diagnostic assessment? In J. P. Leighton & M. J. Gierl (Eds.), *Cognitive diagnostic assessment for education* (pp. 3–18). Cambridge: Cambridge University Press.

MacQueen, J. (1967). Some methods of classification and analysis of multivariate observations. In L. M. Le Cam & J. Neyman (Eds.), *Proceedings of the fifth Berkeley symposium on mathematical statistics and probability* (pp. 281–207). Berkeley, CA: University of California Press.

Milligan, G. W. (1980). An examination of the effects of six types of error perturbation on fifteen clustering algorithms. *Psychometrika, 45*, 325–342.

Mullis, I., Martin, M., Gonzalez, E., & Kennedy, A. (2003). *PIRLS 2001 international report: IEA's study of reading literacy achievement in primary schools in 35 countries.* Chestnut Hill, MA: Boston College.

Pena, J., Lozano, J., & Larranaga, P. (1999). An empirical comparison of four initialization methods for the *K*-means algorithm. *Pattern Recognition Letters, 20*, 1027–1040.

Rupp, A. A., & Templin, J. L. (2007). *Unique characteristics of cognitive diagnosis models.* Paper presented at the annual meeting of the National Council for Measurement in Education, Chicago, IL.

Steinley, D. (2006). *K*-means clustering: A half-century synthesis. *British Journal of Mathematical and Statistical Psychology, 59*, 1–34.

Tatsuoka, K. (1985). A probabilistic model for diagnosing misconceptions by the pattern classification approach. *Journal of Educational Statistics, 10*, 55–73.

Tatsuoka, C. (2002). Data-analytic methods for latent partially ordered classification models. *Applied Statistics (JRSS-C), 5*, 337–350.

Twist, L., Sainsbury, M., Woodthorpe, A., & Whetton, C. (2003). *Reading all over the world: Progress in International Reading Literacy Study: National report for England.* Slough: National Foundation for Educational Research.

Ward, J. H. (1963). Hierarchical grouping to optimize an objective function. *Journal of the American Statistical Association, 58,* 236–244.

Whetton, C., & Twist, L. (2003). *What determines the range of reading attainment in a country?* Paper presented at the 29th International Association for Educational Assessment Conference, Manchester, United Kingdom.

Variance estimation for NAEP data using a comprehensive resampling-based approach: An application of cognitive diagnostic models[1]

Chueh-an Hsieh
Michigan State University, East Lansing, Michigan, United States of America

Xueli Xu and Matthias von Davier
Educational Testing Service, Princeton, New Jersey, United States of America

This article presents an application of the jackknifing re-sampling approach (Efron, 1982) to error variance estimation for ability distributions of groups of students, using a multidimensional discrete model for item response data. The data utilized to examine the approach came from the National Assessment of Educational Progress (NAEP). In contrast to the operational approach used in NAEP, where plausible values are generated using the complete sample and are then subjected to a resampling scheme, the proposed approach re-estimated all model parameters for each of the replicate samples during the jackknife. The resampling approach proposed here is therefore a more comprehensive one because of its expected ability to represent the uncertainty due to sampling more appropriately. Results for the comprehensive resampling and re-estimation-based standard errors are presented for estimates of group means, total means, and other statistics used in NAEP for official reporting. Differences in results between the proposed approach and the operational approach are discussed.

---

1 The authors thank Dan Eignor, Yue Jia, Frank Rijman, and Andreas Oranje for their comments and suggestions, and Kim Fryer for her assistance in copyediting. The authors also thank Steve Isham for providing the data used in this study.

INTRODUCTION

The statistics reported in educational surveys form the basis for secondary analyses and policy research, the outcomes of which guide educational planning. As an ongoing national survey, the National Assessment of Educational Progress (NAEP) is designed to provide national and state information on the academic performance of United States students (fourth-, eighth-, and twelfth-graders) in various subjects, such as reading, mathematics, writing, science, and other subject areas. Often referred to as the Nation's Report Card, NAEP is administered by the United States Department of Education's National Center for Education Statistics (NCES), and includes a range of surveys and assessments that provide information on students' educational experiences, teachers' characteristics and practices, and school climate.

As is the case with many national surveys, NAEP has adopted a complex sampling design for selecting student participants to the assessments. The major feature of the complex sample design includes cluster sampling (utilizing the differential sample selection characteristics) and sampling weights (including adjustments for school and student non-response and post-stratification). As a major source of uncertainty, sampling variability provides information about how much variation in a given statistic would likely occur if another equivalent sample of individuals was observed (Qian, Kaplan, Johnson, Krenzke, & Rust, 2001). Another important source of variability of NAEP scores is measurement error. Because items in NAEP assessments are administered according to a partially balanced incomplete block (pBIB) design, each student responds to relatively few items. Thus, the uncertainty in estimation of proficiency is also a variability component due to the imprecision in the measurement of the scale scores (Johnson, 1989; Li & Oranje, 2007; Mazzeo, Donoghue, & Johnson, 2006; Qian et al., 2001).

A major goal of NAEP is to provide estimates of group-level distributions of student proficiencies in the target population as well as in subpopulations of United States youth. Since 1984, NAEP has reported these academic results using item response theory (IRT) models (Lord & Novick, 1968; Rasch, 1960) and latent regression models (Mislevy, 1991). The IRT models are used to calibrate the cognitive items, and the latent regression models are used to make inferences on the latent abilities. Operationally, through the use of the software CGROUP,[2] population-related ability estimates, such as subpopulation means, achievement levels, and score distributions for various reporting groups, are obtained from examinees' item response data and background data (Mazzeo et al., 2006; Mislevy, 1991; von Davier, Sinharay, Oranje, & Beaton, 2007). This marginal estimation approach involves two stages in which the parameters of a latent regression model are estimated in the first stage, assuming the item parameters are fixed. This model, with its estimated parameters, is then used to generate a set of plausible values (Mislevy, 1991) that can be considered multiple imputations from the posterior distribution, given students' responses to cognitive

---

2   CGROUP uses a Laplace approximation and is designed to be computationally feasible for a test with more than two dimensions (Thomas, 1993; von Davier & Sinharay, 2007).

items and background data. These plausible values, in turn, are used to obtain the estimates of interest, for example, group means, standard deviations, percentiles, and other summary statistics. A jackknifing approach based on the single, operational, set of plausible values is adopted in NAEP to obtain estimates of variability for the different statistics of interest.

One consequence of ignoring the complex sample design is that the magnitude of the standard error of group-level statistics tends to be underestimated. It has been argued that the effect of ignoring the complex structure on the parameters of interest is relatively large in an NAEP operationally saturated model. In some situations, the effect may be substantial (Mazzeo et al., 2006, pp. 68–69). This finding may be the result of assuming common variance across subpopulations embedded in the latent regression models, and this effect may be alleviated by using a model that allows for the estimation of group-specific variances (Mazzeo et al., 2006; Thomas, 2000; von Davier, 2003). The general diagnostic model (GDM) (von Davier, 2005) is one such model that allows different ability variances in different subgroups (Xu & von Davier, 2006, 2008). In addition, the GDM allows a quite parsimonious specification of multiple-group models by utilizing constraints, making it possible to estimate the item parameters and the parameters in the regression models simultaneously. This allows one to utilize the GDM for the required repeated estimation of all model parameters for each of the jackknifing samples in resampling-based variance estimation. In contrast, the current NAEP operation does not allow simultaneous estimation of all model parameters for each jackknifing sample. Thus, the primary goal of this study is to use GDM, assuming a multiple-group population model, to obtain the estimation error based on a jackknife resampling procedure, and to compare the variance estimates obtained with the operational results.

GENERAL DIAGNOSTIC MODELS (GDM)

The GDM (von Davier, 2005) contains a large array of psychometric models, such as the latent class analysis (LCA) (Goodman, 1974; Lazarsfeld, & Henry, 1968; McCutcheon, 1987), as well as discrete latent trait models, with pre-specified skill profiles and levels, and multidimensional IRT models (MIRT) (Ackerman, 1994, 1996). For instance, the GDM can be used to perform multiple classifications of examinees based on their response patterns with respect to skill attributes. Using ideas from IRT, log-linear models, and latent class analysis, GDM can be viewed as a general modeling framework for confirmatory multidimensional item response models (von Davier, 2005, 2007; von Davier & Rost, 2006; von Davier & Yamamoto, 2004). Within this comprehensive framework, many well-known models in measurement and educational testing, such as the unidimensional and multidimensional versions of the Rasch model (RM) (Rasch, 1960), the two-parameter logistic item response theory model (2PL-IRT) (Lord & Novick, 1968), the generalized partial credit model (GPCM) (Muraki, 1992), together with a variety of skill-profile models, are special cases of the GDM (von Davier, 2005).

In the following analyses, we applied a compensatory GDM and used the software *mdltm* (von Davier, 2005) to estimate a MIRT model for NAEP data. In addition, we adopted a log-linear smoothing technique to facilitate the estimation of the latent skill space (Xu & von Davier, 2008). Using a log-linear smoothing method allowed us not only to substantially reduce the number of estimated parameters (associated with the latent skill distribution) but also to account for the interrelationship among distinct latent skills. In the software *mdltm*, the expectation-maximization algorithm (EM; Dempster, Laird, & Rubin, 1977) is implemented and used for parameter estimation. This implementation enables one to use standard tools from IRT for scale linking, deriving measures of model goodness of fit, assessing item and person fit, and estimating parameters (von Davier, 2005).

The Logistic Formulation of a Compensatory GDM

In this section, we introduce the logistic formulation of the compensatory GDM applied in this study. The probability of obtaining a response in the GDM is given as follows:

$$P(X_i = x \mid \vec{\beta}_i, \vec{q}_i, \vec{\gamma}_i, \vec{a}, c) = \frac{exp\left[\beta_{xic} = \sum_{k=1}^{K} x\, \gamma_{ikc}\, q_{ik}\, a_k\right]}{1 + \sum_{y=1}^{m_i} exp\left[\beta_{yic} = \sum_{k=1}^{K} y\, \gamma_{ikc}\, q_{ik}\, a_k\right]} \quad (1)$$

where x is the response category for each item i ($x \in \{1,2,...m_i\}$); $\vec{a} = (a_1,...,a_K)$ represents a K-dimensional skill profile containing discrete, user-defined skill levels $a_k \in \{s_{k1},...,s_{kl},...,s_{kL_k}\}$ for $k = 1,...,K$; $\vec{q}_i = (q_{i1},...,q_{iK})$ are the corresponding Q-matrix entries relating item i to skill k ($q_{ik} \in (0,1,2...)$, for $k = 1,...K$); the parameters β_{xic} and $\gamma_{ikc} = (\gamma_{i1c},...,\gamma_{iKc})$ are real-valued thresholds and K-dimensional slope parameters, respectively, and c is the group membership indicator. For model identification purposes, some necessary constraints on $\Sigma_k\, \gamma_{ikc}$ and $\Sigma\beta_{ikc}$ have to be imposed, much like the constraints needed to remove indeterminacy in unidimensional IRT models. Note that a non-zero Q-matrix entry implies that a slope parameter γ_{ikc} is estimated. These slope parameters quantify how much a particular skill component in $\vec{a} = (a_1,...,a_K)$ contributes to the conditional response probabilities for item i given membership in group c. For multiple-group models with a common scale across populations, the item parameters are constrained to be equal across groups, so that $\beta_{ixc} = \beta_{ixg} = \beta_{ix}$ for all items i and thresholds x as well as $\gamma_{ikc} = \gamma_{ikg} = \gamma_{ik}$ for all items i and skill dimensions k.

Loglinear Smoothing of Latent Class Space

In this section, we introduce the log-linear smoothing of the latent skill space predefined by the design matrix. Suppose we have k skills/attributes, the probability of a certain combination of these skills can be approximated by:

$$log(P_g(a_1, a_2, ...,a_k)) = \mu + \sum_k \beta_{k,g}\, a_k + \sum_k \gamma_k\, a_k^2 + \sum_{i \neq j} \delta_{ij}\, a_i\, a_j \quad (2)$$

where μ, β_k, γ_k and δ_{ij} are parameters in this log-linear smoothing model, and g is a group index (Haberman, von Davier, & Lee, 2008; Xu & von Davier, 2008). While the GDM and the *mdltm* software allow higher order moments to be estimated, the model in (2) indicates that, in our application to NAEP data, we used only linear and quadratic terms.

SAMPLE AND DATA SOURCES

Data from NAEP 2003 and 2005 fourth-grade reading assessments were used in this study. A representative sample of approximately 191,000 fourth-graders from 7,600 schools was drawn in 2003 by the consortium conducting the NAEP. The operational reporting includes results presented for the nation, 50 states, and three jurisdictions that participated in the 2003 assessment, and for nine districts that participated in the Trial Urban District Assessment (TUDA) (Donahue, Daane, & Jin, 2005). In addition, unlike the results obtained from participating states and other jurisdictions, the national results reflect both public and non-public school student performance. Generally, NAEP reports not only the overall results but also the performance of various subgroups of students, where statistics such as average scores and achievement-level percentages are the foci of interest.

Developed by the National Assessment Governing Board (NAGB), two reading contexts[3] and four reading aspects[4] were specified in the framework of the 2003 reading assessment to evaluate fourth-graders' reading performance, such as population-related means, standard deviations, and percentiles. In order to minimize the burden on any individual student, NAEP uses matrix sampling, where each student is administered a small portion of the entire assessment. For instance, in 2003, the Grade 4 students were given a test booklet consisting of two 25-minute blocks, where reading scales were summarized by three types of questions (i.e., multiple-choice, short constructed-response, and extended constructed-response; see Table 1). In addition, students were asked to complete two sections of background information questions (Donahue et al., 2005). The two reading contexts—reading for literary experience and reading to gain information—are currently taken as two subscales of psychometric analysis of NAEP Grade 4 assessments. These two subscales are denoted by Skill 1 and Skill 2 in this study, respectively.

Table 1: The number of items in the NAEP 2003 and 2005 reading assessments

Year	Subscales	Response categories in the item			Total
		Multiple-choice	Short construct	Extended construct	
2003	Reading for literary experience	40	8	3	51
	Reading to gain information	40	8	3	51
2005	Reading for literary experience	41	5	4	50
	Reading to gain information	35	11	3	49

---

3 Namely, reading for literary experience and reading to gain information.

4 Namely, forming a general understanding, developing interpretation, making reader/text connections, and examining content and structure.

In similar manner to the 2003 procedure, a nationally representative sample of more than 165,000 fourth-grade students participated in the 2005 assessment. The national results were based on a representative sample of students in both public and non-public schools.[5] The framework used for the NAEP 2005 reading assessment was the same as that used in 2003 (Perie, Grigg, & Donahue, 2005).

VARIANCE ESTIMATION

Estimation of the sampling variability of any statistics should take account of the sample design. In survey practice, the simple random sampling assumption is often violated. Thus, the proper estimation of the sampling variability of a statistic in survey data requires techniques beyond those commonly available in standard packages. There are two commonly used approaches for estimating variances in the analysis of surveys. One is the Taylor series linearization method used to account for complex sample design (Binder, 1983; Li & Oranje, 2007; Williams, 2000); the other is the replication method, which involves recomputing the statistic of interest through use of subsets of data different from but comparable to the original sample and thereby measuring the variance of the parameter estimator (Fay, 1989; Rust, 1985).

In the present study, we applied the resampling-based approach. Resampling techniques, such as the jackknife, balanced repeated replication (BRR), the methods of random groups, and the bootstrap, were used in earlier developments in variance estimation (Efron, 1982; Rust, 1985; Rust & Rao, 1996). By permitting fractional weighting of observations, the class of replication methods becomes considerably broader and more flexible (Fay, 1989). By associating replicate weights with the characteristics of the observed sample cases, the replicate weighting approach lends itself particularly well to analysis of data with highly complex design features (Dippo, Fay, & Morganstein, 1984).

NAEP uses a modified BRR, derived from the jackknife procedure (Miller, 1974), to obtain the variance estimate of a statistic. There are 62[6] jackknife samples with different sets of student replicate weights (*SRWTs*). The *SRWTs* are derived from adjustments to the initial base weight. Examples of the adjustments may include non-response, trimming, post-stratification, and the probability of selection for each primary sampling unit (Allen, Donoghue, & Schoeps, 2001). The estimated sampling variance of an estimator, t, is calculated by aggregating these 62 squared differences, $\hat{v}(t) = \sum_{i=1}^{62}(t_i - t)^2$, where t_i denotes the estimator of the parameter obtained from the ith jackknife sample (Qian et al., 2001). For further discussion of the variance estimation procedure used by NAEP, interested readers can refer to the paper by Johnson (1989, p. 315).

---

5 In 2005, the definition of the national sample was changed: it now includes all of the international Department of Defense schools (Perie, Grigg, & Donahue, 2005).

6 This number is used in NAEP operational analysis.

EMPIRICAL EVALUATION

The GDM with both a single-group and a multiple-group assumption was applied to analyze the data. Under a single-group assumption, all students are assumed to belong to a single population with one latent skill distribution; under a multiple-group assumption, different latent skill distributions are allowed for different groups. In this study, the multiple-group variable was defined by race/ethnicity. Four ethnicity groups were distinguished to form the different levels of this variable: White, Black, Hispanic, and Asian/Pacific Islander. As shown in Tables 2 and 5, the results from using the multiple-group assumption, when compared to the results from the single-group assumption, showed better fit in terms of the several fit indices, such as the Bayesian information criterion (BIC; Schwarz, 1978), Akaike's information criterion (AIC; Akaike, 1974), and log-likelihood. Hence, in our study, we compared the results from the multiple-group assumption, such as group means and standard deviations as well as the estimation error of the group mean, with the results from the NAEP operational analysis. The scale used in these comparisons is the one obtained from IRT calibrations, not the one converted to the NAEP reporting scale.

NAEP 2003 Reading Assessment for Fourth-grade Students

Table 2 shows the model fit indices under different assumptions. What is evident here is that the multiple-group GDM with race/ethnicity has the better model fit. Thus, this multiple-group GDM will be used and estimates obtained from this model will be compared to the operational results.

Table 2: Model evaluation based on the NAEP 2003 reading assessment

Model	Number of parameters	-2*Log-likelihood	AIC per person	BIC
Single-group analysis	240	4,247,410	.607	4,250,328
Race-group analysis	960	4,215,853	.603	4,227,528

Table 3 presents the mean and standard deviation for the race/ethnicity subgroups. As is evident, the results that emerged from using the GDM with the race-group assumption and those that emerged from the NAEP operation have a similar pattern: from high score to low score, the four racial groups have the following order—White, Asian, Hispanic, and African American. We can also observe differences in the means for the subgroups: the differences are relatively large in the subgroups of small sample size (such as in the Asian group). Moreover, the standard deviation estimates obtained from the current approach were smaller for the White and the Asian students and larger for the African American and the Hispanic students.

Table 3: Means and standard deviations for ethnicity subgroups in the 2003 assessment

	GDM				NAEP*			
	Literary subscale		Information subscale		Literary subscale		Information subscale	
	Mean	SD	Mean	SD	Mean	SD	Mean	SD
White	0.689	0.938	0.577	0.982	0.691	0.956	0.575	1.002
African American	- 0.140	1.054	- 0.351	1.070	- 0.144	1.016	- 0.349	1.031
Hispanic	- 0.046	1.065	- 0.290	1.099	- 0.059	1.034	- 0.282	1.051
Asian	0.571	0.991	0.495	0.987	0.613	1.030	0.478	1.083

Note: * These results are already on the same scale as those from the GDM runs.

Table 4 shows the comparison between the standard errors associated with the group mean estimates. Here, we can see that the standard errors obtained from using the current approach are slightly larger than those obtained from the operational approach.

Table 4: Standard errors for subgroup mean estimates in the 2003 assessment

White (N = 118,061)			
	GDM	NAEP*	Ratio of GDM to operation
Literary	0.007	0.006	1.167
Information	0.008	0.006	1.333
African American (N = 35,308)			
	GDM	NAEP	Ratio
Literary	0.017	0.011	1.545
Information	0.018	0.011	1.636
Hispanic (N = 23,839)			
	GDM	NAEP	Ratio
Literary	0.021	0.016	1.312
Information	0.019	0.017	1.118
Asian (N = 8,223)			
	GDM	NAEP	Ratio
Literary	0.032	0.033	0.970
Information	0.038	0.033	1.151

Note: *These results are not readily available from the NAEP report because the reporting of NAEP is on a scale score metric, not on the θ metric. Instead, these results are derived from the NAEP reporting that involved inversing the transformation.

NAEP 2005 Reading Assessment for Fourth-grade Students

Table 5, which presents the model fit indices, shows that the GDM with a race-group assumption has a better fit than a single-group assumption. Hence, the race-group analysis is used in the comparison with the operational results. The presentation of the means and the standard deviations for the racial subgroups (Table 6) shows some differences in the ability estimates between the current and the operational approaches with respect to the literary-experience subscale. In addition, the standard deviations for the White and the Asian students tend to be somewhat smaller relative to the current approach than to the operational approach, while the standard deviations for the Hispanic and the African American students are larger for the current than for the operational approach. Note, however, that the patterns of results between the 2003 and 2005 assessments are quite similar.

Table 5: Model evaluation based on the NAEP 2005 reading assessment

Model	Number of parameters	-2* Log-likelihood	AIC per person	BIC
Single-group analysis	235	3,650,627	.610	3,653,452
Race-group analysis	940	3,625,153	.606	3,636,450

Table 6: Means and standard deviations for subgroups in the 2005 assessment

	GDM				NAEP			
	Literary subscale		Information subscale		Literary subscale		Information subscale	
	Mean	SD	Mean	SD	Mean	SD	Mean	SD
White	0.880	0.872	0.501	1.027	0.910	0.930	0.500	1.028
African American	0.177	1.081	- 0.422	1.067	0.119	0.970	- 0.410	1.049
Hispanic	0.264	1.087	- 0.340	1.112	0.206	1.007	- 0.341	1.102
Asian	0.866	0.921	0.482	1.020	0.917	1.000	0.462	1.114

Table 7 shows the comparison between the estimation errors for the group means from the 2005 data. Again, we observe that the standard errors for the group means obtained from the current approach are slightly larger than those obtained from the NAEP operational approach.

Table 7: Standard errors for subgroup means in the 2005 assessment

White (N = 99,425)		
GDM	NAEP	Ratio of GDM to operation
Literary	0.007	0.005	1.400
Information	0.008	0.006	1.333

African American (N = 27,897)		
GDM	NAEP	Ratio
Literary	0.012	0.008	1.500
Information	0.014	0.009	1.555

Hispanic (N = 25,122)		
GDM	NAEP	Ratio
Literary	0.016	0.014	1.143
Information	0.016	0.015	1.067

Asian (N = 7,706)		
GDM	NAEP	Ratio
Literary	0.024	0.019	1.263
Information	0.026	0.022	1.182

SUMMARY AND DISCUSSION

The application of the GDM in this article focused not on detecting the skills measured by the NAEP assessment but on improving the estimation of error variances by using a more comprehensive jackknife procedure. The proposed approach accomplishes this by requiring a complete re-estimation of model parameters (item parameters and ability distributions) in jackknife samples, using a multiple-group MIRT model implemented in the GDM framework. Compared to the NAEP operational analysis, where hundreds of background variables are used to extract group ability estimates, the approach chosen for the GDM utilizing only a single grouping variable with four levels is much more parsimonious. In addition, the IRT model used in the GDM analysis does not assume a guessing parameter for multiple-choice items. Given these differences, the results obtained with the two approaches are quite similar. However, the main focus of this paper was to compare the error variance estimation based on one set of (operational) plausible values used in a jackknife scheme, versus a comprehensive re-estimation utilized in the GDM-based jackknife.

Thus, the primary goal of our study was to obtain the estimation error of the subgroup ability means and the standard deviations obtained under the GDM framework. Specifically, we used, in our current procedure, 62 jackknife samples coupled with different sets of weights utilized in the NAEP operational analysis. The results showed that the estimation errors for the ethnicity subgroup means were slightly larger in the proposed approach than were those in the operational. This may be because NAEP operational procedures ignore uncertainty in the item parameters due to sampling.

There are a number of differences between the approach taken using the GDM and that taken using operational procedures. The operational approach assumes normality in the conditional distribution of the latent trait because of the item responses and the large number of background variables (von Davier, 2003). In contrast, the GDM approach does not assume a particular form of the multidimensional ability distributions. Most importantly, the item parameters in the operational analysis are assumed to be fixed and known for the purpose of estimating both the population model and the jackknife replications; our proposed approach re-estimated the item parameters and population distributions for each of the 62 jackknife samples. The capability to re-estimate all parameters used in the GDM enables one to implement a complete jackknife procedure, which results in relatively larger error variance estimates for the group ability means.

Application of the GDM to the NAEP assessment data is not limited to what we have shown in this article.[7] The GDM is able not only to facilitate dimensionality exploration of the NAEP assessment (von Davier, 2005) but also to reduce the number of background covariates when one makes inferences about the group ability estimates. For example, the multiple-group variant of the GDM allows for possible different ability distributions (with potentially different covariance structures) across groups. This heterogeneity of variance structure may reduce the secondary bias in the group mean estimates (Thomas, 2000).

The complexity of the latent ability space introduces corresponding complexities into the statistical modeling and score reporting. In practice, because data-driven model specification is often not straightforward, a careful judgment process involving content experts and psychometricians is needed during formulation of appropriate models. Moreover, results and inferences must be suitable to be communicated in ways that are useful to stakeholders. For instance, Xu (2007) recently conducted an investigation to examine whether the monotonicity property can generally be sustained in GDM so that simple data summaries (e.g., the observed total score) can help inform the ordered categories of the latent trait and lead to the reporting of valid and reliable scaled scores. In recent years, there have been calls for more and more subscales and skills to be reported in large-scale surveys. This call leads to models that are parametrically complex, potentially involving multiple, but potentially redundant, subdomains. The principle of parsimony would indicate that the model used for reporting must be complex enough to provide sufficient skill information but still parsimonious enough for the obtained skill information to be non-redundant and reliable (Haberman & von Davier, 2007).

Finally, the question of whether the larger variance estimates were observed because the GDM approach was carried out with a complete jackknife (i.e., using recalibrations of item parameters and re-estimated population models) rather than with a jackknife based on imputations from a model using the complete sample needs further investigation. If this was indeed the reason for observing larger variance estimates

---

7 What is presented here is part of an ongoing program of research geared toward expanding the analysis and reporting alternatives for NAEP.

during use of the GDM rather than of the operation approach, then an inquiry is needed into whether the added portion of variance reflects the true sampling variance of the parameters. If this proves true, then the feasibility of implementing a more complete jackknifing approach into operational analysis procedures should be studied.

References

Akaike, H. (1974). A new look at the statistical model identification. *IEEE Transactions on Automatic Control, 19*(6): 716–723.

Allen, N. A., Donoghue, J. R., & Schoeps, T. L. (2001). *The NAEP 1998 technical report* (NCES 2001-452). Washington DC: United States Department of Education, Institute of Education Sciences, Department of Education, Office for Educational Research and Improvement.

Ackerman, T. A. (1994). Using multidimensional item response theory to understand what items and tests are measuring. *Applied Measurement in Education, 7*, 255–278.

Ackerman, T. A. (1996). Graphical representation of multidimensional item response theory analyses. *Applied Psychological Measurement, 20*, 311–329.

Binder, D. A. (1983). On the variances of asymptotically normal estimators from complex surveys. *International Statistical Review, 51*(3), 279–292.

Dempster, A. P., Laird, N. M., & Rubin, R. D. (1977). Maximum likelihood from incomplete data via the EM algorithm (with discussion). *Journal of the Royal Statistical Society, Series B, 39*, 1–38.

Dippo, S., Fay, R. E., & Morganstein, D. H. (1984). Computing variances from complex samples with replicate weights. In *Proceedings of the American Statistical Association Survey Research Methods Section* (pp. 113–121). Alexandria, VA: American Statistical Association.

Donahue, P. L., Daane, M. C., & Jin, Y. (2005). *The Nation's Report Card: Reading 2003* (NCES 2005-453). Washington, DC: United States Department of Education, Institute of Education Sciences, National Center for Education Statistics.

Efron, B. (1982). *The jackknife, the bootstrap and other re-sampling plans*. Philadelphia, PA: Society for Industry and Applied Mathematics.

Fay, R. E. (1989). Theory and application of replicate weighting for variance calculations. In *Proceedings of the Section on Survey Research Methods, American Statistical Association* (pp. 212–217). Alexandria, VA: American Statistical Association.

Goodman, L. A. (1974). Exploratory latent structure analysis using both identifiable and unidentifiable models. *Biometrika, 61*, 215–231.

Haberman, S. J., & von Davier, M. (2007). Some notes on models for cognitively based skills diagnosis. In C. R. Rao & S. Sinharay (Eds.), *Handbook of statistics: Vol. 26. Psychometrics* (pp. 1031–1038). Amsterdam: Elsevier.

Haberman, S. J., von Davier, M., & Lee, Y. H. (2008). *Comparison of multidimensional item response models: Multivariate normal ability distributions versus multivariate polytomous ability distributions*. Princeton, NJ: Educational Testing Service.

Johnson, E. G. (1989). Considerations and techniques for the analysis of NAEP data. *Journal of Educational Statistics, 14*(4), 303–334.

Lazarsfeld, P. F, & Henry, N. W. (1968). *Latent structure analysis*. Boston, MA: Houghton Mifflin.

Li, D., & Oranje, A. (2007). *Estimation of standard error of regression effects in latent regression models using Binder's linearization* (ETS Research Rep. No. RR-07-09). Princeton, NJ: Educational Testing Service.

Lord, F. M., & Novick, M. R. (1968). *Statistical theories of mental test scores*. Reading, MA: Addison-Wesley Publishing Company.

Mazzeo, J., Donoghue, J. R., Li, D., & Johnson, M. (2006). *Marginal estimation in NAEP: Current operational procedures and AM*. Prepared for the National Center for Education Statistics (NCES) under Task 2.2.8 of the NAEP in the New Millennium, Continuity and Innovation contract.

McCutcheon, A. L. (1987). *Latent class analysis: Quantitative applications in the social sciences*. Thousand Oaks, CA: Sage Publications.

Miller, R. G. (1974). The jackknife: A review. *Biometrika, 61*(1), 1–15.

Mislevy, R. J. (1991). Randomization-based inference about latent variables from complex samples. *Psychometrika, 56,* 177–196.

Muraki, E. (1992). A generalized partial credit model: Application of an EM algorithm. *Applied Psychological Measurement, 16,* 159–176.

Perie, M., Grigg, W., & Donahue, P. (2005). *The Nation's Report Card: Reading 2005* (NCES 2006–451). Washington, DC: United States Department of Education, National Center for Education Statistics.

Qian, J., Kaplan, B. A., Johnson, E. G., Krenzke, T., & Rust, K. F. (2001). Weighting procedures and estimation of sampling variance for the national assessment. In N. A. Allen, J. R. Donoghue, & T. L. Schoeps (Eds.), *The NAEP 1998 technical report* (NCES 2001-452). Washington, DC: United States Department of Education, Institute of Education Sciences, Department of Education, Office for Educational Research and Improvement.

Rasch, G. (1960). *Probabilistic models for some intelligence and attainment tests*. Chicago: University of Chicago Press.

Rust, K. F. (1985). Variance estimation for complex estimators in sample surveys. *Journal of Official Statistics, 1*(4), 381–397.

Rust, K. F., & Rao, J. N. K. (1996). Variance estimation for complex surveys using replication techniques. *Statistical Methods in Medical Research, 5,* 283–310.

Schwarz, G. (1978). Estimating the dimension of a model. *Annals of Statistics, 6*(2), 461–464.

Thomas, N. (1993). *The E-step of the MGROUP EM algorithm* (ETSRR-95-05). Princeton, NJ: Educational Testing Service.

Thomas, N. (2000). Assessing model sensitivity of the imputation methods used in the National Assessment of Educational Progress. *Journal of Educational and Behavioral Statistics, 25*, 351–372.

von Davier, M. (2003). *Comparing conditional and marginal direct estimation of subgroup distributions* (ETS Research Rep. No. RR-03-02). Princeton, NJ: Educational Testing Service.

von Davier, M. (2005). *A general diagnostic model applied to language testing data* (ETS Research Rep. No. RR-05-16). Princeton, NJ: Educational Testing Service.

von Davier, M. (2007). *Mixture of general diagnostic models* (ETS Research Rep. No. RR-07-32). Princeton, NJ: Educational Testing Service.

von Davier, M., & Rost, J. (2006). *Mixture distribution item response models*. In C. R. Rao & S. Sinharay (Eds.), H*andbook of statistics: Vol. 26. Psychometrics* (pp. 643–768). Amsterdam: Elsevier.

von Davier, M., & Sinharay, S. (2007). An importance sampling EM alogorithm for latent regressional models. *Journal of Educational and Behavioural Statistics, 32*(3), 233–251.

von Davier, M., Sinharay, S., Oranje, A., & Beaton, A. (2007). Statistical procedures used in the National Assessment of Educational Progress (NAEP): Recent developments and future directions. In C. R. Rao & S. Sinharay (Eds.), *Handbook of Statistics: Vol. 26. Psychometrics* (pp. 1039–1055). Amsterdam: Elsevier.

von Davier, M., & Yamamoto, K. (2004). Partially observed mixtures of IRT models: An extension of the generalized partial credit model. *Applied Psychological Measurement, 28*(6), 389–406.

Williams, R. L. (2000). A note on robust variance estimation for cluster-correlated data. *Biometrics, 56*(2), 645–646.

Xu, X. (2007). *Monotone properties of a general diagnostic model* (ETS Research Rep. No. RR-07-25). Princeton, NJ: Educational Testing Service.

Xu, X., & von Davier, M. (2006). *General diagnosis for NAEP proficiency data* (ETS Research Rep. No. RR-06-08). Princeton, NJ: Educational Testing Service.

Xu, X., & von Davier, M. (2008). *Fitting the structural general diagnostic model to NAEP data* (ETS Research Rep. No. RR-08-27). Princeton, NJ: Educational Testing Service.

INFORMATION FOR CONTRIBUTORS

Content

IERI Monograph Series: Issues and Methodologies in Large-Scale Assessments is a joint publication between the International Association for the Evaluation of Educational Achievement (IEA) and Educational Testing Service (ETS). The goal of the publication is to contribute to the science of large-scale assessments so that the best available information is provided to policy-makers and researchers from around the world. Papers accepted for this publication are those that focus on improving the science of large-scale assessments and that make use of data collected by programs such as IEA-TIMSS, IEA-PIRLS, IEA-Civics, IEA-SITES, US-NAEP, OECD-PISA, OECD-PIAAC, IALS, ALL, etc.

If you have questions or concerns about whether your paper adheres to the purpose of the series, please contact us at IERInstitute@iea-dpc.de.

Style

The style guide for all IERI publications is the *Publication Manual of the American Psychological Association* (5th ed., 2001). Manuscripts should be typed on letter or A4 format, upper and lower case, double spaced in its entirety, with one-inch margins on all sides. The type size should be 12 point. Subheads should be at reasonable intervals to break the monotony of lengthy text. Pages should be numbered consecutively at the bottom of the page, beginning with the page after the title page. Mathematical symbols and Greek letters should be clearly marked to indicate italics, boldface, superscript, and subscript.

Please submit all manuscripts electronically, preferably in MS-Word format and with figures and tables in editable form (e.g., Word, Excel) to the editorial team at IERInstitute@iea-dpc.de and attach the Manuscript Submission Form, which can be obtained from the IERI website: www.ierinstitute.org. For specific questions or inquiries, send emails to editors at the same address. Only electronic submissions are accepted.

Author Identification

The complete title of the article and the name of the author(s) should be typed only on the submission form to ensure anonymity in the review process. The pages of the paper should have no author names, but may carry a short title at the top. Information in the text or references that would identify the author should be deleted from the manuscript (e.g., text citations of "my previous work," especially when accompanied by a self-citation; a preponderance of the author's own work in the reference list). These may be reinserted in the final draft. The author (whether first-named or co-author) who will be handling the correspondence with the editor and working with the publications people should submit complete contact information, including a full mailing address, telephone number, and email addresses.

Review Process

Papers will be acknowledged by the managing editor upon receipt. After a preliminary internal editorial review by IERI staff, articles will be sent to two external reviewers who have expertise in the subject of the manuscript. The review process takes anywhere from three to six months. You should expect to hear from the editor within that time regarding the status of your manuscript. IERI uses a blind review system, which means the identity of the authors is not revealed to the reviewers. In order to be published as part of the monograph series, the work will undergo and receive favorable technical, substantive, and editorial review.

Originality of Manuscript and Copyright

Manuscripts are accepted for consideration with the understanding that they are original material and are not under consideration for publication elsewhere.

To protect the works of authors and the institute, we copyright all of our publications. Rights and permissions regarding the uses of IERI-copyrighted materials are handled by the IERI executive board. Authors who wish to use material, such as figures or tables, for which they do not own the copyright must obtain written permission from IERI and submit it to IERI with their manuscripts.

Comments and Grievances

The Publications Committee welcomes comments and suggestions from authors. Please send these to the committee at IERInstitute@iea-dpc.de.

The right-of-reply policy encourages comments on articles recently published in an IERI publication. Such comments are subject to editorial review and decision. If the comment is accepted for publication, the editor will inform the author of the original article. If the author submits a reply to the comment, the reply is also subject to editorial review and decision.

If you think that your manuscript is not reviewed in a careful or timely manner and in accordance with standard practices, please call the matter to the attention of the institute's executive board.

Publication Schedule

There is one publication per year. This publication will consist of five to seven research papers. Manuscripts will be reviewed and processed as soon as they are received and will be published in the next available monograph series. In the event that, in a single year, there are more than seven accepted manuscripts, the editorial committee determines whether the manuscript(s) will be published the next year or in an additional monograph in the same year. Manuscripts are accepted any time of the year.